From Quantitative to Qualitative Change in Ontario Education

A FESTSCHRIFT FOR R.W.B. JACKSON

Garnet McDiarmid, editor

Symposium Series/6 • The Ontario Institute for Studies in Education

MINISTRY OF EDUCATION, ONTARIO
COMMUNICATION SERVICES BRANCH
13TH FLOOR, MOWAT BLOCK
TORONTO, ONTARIO M7A 1L3

MINISTRY OF EDUCATION, ONTARIO
COMMUNICATION SERVICES BRANCH
13TH FLOOR, MOWAT BLOCK
TORONTO, ONTARIO M7A 1L3

THE ONTARIO INSTITUTE FOR STUDIES IN EDUCATION has three prime functions: to conduct programs of graduate study in education, to undertake research in education, and to assist in the implementation of the findings of educational studies. The Institute is a college chartered by an Act of the Ontario Legislature in 1965. It is affiliated with the University of Toronto for graduate studies purposes.

The publications program of the Institute has been established to make available information and materials arising from studies in education, to foster the spirit of critical inquiry, and to provide a forum for the exchange of ideas about education. The opinions expressed should be viewed as those of the contributors.

© The Ontario Institute for Studies in Education 1976
252 Bloor Street West, Toronto, Ontario M5S 1V6

All rights reserved. No part of this publication may be reproduced in any form without permission from the publisher, except for brief passages quoted for review purposes.

ISBN 0-7744-0121-4   Printed in Canada

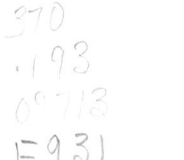

1 2 3 4 5 BP 08 97 87 77 67

CONTENTS

Foreword   v

Preface   xi

Edward B. Harvey
   Dimensions of a Decade: Canadian Higher Education in the Sixties   1

George E. Flower
   Graduate Studies in Ontario Education at the Three-Quarter-Century Mark   29

William E. Alexander
   Policy Research and the Concept of Goal   45

John W. Holland
   Education, Public Policy, and Personal Choice   67

Alan M. Thomas
   Funny Things Happen on the Way to Parnassus   101

Jack Quarter
   Shifting Ideologies among Youth in Canada   119

Clive Beck
   Education and Basic Human Values   137

Garnet McDiarmid
   Trends in Society, Trends in Curriculum   149

Foreword

Born in the picturesquely named Alberta hamlet of Seven Persons, [his] preparation for a lifetime of distinguished service to education began as a boy from a homesteading family in a one-room rural school; graduate of the Universities of Alberta and London; for three decades a leading figure in the development of educational policy in Ontario, first as Secretary of the postwar Royal Commission on Education, then as Director of the Department of Educational Research at the University of Toronto, and then as early prophet of the expansion required of universities to accommodate the rising tide of students in the sixties; convinced that the chasm between educational research and classroom practice must somehow be bridged, he brought the weight of an impressive reputation and richly varied experience to bear in persuading the Ontario government to establish The Ontario Institute for Studies in Education—a unique institution through which graduate studies, research and application are combined for their mutual support, and which, in ten short years, has gained international recognition indicating the imaginative judgment of its founding father.

So ran the formal citation of May 23, 1975, as the Chancellor of Queen's University conferred on Robert W. B. Jackson the university's highest honor, the Doctor of Laws, *honoris causa*. It was not the first such honor to come his way, for his alma mater, the University of Alberta, had also bestowed the LL.D. upon him in 1967. Fellow of the Royal Statistical Society of England, Fellow of London, England's College of Preceptors, Fellow of the Ontario Teachers' Federation, recipient of the Canadian Council for Research in Education Whitworth Award, informal accolade as Canada's Mr. Educational Research: these are just some of the other honors Dr. Jackson has worthily won over a long and quietly distinguished career.

Like so many outstanding Canadians of his era, Dr. Jackson was indeed the product of a rural background and a one-room schoolhouse. Following attendance at a high school which was not much larger, he went on to graduate from the Calgary Normal School, and this by his sixteenth birthday. After teaching for two years in a rural school, he continued his formal education, graduating from the University of Alberta with a B.A. in honors mathematics and from the University of London with a Ph.D. in statistics. For two years Dr. Jackson worked in England with the Colonial Office and the London Institute of Education, returning to Canada in 1939 to take up an appointment with the Department of Educational Research in the University of Toronto's College of Education. He became Assistant Director of the Department of Educational Research in 1947 and Director ten years later, a post he held for some eight years. On July 1, 1965, Dr. Jackson became the founding Director of the Ontario Institute for Studies in Education.

The creation of the Institute marked the culmination of a quarter century of steady expansion in the amount and kinds of research carried out by the Department of Educational Research. When Dr. Jackson joined the Department, the staff's main task had been the establishment of Canadian norms for American standardized tests. Housed in the basement of the Ontario College of Education, the staff found working conditions barely tolerable: summers in the cramped offices were thoroughly uncomfortable, and overhead could be heard the thumping of the College's industrial arts students. Despite such disadvantages, Dr. Jackson developed a legendary reputation as an indefatigable worker, often spending seven days a week at the office. His work ranged from the conceptualization of major research studies to the application of a fresh coat of paint to the filing cabinets.

Over those years Dr. Jackson also wrote steadily and prolifically; besides publishing innumerable articles in British, American, Canadian, and Unesco publications, he produced over a score of books and monographs, among them several college texts—*Manual of Educational Statistics: Parts I and II*, with George A. Ferguson, and *Introduction to Statistical Methods* and *Modern Statistical Methods: Descriptive and Inductive*, with Palmer O. Johnson. A sampling of the titles of books he has written indicates the wide range of his interests: *Predicting Reading Achievement in First Grade*, *Emergent Needs in Australian Education*, *Educational Research in Canada: Today and Tomorrow*, and *The Problem of Numbers in University Enrolment*.

Despite his eminence in his own academic field and his pervasive contribution to education in Ontario, Dr. Jackson has never been in any way a public figure. He never wished to be. Indeed, it is only over the past ten years, in his capacity as Director of OISE, that he has become at all known to the general public. However, he was certainly well acquainted for years with the provincial bodies responsible for education and with most of Ontario's leaders in education. For over two decades he enjoyed an influential relationship with many of these leaders, especially with the deputy ministers and other senior officials of the Ministry (formerly the Department) of Education.

The extent of his involvement in education may come as a surprise to many, for he always preferred to work in the background, often as an unofficial advisor to governments and other bodies. A colleague who has known Dr. Jackson since the 1950s recalls, "He kept out of the spotlight, even to the point of deliberately avoiding attendance at conferences. He felt he could be more effective working behind the scenes, and was always ready to give the credit for improvements and new policies to others." Nevertheless, with the help of his colleagues in the Department of Educational Research, he quietly initiated innumerable research studies that were to have far-reaching effects upon educational policy development. Perhaps it was his preference for anonymity which inspired the Toronto *Globe and Mail*'s label "The Pussycats," an appellation applied to an informal but powerful group of leaders in industry, government, and education. Besides Jackson, the term was applied to Public Pussycat Premier William Davis and his Executive Assistant, Clare Westcott; the Economic Council of Canada's John Deutsch; Donald H. MacLaren of Air Canada; Quebec's Minister of Education, Paul Gérin-Lajoie; and North York's Director of Education, Dr. Frederick Minkler. This group was interested in educational strategies at a national level; and in these affairs Jackson was clearly an influential figure. Together with some of his senior staff, among them professors Brock Rideout and Gerry Fleming, Bob Jackson had become a major source of ideas when it came to the formulation of broad policies to be implemented by government. A succession of ministers of education—William Dunlop, John Robarts, and William Davis—came to depend heavily on him.

It was during his quarter century with the Department of Educational Research that Dr. Jackson's relationship with government evolved. No doubt it was this relationship that gave the Department of Educational Research program its strong practical emphasis; in fact, the DER came to be viewed by many as the research arm of Ontario's Department of Education. As early as 1944, Jackson worked with the province's Superintendent of Elementary Education, Dr. V. K. Greer, in developing legislative grant systems for elementary and secondary schools. The grant formulas, now very elaborate, were at that time in a very primitive stage of development. This was perhaps the beginning of Dr. Jackson's relationship with government, for after Dr. Greer died in 1945, Jackson became the Ontario Cabinet's chief advisor on school grants and, later, on other policies as well.

From 1945 to 1950 Dr. Jackson served as Secretary of the Royal Commission on Education in Ontario, popularly known as the Hope Commission. This assignment provided him with a unique and invaluable opportunity to study all aspects of education in Ontario and to work with numerous civil servants and educators at every level. The preface of the report of the Commission, published in 1950, singled out Dr. Jackson for special commendation for his "unremitting zeal, great organizing ability, clear judgment, and ... complete grasp of the problems involved." The members of the Commission clearly appreciated his conspicuous research ability, and they expressed the hope that Ontario would find ways to take advantage of his valuable services.

Dr. Jackson's outstanding service to the Commission and his subsequent role as advisor to the provincial government marked the first step in the expansion of the Department of Educational Research, a development that led to the establishment of OISE many years later. Over the years, his specialized scholarship in statistics, measurement, and research methodology had earned Dr. Jackson an international reputation. During the 1950s, he was therefore able to obtain substantial grants from both the Atkinson and Carnegie foundations for the conduct of long-term studies in Ontario education. Both studies had essentially the same purposes—to measure student aptitudes, to demonstrate how effectively these were being used, and to recommend improvements. In terms of the volume of statistics compiled and reports written, the Atkinson Studies constituted the largest research project ever carried out in Canada. They stimulated wide public interest in the grade 13 program and examinations, and led to the reform of both.

Other projects of the Department included the experimental development and scoring, in 1957, of objective aptitude and achievement tests for grade 12 students, a program that in the next year became a regular aspect of the provincial examination system. In addition, the Department gradually assumed responsibility for the machine scoring and reporting of the grade 13 departmental examinations, until their abolition in the mid-sixties.

But back to government. As mentioned earlier, Dr. Jackson had attracted the attention of the policy makers in Ontario education, who were impressed by his capacity to anticipate events and support his predictions with solid research. There was scarcely an educational development from the 1950s onward that did not bear his stamp: the consolidation of the Toronto and area school boards into the unique Metropolitan Toronto school system, the expansion of the Ontario system of universities and the creation of a formula for distributing funds to them equitably, the reforms in grade 13 examinations, and the development of a provincewide network of colleges of applied arts and technology (CAATs). Dr. Jackson provided the government with enrollment forecasts that enabled it to anticipate the massive education needs of the 1960s and plan for them by building the colleges and universities to accommodate the thousands of students who were to seek higher education. He also worked closely with the Honourable William Davis, then Minister of Education, in planning the CAATs, even to the point of helping to draft the legislation.

The reputation of Dr. Jackson and his associates in the Department of

Educational Research was unquestionably a prime factor in the decision to create OISE, a decision supported by all parties in the Ontario legislature. This was a deliberate experiment in a kind of institute new not only to Ontario but to all of Canada—a melding of graduate studies in education with research and development and with an even more innovative concept that came to be known as field development. On July 1, 1965, the Department of Educational Research merged with the Department of Educational Theory of the University of Toronto's School of Graduate Studies to form the Ontario Institute for Studies in Education. A year later, the Ontario Curriculum Institute broadened the scope of the new institute with the addition of its resources in curriculum development.

The decade in which Dr. Jackson served as Director of OISE saw the Institute's faculty grow in number from 25 professors to 160. The 1960s were turbulent years for colleges and universities everywhere, and OISE faced as well the growing pains of a young and innovative organization. To Dr. Jackson's wisdom and patience during these formative years, all of us at OISE are indebted, and—although they may be unaware of it—so are all those in the educational community that OISE strives to serve.

Perhaps this is a good place to end, with the ideal of service. It is an ideal that Dr. Jackson has aspired to in all his work—service to government, service to education, and ultimately, service to the people, children and adults both, for whom our schools, colleges, and universities exist. Dr. Jackson's special competence has lain in the effective application of statistical methods to problems in education. He is a scholar of the first rank, but he has never lost touch with his roots: the prairie homestead, the one-room schoolhouse, the country children who had the distinction of being his first pupils. With all the honors and esteem that his achievements have brought him, Dr. Jackson has remained a quiet, modest man, content in seeing that he has, indeed, served well the cause of quality education in Ontario.

Clifford C. Pitt

Preface

Two events in OISE coincided in 1975. Canada's first educational research, development, and graduate teaching institute celebrated its tenth anniversary, and its founding director retired. Published in honor of Dr. Robert William Brierley Jackson, who has made an outstanding contribution to his field, this *Festschrift* grows out of a tradition to which the academic side of the Ontario Institute for Studies in Education owes its allegiance. In the foreword to this volume, Clifford Pitt, the incoming director and a long-time colleague of R. W. B. Jackson, describes the extent of that contribution as it applies generally to the field of knowledge and more particularly to Dr. Jackson's involvement in the changing appearance and structure of Ontario education over more than twenty years.

Laymen whose views of the world of ideas are shaped by the traditional disciplines and professions are often unwilling to grant legitimacy to the specialization of educational studies. Nevertheless, the translation of an insistent, popular ideology of equality into educational practice has required, and continues to demand, a search for knowledge, for determinants, for procedures, indeed for a sophisticated conceptualization in which tradition has seldom offered a precedent. Accessibility to education, a long-sought goal in our society, is now a reality for more people in Ontario than ever before. Obviously this could not have happened without the efforts of successive ministers of education and the Ontario legislature. It does not diminish the instrumental role of the government, however, if we recognize Dr. Jackson's part in the achievement of this highly desirable social goal.

By the early 1950s there was a growing consciousness in Ontario that there was a dearth of information about education, and decision making was suffering because of this dearth. The earlier diversions of money from the construction and maintenance of schools to armaments to fight a second world war, the influx of immigrants following the war, and the inevitable rise in the birthrate after the return of the veterans placed serious financial and logistical pressures on the Ontario school system. Assuredly, even this quantitative problem had its qualitative aspects. But the church basements that were pressed into use and the portables that were placed discreetly behind old buildings and new bespoke the most insistent problem of the decade. Where could Ontario find enough teachers and sufficient classrooms to cope with this vast and growing quantity of students? All of these problems were widely discussed in the province, while the province was becoming a sort of natural laboratory without any staff to collect and organize the data.

Dr. Pitt documents the many ways in which R. W. B. Jackson guided Ontario toward the development of the infrastructure that made it possible to institute and then to utilize, rationally rather than haphazardly, research, planning, and development in education.

The last component to be added to that structure before Dr. Jackson's retirement was OISE. It was his firm hand as director that placed the onus for the integration of theory and practice on individual professors. It would have been easier to bureaucratically assign staff to one or another of the Institute's three functions—graduate studies, research, and development—and it would have been disastrous.

The construction of theoretical models, the identification and clarification of societal values, and the derivation of appropriate policy and school practices may seem to be esoteric ventures; nonetheless, they are interrelated skills that are prerequisites for those who look forward to serving the public as responsible educators. It may be true that education is everybody's business, as the slogan informed us in the 1950s, but it is not everyone's profession. It is the double helix of the acquisition of knowledge and the derivation of changing practice that constitutes the base laid by educational studies in this generation.

On the surface it often appears that social scientists are interested only in numbers. The papers that follow expose this fallacy by illustrating how Dr. Jackson's policy has resulted in rigorous examinations of the culture that serve as a prelude to the satisfaction of human concerns. Empirical measures are only part of such analyses.

Edward Harvey describes the role that postsecondary education has played in efforts to achieve a greater measure of equality of educational opportunity. In doing so, he examines the interacting effects of student politics and life styles and then the changing relationships between education and employment.

Much closer to home, George Flower, OISE's retiring coordinator of graduate studies, focuses on the problems that have faced graduate studies in Ontario. He discusses the role that OISE has played in trying to meet the practical needs of the education system.

Unlike traditional societies, where deliberation is aimed more at the interpretation of established norms than at the formulation of new ones, technological cultures have universally adopted the language of goal setting. Indeed, the identification of goals is a preoccupation of educators and, as William Alexander tells us, of researchers also. Since it is not just a question of what the goals should be, no mean problem in itself, Alexander takes us on a mental tour of various definitions of goals and how people attempt to measure and achieve them. We become aware of the fact that rational decision making, based as it must be on the collection of reliable and valid data, is a primitive art in spite of the availability of sophisticated technologies of analysis.

Of course, it is possible that we might yet come to understand that the Western European ideal of rationality in decision making is as great a fallacy as the mind/body dichotomy has been shown to be in the healing sciences. John Holland's historical analysis of economics and education ties the development of public policy to something very deep in the social psyche. Holland shows us how the once widely held belief in the perfectability of the nation state—an unexamined belief in progress—and the Western world's consensus that compulsory schooling was to be the instrument of that progress have now come to a resounding and very confused impasse. One hundred years after these assumptions started to spread, the institution that Dr. Jackson founded so that more sophisticated questions could be researched now "faces the challenge of accommodating to a remarkable environmental change."

No one writes more eloquently of the implications of this environmental change than does Alan Thomas. Like Edward Harvey and John Holland, Thomas notes the intimate relationship between the realms of economics and education. He makes the point that the system of elementary and secondary education has drawn attention away from the legitimate needs of groups in our society. The wisdom of a deliberate policy of maintaining economic growth, and its correlative indexing of funds to the self-serving education of the young, must now be challenged because the elementary/secondary school system "seems hopelessly adrift."

Thomas devotes most of his attention to the imputed economic benefits of education. His analysis, along with most other analyses in this volume, indicates that the pull of economic factors, mediated through human expectations, inexorably shapes broad educational practice. The nature of his discussion precludes an elaboration of possible alternative aims of education, although he does refer to a diversity of social needs. But social needs manifest themselves through people, the mediating factor between dominant economic forces and the school system. It is Thomas's contention that people are too diverse to be satisfied with the relatively homogeneous system we have today.

Some of the ways in which at least the young differ in their approach to schooling are described by Edward Harvey in his article. Jack Quarter takes the matter a great deal further. For him, it is not only varied approaches to the training function of schools that are needed; we must also come to terms with young people's very different perception of work. By analyzing attitudinal responses he identifies a "youth revolt." Although less strident than in its early years, when it was establishing a qualitatively different set of expectations in the culture, it constitutes a potential for changes as occasion permits.

As both Quarter and Harvey note, problems of unemployment have tempered somewhat the publicly expressed dissatisfaction with education. Nevertheless, it would be rash to maintain that older perceptions of authority and of the assumed intrinsic worthiness of work have returned to the status they held in the popular mind during the 1950s.

True, many people have questioned the legitimacy of an amorphous demand for change among large segments within our culture, but few have doubted its existence. In spite of the fact that it pleases some critics to focus on a group that can be easily identified by a common element—age—it is not solely among youth that new values are emerging. Alan Thomas and Edward Harvey indicate a major concern for economic justice. Jack Quarter writes of a desire for humanism. Clive Beck brings both these intentions to the context of the classroom.

According to Beck, we have moved through the more mechanistic phases of human interaction associated with industrialization, production, and efficiency. As important as our preoccupations with predictability and allegiance to hierarchical authority were in our historical development, higher-order questions are being asked now. Value education derives from a concern for fulfillment of personal and interpersonal potential. It is not a return to individualism in its economic sense, as is often mistakenly assumed, but rather a reflection of an individual consciousness in morality. When many avenues can be pursued in an open society, which is the best and how do we know it is the best?

It is an irony that such questions could not be asked in school—and thus set the stage for greater adult introspection—until a significant portion of the adult population had abandoned a relatively uniform institutionalized response and had arrived at the level of consciousness where the questions came to the fore.

The paradox of which comes first, the school or the society, is pursued in my own article. By identifying five broad historical periods I have tried to show the changing nature of the press for change that the public has exerted upon the schools. Only for a very brief period in the 1960s was there a neglect of the moral factor. At that time an infiltrating war psychosis diverted Ontario's attention in education away from slowly evolving change in the nature of interpersonal relationships and toward the production of larger numbers of scientists and other technologists.

But we returned quickly to problems that are less amenable to quantification, problems whose very existence is legitimated or denied according to public sentiment.

We should take hope from the fact that we have arrived at the point where we are willing to resolve—or, alternatively, are unable to avoid resolving—such value problems as moral development (distinguished from religious development), sex education, and ethnic diversity. We have even acknowledged the fact that we have all played a role in keeping Canada's indigenous people repressed and out of mind.

The articles in this volume make much of the economic context as a shaper of educational events. But there is a human proclivity toward enlarging the personal sphere. Each writer has written of this antithesis, each in his own context. I see Ontario engaged in a long-term process of discussion, thinking, and debate about education. Even if this dialogue is limited by considerations of money, it will not be focused primarily on quantitive matters; as the synthesis occurs, it will speak to a quality of life for present and succeeding generations.

There is ample reason for acknowledging the assistance of people without whose help few books would ever get printed. My secretary, Ina Dumphie, has been patient and tireless, and I am grateful. Shelagh Towson and Frank Quinlan both assisted in editorial work for which there is no other kind of public recognition except in these pages. All of the authors have described similar assistance in their respective departments.

Dr. C. C. Pitt was a member of the faculty when OISE received its charter in 1965. He spent four years as Director of the Ontario College of Art and in 1975 returned to OISE to become its second director. Edward Harvey is Chairman of the Department of Sociology in Education.

George Flower was Coordinator of Graduate Studies at the inception of the Institute, but left in September 1975 to become Dean of Education of McGill University. William Alexander and John Holland are members of the faculty in the Department of Educational Planning. Alan Thomas is Chairman of the Department of Adult Education. Jack Quarter is a member of the Department of Applied Psychology.

Clive Beck, who was a member of the Department of History and Philosophy of Education when he wrote the article, is now the Coordinator of Graduate Studies. My home base is the Department of Curriculum.

Garnet L. McDiarmid

Dimensions of a Decade: Canadian Higher Education in the Sixties

Edward B. Harvey

INTRODUCTION

There are a number of reasons why it is especially appropriate to focus on the sweeping educational changes of the 1960s in Canada when one writes to honour Dr. R. W. B. Jackson. Bob Jackson was the author of studies that constituted pioneering contributions to our understanding of the educational boom that was to come in the sixties.[1] He recognized the need for providing a more adequate basis for research and development in the field of education and the postgraduate training of the highly qualified individuals who would carry on such work. The effective synthesis of these two objectives became the hallmark of the Ontario Institute for Studies in Education, the institution that Jackson was instrumental in bringing into existence, the Institute to which he gave his informed leadership for nine years. Both within and outside the Institute, Jackson was deeply involved in the development and design of education in Ontario during the turbulent but exciting decade of the sixties. It was a decade synonymous with change, both quantitative and qualitative. This essay explores a few of those changes, including the growth process itself and other associated patterns that characterized the decade, including the growing concern with equality of access, changing patterns of student politics and life styles, and the changing relationships between education and employment.

GROWTH AND DIVERSIFICATION

For the educational system of Canada, the decade of the 1960s was a period of dramatic growth and diversification. Enrolments and expenditures rose in a sharp trajectory. Teaching staffs were expanded. New universities were created and a new approach to post-secondary schooling, the community colleges, emerged. A recent publication of Statistics Canada, *Education in Canada*, observes

> ... the 1960's were indeed a period of rapid enrolment growth, especially at the Pre-grade 1, secondary and post-secondary levels. The average annual growth rate during the 1960's came to 8% for secondary and 11% for full-time post-secondary. The total full-time enrolment aggregated from Pre-grade 1 to the graduate school level increased from 4.4 million in 1960–61 to 6.4 million in 1970–71. Related to the total population, full-time students comprised 24% in 1960–61 and 30% by the end of the 1960's.
>
> In order to provide instruction to these students, whose numbers kept increasing year after year, the educational institutions expanded their teaching staff from about 175,000 to nearly 320,000. Teachers improved their academic qualifications. Billions of dollars were spent annually and in ever increasing amounts, starting at $1.7 billion in 1960 and rising to an estimated $6.6 billion by 1969 and to an estimated $7.4 billion the year after. These amounts represented 4.5% of the GNP in 1960 but 8.3 and 8.8% in the two latter years.[2]

This process of dramatic growth gave rise to many issues and problems, some of which I shall examine here. To keep the discussion within reasonable limits, the following analysis will be restricted to post-secondary education, and, within that sector, primarily to the universities. Certainly if the 1960s were a period of growth for education in general, this growth was particularly dramatic in the university sector. To again quote the Statistics Canada report,

> The total enrolment at the university level increased by 213% over the 11-year period (1961–1971) from 114,000 to 357,000. This represents an average annual growth rate of 11% which was exceeded in post-war years only by the annual growth rate of 59% between 1944–45 and 1945–46 and 25% between 1945–46 and 1946–47, when the veterans came home and flooded the universities.
>
> Clearly, the trend for the 1960's had been set in the 1950's when the university enrolment started to rise once more from a low of 63,000 in 1952–53, by which time the bulk of World War II veterans had passed through the university system. Between 1952–53 and 1960–61 there was an 81% increase in enrolment, or an average annual increase of 8%.[3]

The growth process the statistics describe was, of course, a result of a complex series of policy decisions which were a response to changing social and economic considerations. For example, the veterans' benefit programmes permitted many to attend universities who might otherwise never have gone. This served to increase in Canadian society the general levels of aspiration for higher education. As Canada continued to industrialize, there was also an obvious need to become more self-sufficient in the training and development of highly qualified human resources. In addition, the post-war baby boom created a great increase in the number of young people who would require schooling over the years to come.[4]

But rapid growth is never an unproblematic process. Rapid growth is disruptive of existing institutional arrangements. It calls for the development of new approaches, innovations, and solutions. Such processes afford as much opportunity for conflict as they do for creative problem solving. Also, although major processes of institutional change can in some measure be planned, it is doubtful if they can ever be planned perfectly. Unanticipated consequences are inevitable.

I shall discuss this decade of educational growth and change in terms of three major dimensions of the decade: the efforts to create a greater measure of equality of educational opportunity, patterns of change in student politics and life styles, and changing relationships between education and employment. These three dimensions are critical to any understanding of what happened in Canadian higher education during the decade of the sixties. Each of these dimensions presented problems without precedent and posed complex policy questions. Although each, in its own right, constitutes a major issue in Canadian higher education in the sixties, these dimensions interacted with the rapid growth of education to produce major problems. For example, as will be discussed below, the expansion of the universities contributed to the student power movement. Later in the decade, the nature of relationships between education and employment began to change as the continuing expansion of enrolments that characterized the decade produced an oversupply of graduate job seekers.

EQUALITY OF EDUCATIONAL OPPORTUNITY

Reference has been made to the billions of dollars in taxpayers' money that were poured into educational growth and diversification across Canada during the 1960s. Prior to the 1960s the higher reaches of the educational systems, notably the universities, had recruited students principally from the more privileged socio-economic strata of the nation. There were a number of considerations behind the growing concern with equality of educational access during the decade of the sixties. In part, it would have been extremely difficult to continue to justify large expenditures on education if the public felt that a very strategic part of that education, the post-secondary schools, were only open to those already privileged. In addition, in order to become nationally self-sufficient in matters of highly qualified human resources talented people regardless of class background had to be encouraged to pursue post-secondary training.

It was not until the mid-sixties, however, that government-supported loan schemes permitted students to borrow for the purposes of pursuing post-secondary education without their being required to provide parental guarantees and being liable for accrued interest on such loans until after graduation or otherwise leaving the programme.

A study paper published by the Department of University Affairs (DUA) in 1971 presented statistics to suggest that the Ontario Students Awards Programme had achieved the objective of equalizing access to post-secondary education in Ontario.[5] The argument rested upon observed similarities between the distribution of incomes in Ontario and the distribution of the parental incomes of students in post-secondary institutions. This report has been extensively criticized and justifiably so.[6] Quite apart from various methodological difficulties with the analysis, even simple controls for type of post-secondary programme (e.g., university versus community college) and sex reveal that the attainment of equality of opportunity is not as far advanced as one might hope, at least upon those dimensions.

Furthermore, attempting to remove financial barriers is only one way, and by no means a totally effective way, of increasing equality of educational opportunity. It is of course obvious that many potentially capable people from disadvantaged backgrounds do not ever reach the point where they would seek financial assistance for post-secondary schooling. Many never come to believe that post-secondary schooling is even a possibility. Such considerations inform the following discussion of alternative considerations in the equality of access issue.

Money Isn't Everything: An Alternative View of Equality of Access
This section discusses the meaning of equality of access as it pertains to post-secondary education in Ontario and presents hypotheses about alternative bases for the measurement of equality. First, I discuss some of the relevant literature on the subject. Next, from the literature, I advance an alternative model for the measurement of equality of access.

The goal of the discussion that follows is not to belittle the importance of financial aids in access to post-secondary institutions in Ontario.[7] It is, rather, to suggest that there are biases built into the discussion of financial access for both structural and functional reasons. I propose that we reconsider our goals in post-secondary education and our meaning of equality.

The emphasis on the financial factor in access to programmes of post-secondary education in the province is not the major concern only of the aforementioned DUA report. A review of the literature on access to post-secondary education in Ontario reveals that much of it deals with financial concerns.[8]

In order to deal with the broader concerns of access, I propose first to define access simply as the entry to a post-secondary institution. The difficult concept to cope with politically, theoretically, and methodologically is "equality" of access.[9] The major decision as to the meaning of "equality" is left to the policy maker who determines upon some basis the ideology of the society with regard to the meaning of equality and the philosophy of the Ministry of Education. But there is some question as to how policy makers arrive at such interpretations. Aucoin has pointed out that important policy decisions are often taken on technical bases that solve the problem without considering the philosophy lying behind it.[10] In the apparent preoccupation with equalizing the financial opportunity to enter a post-secondary institution in the province one finds a legitimate concern with a real problem, but, at the same time, the possibility of a methodological triumph buries a fundamental confusion. It is satisfying to measure and make decisions about money. Money may be fairly easily divided up and decided upon. But in many important ways, equalizing financial opportunity begs the question about equality of access to post-secondary institutions.

In order to put the question of defining equality of access into perspective, I first briefly review some literature and then offer a view of how equality of access might be approached in Ontario.

In the literature concerned with the way in which education is distributed throughout the population, one finds the broad concept of equal educational opportunity and the more specific concept of equal access to education. The former concept has been discussed from many perspectives—the approach of international comparisons,[11] and the domestic concerns of Americans and British, as evidenced in the work of Coleman[12] and Musgrave,[13] for example. Various authors have argued the necessity for equality of educational opportunity, from the ideological or philosophical foundations of the social order[14] to the economic considerations sometimes called the equality of economic opportunity.[15]

Not so frequently does one come across a definition of equal educational opportunity or a discussion of the measurement of equal educational opportunity. In his discussion of social class and education in Britain, Musgrave expresses concern for the necessity of defining equality of educational opportunity.[16] He offers the following operational definition: "Equality exists when all children of the same measured intelligence have the same chance of going to a grammar school."[17] He then points to the problems involved in the measurement of IQ, the allocation of places in grammar schools, and distribution of IQ by social class. He offers a model for the measurement of the equality of educational opportunity in any geographical area.

In America, the history of the concept of equal educational opportunity has been recently analyzed by Coleman.[18] In pointing to some of the dilemmas of defining equality of educational opportunity, Coleman clarifies two of the major sources of confusion. First, there is that confusion resulting from using inputs (curriculum, financial aid, facilities, teachers, home background, and school morale), rather than outputs (equality of results, given different inputs and the same outputs) or effects of the educational experience on the child, as the measure of success. Second, Coleman concludes that the concept of equal educational opportunity has moved from considering the educational system as the passive provider of opportunity, which the student must then take advantage of, to considering the educational system as the active element in creating an environment that reduces the inequality among students within the system. Because of the priority of racial integration in the American school system, Coleman's discussion relates primarily to the dilemma of measurement in the United States. Nonetheless, the basic question of how to define and how to measure equality of educational opportunity in Canada is informed by Coleman's analysis of the subject.

A related but much narrower problem is that of equality of access to post-secondary institutions of learning. This subject is equally open to problems of definition and measurement. There is plenty of evidence in Canada, the United Kingdom, and the United States to show that one's chances of entering post-secondary institutions vary with one's social class. These chances are narrowed at each successive educational stage from kindergarten through the college preparatory streams.[19]

A comprehensive consideration of the problem of access to post-secondary institutions in Canada has been that of Pike.[20] In his book *Who Doesn't Get to University ... And Why*, Pike considers all aspects of the problem—financial, social, and ideological. While his emphasis is upon access to universities, he discusses the other post-secondary institutions available to young people in Canada. The factors he highlights as important in the question of access are social class, geographical position in relation to the university, ethnicity, intelligence, scholastic aptitude, and performance. However, the second half of the book is devoted to the question of financial access.

In Ontario, there has been a considerable discussion of the problems of equality of access, and various proposals have been put forward to ameliorate the traditional inequalities in the system. But, as with the DUA report, the discussion somehow quickly narrows to a discussion of financial aid.[21] Mention is made of the other social and psychological factors involved in equality of access, and sometimes there is considerable discussion,[22] but money is the ultimate measure of how we are doing. It is true that there is not a great deal to be said in empirical terms about the climate of the home as it influences access to post-secondary institutions—or the influence of child-rearing and parents' education. But if the Coleman discussion of the emphasis upon the educational system as the active element in equalizing opportunity is to be taken seriously, we should be looking at other measures of equality of access besides financial aid. We can, for example, measure the success of our programmes of counseling students about educational possibilities and motivating students to aspire to certain levels of success.

The danger in ignoring the great but difficult-to-measure aspects of equality, such as those mentioned above, is that we allow a definition of equality of access in monetary terms to be thrust upon us by default by those who seek closure and would prefer to ignore all variables that are not easily quantifiable. In making this statement, I do not deny the great importance of financial aid in achieving gains in equalizing access to post-secondary institutions in Ontario, but one must recognize that financial equalization is not the only change that can be made and that financial opportunity alone is not going to tempt students into high grades in high school or into the post-secondary system.

A second danger of the emphasis upon the financial accessibility of post-secondary education is that we continually fail to reassess the changes in society in relation to access to post-secondary education. We must constantly re-examine the goals of the Ministry of Education, the needs of the labour force, and the changing aspirations and interests of young people. Only by repeatedly carrying out studies of the non-monetary aspects of equality can we assure that the educational system will be responsive to the rapid changes in contemporary Canadian society.

In proposing an approach to equality of access, I would like to suggest that the conclusions of Coleman's study of equal opportunity can be adapted to equality of access. Specifically, the educational system can be regarded as an active agent seeking to equalize the life chances of the students. To make this assertion is hardly controversial since the philosophy of financial aid has precisely that in mind. Next, one can talk about access from the point of view of inputs into the post-secondary system, as we do at the present time. Thus, we say, all those who have achieved a certain grade in secondary school may enter our universities regardless of sex, race, creed, or class. This equality through accomplishment is part of what might be called the "passive" approach of the post-secondary institutions.

Alternatively, we may take the approach of output. Here, output is used in the narrow sense of meaning who enters (is "accessed") from the secondary into the post-secondary institutions. Thus, we examine the characteristics of post-secondary students to see who has actually come when offered the chance. This second approach is comparable to Coleman's definition of equality of opportunity as the equality of results, given different inputs.

I propose that the second approach is preferable in the contemporary climate of post-secondary education in Ontario. However equality of educational opportunity or equality of access is conceptualized, it must in the last resort be specific to the society to which it pertains. The major parameters of equality of opportunity in Ontario involve the recognition of bilingualism, a variety of ethnicities, region, and urban–rural differences.

How, then, should we measure equality of access here? First, we should measure it in terms of outputs as defined above. That is, we should examine the characteristics of our students to see how representative they are of Canadian society. Then, since we can only slowly correct the various stages in the educational system that have built inequality into a student's chances of even being in a position to apply to a post-secondary institution, we should define equality of access *operationally* as having a proportional representation of students based on the measurement of certain relevant characteristics of our society.

What should be regarded as relevant characteristics for the Ontario population? While financial backing may be one important characteristic, I suggest that others are more viable both theoretically and methodologically.

First, the sex of the student should be an important characteristic. It has been known for some time that women perform at least as well as men in secondary school and are, indeed, more likely to finish high school, but they are under-represented in post-secondary institutions.[23] Thus I propose that a number of places be kept in the post-secondary institutions proportional to the sex ratio in Canada in the relevant age groups. Certain patterns of differential accessibility to both post-secondary education in general and to some programmes in particular may be obscured if a control for sex is not made. Not only do the sexes enter different segments of the occupational structure and thus prepare through different means for their careers, but different values are placed upon educating men and women in our society. Increasingly, however, women enter the labour force both before and after child-rearing, and if we are to discuss seriously access to education, differential access on the basis of sex is of some importance.[24] If equality is our aim, then the sex variable is a clear case where inequalities can be redressed.

Second, some characteristics of socio-economic background should be a basis for admission. The measure now is often family income. While this might be retained, I also propose a less labile variable more indicative of the cultural opportunities of the atmosphere in which the child grew up. There are two measures that are highly suitable. One is ethnicity and the other is parents' education.[25] The first measure has been shown to be important in the famous Carnegie Study of Identification and Utilization of Talent in High School and College.[26] Ethnic background was shown to be a crucial factor in retention in the educational system in Ontario. This subject was taken further in the report of the Royal Commission on Bilingualism and Biculturalism.[27] It has also been shown in studies in the United States that different ethnic groups have different patterns of mental ability that might be maximized by the educational system.[28] The second measure, which we pursue further, is the education of the child's parents. Pike[29] and the Report of the Subcommittee[30] have commented on the importance of this variable in the development of the child's motivation to enter post-secondary institutions and indeed to participate in the educational process at all.

While education and occupation are highly correlated,[31] and are therefore useful in combination as an indicator of social class, they are best considered separately as indicators of values held by groups in the society with regard to specific behaviours. In this regard, the support (both economic and psychological) of children in post-secondary education is likely to relate more to the educational level of parents than to their income. For example, as Porter has pointed out, clergy and some other professionals such as teachers and social workers are highly educated and receive low incomes.[32] They have indicated by their occupational choice that they value education more than income, and their children are likely to be influenced by such values. Using father's education as an indicator of socio-economic background not only reflects the family's values with regard to education better, but also indicates something much more pragmatic. Children of parents who have been through the educational system are more likely to know how to enter post-secondary education. Children of parents who have not (and this category would include many immigrants to Canada) have to learn from peers and counselors at school.[33] Access to many post-secondary programmes depends on some very early decisions about courses, streams, one's future in the labour force, and so on. In sum, we would argue that, especially in light of the student award programmes, parents' education is a most suitable measure of socio-economic background.

Both ethnicity and parents' education are rather easily measured characteristics—especially parents' education, which seldom changes throughout the life span. While the number of years of education does not mean the same thing from province to province or country to country, the task of assessment is not an impossible one. Those studying admissions to graduate schools have established equivalencies between the education offered in most of the countries of the world.[34]

But, you argue, what about intelligence? Is that not the most important factor and should not the most intelligent have the first opportunity to benefit by higher education? The studies of financial accessibility assume that the intelligence factor has been taken care of in the entrance procedure.[35] I argue that intelligence, if defined by the IQ test and performance in school (and, in the last resort, the latter), is biased in the direction of the middle and upper classes—a situation that will *never* lead to equality of access.[36]

What is being suggested here, therefore, is that students be allowed into post-secondary institutions, first, on the basis of proportional representation by sex, class, as measured by parents' education, and ethnicity, and second, on the basis of intelligence, by which I mean that those who achieve the best academic results in each of the groups selected according to the first criteria be chosen; third, after this selection process has taken place, we should equalize financial access by a process of loans, bursaries, and other types of assistance.

The reasons for putting forward this admittedly unrefined and one-sided proposal is that there is good reason to believe that an individual's chances of being admitted to post-secondary education in Ontario (and thus his life chances) are affected as deeply by his sex, ethnicity, and parents' education as by intelligence or ability to pay. I am, in effect, arguing for the development of a more quantitatively varied basis for the development of policies related to educational opportunity and access.

Let us now turn to an exploration of a second major dimension that assumed important proportions in many universities in Canada, as in the United States and Europe: the emergence of militant student politics and more general shifts in the life styles and values of students.

STUDENT POLITICS AND LIFE STYLES

While the decade of the sixties was one of growth and diversification for every aspect of Canadian education, for the universities, in particular, it was a time of turbulence and conflict.

The growth of the student power movement was a major theme of American university life during the 1960s. Although the form taken by the movement in Canada was perhaps more circumscribed, the rising voice of students demanding a part in university government was also a major theme in many Canadian universities during the decade.[37]

It is hardly surprising that the 1960s witnessed growing pressures for university reform. The essentially traditional organization of universities was buffeted by growing waves of enrolment, by emerging demands for relevance and accountability, by growing numbers of migrant professors, who sometimes brought with them new and often different political ideals, and by major changes in the composition and outlooks of the student population. Indeed, given the heretofore sheltered existence of most Canadian universities and the magnitude of the changes that affected them during the 1960s, it may be speculated that the form and scope of change and conflict on the campus was really relatively mild.

In addition to the student power movement, the sixties also witnessed a more generally pervasive youth-based cultural movement or, to use the term by which it has been described, "the counter-culture movement."[38] The counter-cultures (for there were a number of variants) constituted a questioning of many aspects of middle-class life styles and norms in many parts of life and experience: sexuality, the use of drugs, norms of dress, material versus spiritual possessions, and so on. It is an oversimplification to label these patterns of social and cultural change "the hippie life style," but that is a term that was not uncommonly used to describe the new values and behaviours. In general, these new values and behaviours (new to most of their proponents, at least) permeated the general style of youth during the sixties. In some cases, and most often in the context of the universities, the new life style was accompanied by radical politics as a way of giving particularly urgent definition to the critique of middle-class values and the *status quo* implied in various of the accompanying behaviours.

Before turning to a more detailed exploration of some of the factors associated with the emergence and growth of university student power and politics, as well as with the more general changes in life styles and values, I emphasize that the patterns of social and cultural change described above are *particularly* likely to produce turbulence in institutions, such as universities, that are in large part inhabited by young people, for young people undergo major psychological and social transformations, which are reflected in such patterned phenomena as identity crises and generational conflicts.

Identity Crises and Generational Conflicts
In his writings on the life cycle, Erik Erikson has argued that as individuals progress through life there are a series of critical points at which unfolding psycho-physiological capabilities intersect with and must adapt to the surrounding socio-cultural environment.[39] One such critical developmental point is the period of adolescence, which in terms of his life-cycle approach Erikson analyses through his conception of the identity crisis. Obviously, the adolescent is neither child nor adult. In the adolescent, sexual capability has emerged, as has the capacity for work, yet there is still a high degree of indeterminacy with regard to what such adolescents will ultimately do in terms of occupation or family formation. In modern and industrial societies, in particular, adolescence provides a relatively unstructured period during which different roles and life plans can be experimented with. This is clearly at variance with traditional societies, where *rites de passage* typically mark an abrupt transition point from child status to adult status.[40]

But if there are marked differences between industrial and traditional societies in this regard, there are also sources of variation in the socio-cultural context of industrialized societies that hold implications for the identity-crisis period. Some industrial societies, such as Britain and France, are characterized by a fairly high degree of specification with regard to the societal expectations held of the adolescent.[41] These expectations do not take the form of amorphous ideologies, but rather are built directly into the very fabric of major social institutions, such as the family, educational system, and occupational structure.

In Canada these societal expectations are less explicitly specified. Here, a less structured socio-cultural context creates special anxieties associated with the period of adolescence. It also serves to facilitate a much wider range of behaviours and role experimentation, which indeed, as recent history suggests, includes experimentation with and the adoption of political and social alternatives divergent from those of a previous generation. In effect, then, we are arguing that the period of the identity crisis lends itself to the types of processes we imply when discussing student politics and life styles.

The identity-crisis perspective is perhaps a somewhat psychological way of looking at the issues we are examining here. However, much the same type of process is noted by those writers who have observed the manifestation of generational crises in industrial societies.[42] The rapid rates of technological change associated with such societies exacerbate differences of life styles, values, and perceptions on an age-specific basis. Generational differences in life styles or perceptions of the world can provide important foundations for widely varying political and social ideologies and practices.

I now examine some socio-cultural patterns of the sixties that, in my view, were influential factors *vis-à-vis* the emergence of new forms of student patterns and life styles.

The Affluent Student
The students born during the "baby-boom" who went on to higher education during the decade of the sixties lived during a period of relative affluence in Canada. During this period the Canadian economy continued to enjoy growth and buoyancy. Among the results was an increasing level of affluence. These conditions of affluence wrought subtle changes in the types of attitudes people held toward life and work. Those young people who went on to higher education were less likely to feel pressured to enter the labour force quickly and start to earn a living. Even the very process of pursuing higher education started to serve goals other than occupational preparation. Higher education represented a route to a good job for the returned veteran of World War 2, but it was more likely to represent a means of finding one's self and meaning in life for the "baby-boom" student. The pursuit of education became less instrumental; that is, education became less a means to other goals and more an end in itself.

The curricula of many colleges and universities reflected this change. Courses concerned with general and perhaps somewhat amorphous goals, such as self-realization, grew in number. Student choice of programmes reflected a similar trend away from programmes more specifically geared to vocational or professional preparation and toward courses that promised understanding of self or the society in which we live. Not surprisingly, it was a period when social science enrolments burgeoned.

Issues and Alternatives
The decade of the sixties in North America witnessed a substantial amount of social questioning and upheaval, much of which involved, in one way or another, college and university students. Although the following issues were stronger and more polarizing in the United States than in Canada, as issues they enjoyed a certain legitimacy and urgency for some sectors of the population in both countries.

During the first half of the 1960s, the great issues of civil rights and America's involvement in Viet Nam emerged and assumed critical proportions in the rising consciousness of many young people. The inconsistencies of urban poverty and racial strife at a time when billions expended on a distant war in Viet Nam could no longer be reconciled in terms of ideologies that assumed a high degree of uncritical patriotism. Civil rights and Viet Nam became critical issues, in terms of which college and university students of the sixties put the life styles and value commitments of their middle- and upper-middle-class parents to the test. On campuses in the United States, organizations such as the SDS (Students for a Democratic Society) provided the necessary organizational infrastructures for university students' concerted efforts at altering the political process. Such campus organizations spread to Canada. During this period, being a campus radical emerged as a distinct and viable life style in its own right.[43] As the number and form of campus political structures proliferated, a widening range of related life styles and values emerged.

In addition to the emergence of the politicized campus, the early sixties also witnessed the emergence of counter-culture patterns revolving around the use of psychedelic drugs, rock music, and Eastern religions. In concrete terms there was often a substantial amount of overlap between the "political" and "psychedelic" life styles. It appears useful to recognize, however, that different degrees of *commitment* to one or the other existed for many young people.

Anomie and Mass Institutions
The burgeoning enrolments in universities and colleges that characterized the decade of the sixties exerted enormous pressure on the carrying capacities existing in educational facilities. During earlier times, the characteristic form assumed by most Canadian universities was the medium-sized or small liberal arts college. Research has shown that closer faculty–student links exist in institutions of this type than in large institutions, where size generates a considerable degree of impersonality. The close degree of faculty–student contact in small or medium-sized liberal arts colleges facilitated the development of faculty as strong role models and as effective sources of social control in the lives of young students. The result was the development of a relatively more conservative student body, with values or beliefs more closely in line with such traditional academic norms as the acquisition of knowledge, as opposed to, say, concerns with political organization or attending demonstrations.

However, the burgeoning enrolments of the sixties exerted pressure for the creation of larger and larger institutions.[44] In addition, the continuing "knowledge explosion" exerted pressure for continuing departmentalization and specialization within colleges and universities and their faculties. It was also during this period that demands for the services of faculty as specialized consultants became more widespread, thus affording such faculty more prestigious and remunerative means of developing their careers than serving as social control agents and role models *vis-à-vis* students. Moreover, during this period in Canada, the institutions where higher education could be pursued came to be more often located in urban centres, or the urban centres they were already located in became larger. These various factors may be seen as coalescing to produce what might be called the multiversity syndrome —that is, large enrolments, a greater emphasis on highly specialized research rather than on teaching, and a tendency to locate higher educational facilities in urban areas.[45] It might further be argued that multiversities are characterized by weak links between faculty and students, therefore offering a weak role model or social control function and generating a high degree of anomie among the students themselves.

Kornhauser has pointed out how mass society conditions arise when meaningful patterns of association break down between individuals.[46] Under conditions of mass society, each individual is atomized, cut off from meaningful social relationships with others, and in consequence lacks the socially reinforced basis for a critical exchange of ideas and opinions in a number of areas, most importantly, in the realm of political beliefs and action. The atomized individual living under conditions of mass society loses his critical capability and becomes more easily mobilized for a wide variety of political purposes. We suggest that many students attending universities in the decade of the sixties suffered from such a state of organizationally induced anomie and were casting about for alternatives or paths of action that could create meaning in a highly normless situation.

The search for alternatives and rejection of the existing order at times took the form of violent protest. Indeed, the issue of campus unrest during the sixties was considered sufficiently important in the United States that a detailed study of the phenomenon was made by the Carnegie Commission on Higher Education.[47] One of the findings of this commission was that, particularly where violent disruptions are concerned, the larger the university or college the greater the propensity for demonstrations to take this form. In Canada, sit-ins occurred, and at one university, a computer installation was wrecked by demonstrators. Commissions were formed to review and reconstruct university government.[48]

The active campus radicals of the sixties represented a relatively small proportion of the total student population. How could such a relatively small group come to exercise such a powerful influence over campus political life during the sixties? The answer consists at least in part in the fact that the conditions of anomie and mass society just described fostered a search for answers among many students. Radical campus politics promised to provide both answers and social change.

As students became more politicized and more conscious of their powers, they successfully demanded a greater role in developing priorities for and the governing of the university. A major result was the proliferation of committees that further complicated an already highly complex and departmentalized structure. A political style, however, was established. When crisis loomed, a stock response became that of establishing a committee to deal with the crisis. Crises that would shatter a traditional liberal arts college were handled with relative equanimity within the multiversity. It was as if the multiversity became an organizational Titanic, with complex multi-constituency committees serving as the air pockets that would keep the enterprise afloat.

The complex multi-constituency decision-making apparatus of today's multiversity represents a response, at least in part, to demands for more democratic decision-making structures. Yet in some important respects the demands have been self-defeating. Complex committee structures often generate stasis rather than real action. Power is not infrequently retained by means of administrative subterfuge; committees appear to make decisions but in reality serve only to ratify that which has already been decided elsewhere; in other cases, issues are simply shifted further up the line to less representative organizational levels.

Extended Adolescence

As societies become more industrialized, demands for specialized training before entering the labour force increase. In addition, technological and industrial societies have less need for the unskilled or semi-skilled workman engaged in direct primary activities, such as agriculture, labouring, mining, fishing, and so on. The nature of the industrial occupational structure and the skill requirements associated with it serve to keep young people in school for increasingly longer periods of time. Thus is extended the "moratorium" period, during which the process of identity formation is explored. This process, of course, is most pronounced among those young people who pursue extended periods of post-secondary education.

The period of identity formation has both psychological and sociological components. In psychological terms, different self-conceptions are explored and experimented with. Sociologically, a greater range of responsibilities and involvement is adopted, typically in the areas of employment and family formation. At some point in time, these psychological and sociological dimensions converge, more or less, and the adolescent enters a relatively greater period of role crystallization as a young adult. Research studies have illustrated the politically conservatizing effect of age, which is generally associated with increased occupational and family responsibilities that typically involve individuals in more constricting normative frameworks.

Colleges and universities have traditionally been places where, among other things, the norms and values of society could be questioned. During the sixties there emerged in the universities a much wider range of political and social movements critical of such norms and values. There was a growing population of energetic and questioning students who were yet to enter a phase of greater role crystallization. There were issues of great international and national significance, and alternative life styles and value systems were in the process of being forged. The essence of the extended adolescence pattern is that *more* students were engaging in this kind of activity *further into* the life cycle. Extended adolescence is perhaps best defined as a grey area with indeterminate beginning and end points sandwiched between "adolescence" and "adulthood." As Canadian society continues to evolve into a post-industrial state, the period of post-adolescence will undoubtedly be further extended.

The burgeoning character of enrolments during the sixties would have been, in its own right, an important source of institutional change in the universities. However, the impact of growth and expansion was magnified by the presence of other important coalescent factors. We have mentioned that many university students of the 1960s had different values from their predecessors, particularly with regard to the perceived purpose of university education. "Self-exploration" became a more important objective for many than "training." General conditions of affluence made such a position more realistic. The American war in Viet Nam, in particular, served as a major "carrier issue" that brought into sharp focus the questioning of authority that characterized many students during this period. The university as a social organization was undergoing major changes in size, composition, and objectives. In consequence, many of the management problems associated with the operation of large and complex organizations were being confronted for the first time. The new arrangements for university government, the new ground rules for political participation, had to be worked out, often in a turbulent setting, often without precedents or models.

I now turn to the final major dimension of higher education in the sixties to be considered here: the changing relationships between education and employment.

EDUCATION AND EMPLOYMENT

In the initial section on growth and diversification, we noted various of the factors underlying the dramatic expansion of Canadian education during the 1960s. Particularly in the case of the growth and diversification of higher education, policy initiatives for expansion were to a significant degree motivated by considerations of making Canada more self-sufficient in terms of the supply of highly qualified human resources. Within the framework of human capital theory, it was argued that investment in education would provide the highly qualified human resources essential for economic growth.[49] The benefits realized from such economic growth would constitute the return on investment.

While I stress the importance of human capital theory for the expansion and diversification of Canadian higher education, I do not intend to minimize the significance of demographic factors—that is, the baby-boom children, who exerted an increasing demand for educational services—or the fact that generally increasing levels of affluence and aspirations expanded the potential market for the consumption of higher education. However, the notion of investment in human resources for the stimulation of economic development remained the major set of principles, in terms of which major policy decisions for the expansion and diversification of higher education were rationalized.

By 1968, however, there were growing indications that university graduates were experiencing greater difficulty in securing the relatively desirable sorts of jobs that earlier graduating cohorts had secured.[50] It was around 1968 and in the years immediately following that the growing supply of university undergraduate degree holders collided with some rather harsh facts about the Canadian occupational structure. The basic problem was that the major expansion of higher education during the first two-thirds of the 1960s had produced many more young people seeking entry-level jobs in the upper echelons of the occupational structure than there were jobs available. Given the ubiquitous nature of scarcity, no society can pursue job creation policies to artificially sustain demand. Indeed, as economic conditions gradually worsened toward the end of the sixties and unemployment was on the rise, university graduates were by no means the population of greatest concern to policy makers. In sum, there was only so much elasticity in the Canadian occupational structure, and by 1968 the supply of university graduates was beginning to exceed demand, particularly in the category of general arts and science graduates. The economic downturn that characterized this period served to further suppress demand.

The same set of patterns were observed in the United States. However, the large population of that country means that, in terms of developing a viable tax base, the American middle class need not be as stringently taxed as its Canadian counterpart. A major consequence of this is a greater availability of disposable income, which often finds its way into the consumption of a broad range of services. The demand for such services has been reflected in the proliferation of semi-professional service occupations in the United States for which, in many cases, there are no exact counterparts in Canada. How many Canadians, for example, can afford to send their pet to a pet psychiatrist?

When job markets are poor for university graduates in the United States and Canada, both groups will find themselves forced to accept jobs below their expectations. For the reasons just alluded to, however, the Canadians are likely to experience a fall that is longer and harder in terms of occupational position.

As the job prospects for university graduates generally worsened during the latter part of the 1960s and into the 1970s, a number of associated patterns emerged. During the first two-thirds of the sixties, the ideology that "education pays" was obviously accepted by a large proportion of the students who swelled the enrolments of university and community colleges across Canada. By the end of the decade and the beginning of the seventies, negative feedback from the labour market was making itself felt and enrolments, while still increasing, did so at a much slower rate. Clearly, a greater proportion of potential students were questioning whether or not the investment in education was really worthwhile when weighed against the prospects of forgone wages, uncertain job opportunities, and the attractive possibility of other experiences such as travel. New terms were added to the educators' vocabulary, including "stop-out" and "drop-out."[51] The uncertainty or absence of clearly defined goals at the end of the educational process led an increasing proportion of students to question the necessity of moving through their programmes in a straight line. A year or two out, possibly more, was an eminently reasonable strategy in the circumstances. For educational administrators, of course, the new patterns created havoc in attempts to forecast enrolment-contingent revenues.

It may be safely estimated that politicians concerned with unemployment statistics welcomed these developments. First, they served to stem the growing supply of graduates experiencing labour market difficulties. Second, students who were travelling around North America, Europe, Africa, Asia, and so on were not recorded on the unemployment rolls. Still, there were graduates who chose to remain at home and seek jobs, this taking place during a period of general employment difficulties for many categories of manpower. It was interesting to note around this period subtle changes in norms relating to attitudes about the counter-culture or alternative life styles referred to in an earlier section. Unemployed or otherwise disgruntled university graduates represent a potential political threat in any society.

Programmes such as Opportunities for Youth and the Local Initiatives Program represented highly effective strategies to build upon the new ethic of "do your own thing" prevalent among many young people. Instead of simply decrying the counter-cultures and alternative life styles, new initiatives emerged in an effort to effectively co-opt such patterns to what was deemed to be constructive activity. The Opportunities for Youth programme is a good example. Young people could exercise a considerable measure of autonomy in the design and management of projects for which they were paid by government; however, sophisticated use was made of peer-control techniques in the evaluation and approval of such projects and their subsequent supervision. In many respects OFY and LIP were sophisticated adaptations of more traditional "make-work" programmes.

Another pattern emerging out of changed relationships between education and employment, particularly in the higher education sector, is seen in the growth of nationalist sentiments in Canadian society.[52] In the case of Canadian universities, during the period of rapid expansion and growth, escalating requirements for professorial manpower had to be met through a reliance on foreign-born migrants. Migrants typically tend to be younger individuals in the early processes of family formation. A large proportion of the migrant professors who came to Canadian universities during this period were no exception. With academic conventions such as tenure, the large proportion of such individuals more or less have a lifetime of guaranteed employment in Canadian universities ahead of them. This situation did not create much concern, nor was it indeed even noticed during the period of rapid growth, expansion, and, of course, substantial labour market mobility.

With the contraction of such growth and expansion in the seventies, labour markets for highly qualified manpower have become far less elastic and entry-level jobs are increasingly hard to come by.

It is generally true that the careers of the highly qualified are developed in institutional settings. It is difficult to be a teacher without a school, a professor without a university, a research scientist without a laboratory. In the past, the universities provided the typical employment contexts for such individuals. Now that the brakes are being applied on further university growth and expansion and most of the existing positions are filled by individuals with little incentive or few opportunities to move, the career development prospects for many graduates have become bleak indeed. In the circumstances, it is not highly surprising that when academic appointments do become available in Canada nowadays, greater effort is made to locate qualified Canadians. It is also true that increased hiring in the public sector is creating alternative career lines for a number of graduates. However, it should be pointed out that there has been a substantial hiatus between the diminishment of university-related opportunities and the emergence of these new prospects. In addition, as we suggested earlier, there is undoubtedly an upward limit on the number of university graduates who can be absorbed into the Canadian occupational structure of to-day at the levels of employment they might have anticipated a decade ago, given, of course, the much smaller supply.

Under these sorts of circumstances it is evident that the job and career expectations of university graduates will change. However, such a process of change is by no means automatic, particularly when there are strong historical precedents. When a graduate of 1971 experiences great difficulty in getting a job and is aware of the fact that a graduate of 1967 secured the same sort of job easily, the tendency is not to simply adjust one's expectations downward, however inevitable that process may be, but rather to feel let down, to feel that somehow "the system has failed."

These patterns also have implications for the financing of higher education. The fees paid by students actually cover only a small proportion of the total expense involved in the operation of a modern university. In the past, substantial public subsidies required by such institutions were justified on the basis that graduates contributed to national economic growth and that the generally higher incomes they would earn would bring an adequate return, by way of income taxes, on investment. Although the data on changing rates of return are still sketchy, there are some indications that the rates of return on some forms of higher education are declining.[53] This would particularly be the case for general arts and science graduates, who still constitute a large proportion of the total population of university graduates. This situation implies some complex policy questions.

On the one hand, should such education increasingly be viewed as a consumption rather than an investment good, with the associated expectation that students will bear an increased portion of the costs or indeed even assume the total cost? Also, if this expectation became a policy, how would it relate to other goals of higher education, such as the provision of a mechanism for equalizing opportunity?

On the other hand, should higher education be viewed as yielding tangible benefits to the society through producing individuals who are more flexible, more able to solve their problems on their own, more keenly aware of and committed to their citizenship responsibilities? It goes without saying that these kinds of benefits are infinitely harder to measure in any systematic way, compared, for example, to the measurement of income returns on investment in education. Still, it seems reasonable to assert that higher education is not simply a consumption good and that it is an important policy priority to develop the sorts of social indicators and systems of social indicators that would permit a more effective assessment of the non-economic returns on educational investment.[54]

REFLECTIONS AND FORECASTS

As one reflects upon the evolution of higher education during the decade of the sixties, a scenario of inter-related policy events begins to emerge. Initially, policies to expand and diversify post-secondary education were informed by human capital theory and demographic pressures. As post-secondary education expanded and diversified, and took an increasingly large share of the tax dollar, it became essential to diversify the base of recruitment to such institutions in order to attract the most talented individuals, regardless of their socio-economic origin, and in order to ensure that reasonable norms of social justice were being observed. The need to encourage talented migrants to staff the newly emerging post-secondary programmes was reflected in the rising pay scales for university professors during the 1960s and the liberal tax concessions for those who chose to come to Canada to teach. All of these policy initiatives were related to the growth phase of post-secondary education.

By 1968 there were growing indications that the expansion was beginning to overshoot its goals. Graduates were experiencing more employment difficulties, and the public was beginning to become restive over ever-increasing educational expenditures. Dissent and disruption on the campuses further complicated the matter. Just as policies can be developed to "wind up" a system, policies can be developed to wind it down. University building grants were frozen. A greater proportion of the fiscal burden of post-secondary education was transferred to students in the form of fee increases. Programmes such as Opportunities for Youth and the Local Initiatives Program were designed in an attempt to alleviate some of the pressures being created by graduate unemployment. Subsequently, stronger guidelines designed to orient recruiting activities toward the search for qualified Canadians were issued by government agencies and reinforced by university administrations. But now there were few openings.

It is of course easy in retrospect to identify the many planning failures in the expansion of post-secondary education during the sixties. It is not difficult to note that many of the decisions taken were ad hoc and that more could have been done to develop systems models to guide forward planning and decision making. However, it must also be observed that one of the major reasons for post-secondary educational expansion in Canada during the sixties was precisely to generate domestically the sorts of highly qualified human resources that would increase the planning capabilities of the nation.

This essay has served only to set forth some of the major dimensions associated with the growth and expansion of Canadian post-secondary education during the sixties. This period deserves further and more intensive historical analysis, particularly from the point of view of identifying the kinds of mechanisms and thinking involved in major policy decisions. Such a critical appraisal of decisions is essential to learn more, at a theoretical level, about how institutional change is orchestrated in Canadian society and, at a pragmatic level, about how future processes of institutional change may be better planned and more adequately executed. In view of what has just been said, it is obviously risky to offer forecasts about the future of post-secondary education in Canada. The following seem to be among the more likely.

The debate over post-secondary education as a consumption good or as an investment good will undoubtedly continue. New data sets are available in Canada which will permit a more rigorous and current assessment of the change in relationships between education, occupation, and income.[55] However, learning more about these relationships will not resolve the contentious issues involved. On the investment side of the argument, it will probably have to be conceded that certain varieties of post-secondary education do not make much by way of a direct contribution to national economic development. It remains to be seen whether or not viable indicators of social benefit can be evolved and put to meaningful use in connection with the planning and policy-making process. On the consumption side, there is obviously much room for structural change and innovation. The "open sector" discussed in the report of the Commission on Post-Secondary Education in Ontario represents an important arena in which new forms of post-secondary education can be explored.[56] We will undoubtedly see increasing emphasis on the elimination or minimization of the need for antecedent credentials in many programmes. Individuals from all walks of life and age groups will be encouraged to have more to do with post-secondary educational experiences, but in much broader and more divergent settings than the traditional university setting of the 1950s.

Still, there will be a continuous need for the preparation of highly qualified human resources in the post-secondary sector. It is well known that supply and demand fluctuations can be rather sharp where highly qualified human resources are concerned. To suggest only one example among many, a 1971 report of the Science Council of Canada underscored what appeared to be a growing oversupply of engineers.[57] In 1974 the Science Council held a symposium in Thunder Bay to discuss what now appears to be an increasing undersupply of engineers. There is probably no resolution for such fluctuations. However, one clear set of implications is the need to develop more precise linkages, where highly qualified and specialized human resources are concerned, between the outputs of the educational system and the requirements of the labour market. Improved systems of occupational information for use in career guidance represents one important way of gaining greater control over such linkages.

It can be suggested that post-secondary education can serve as a mechanism for achieving three general goals in a society: economic development, equality of opportunity, and general social and cultural development. Prior to the expansion of the sixties, Canadian higher education tended to provide social and cultural development for the few. As for the expansion, this was extensively justified in terms of the potential contributions to national economic development. The concern with equality of opportunity appears to have followed somewhat later in the decade. Toward the end of the decade, a number of commissions were held across Canada to reconsider the form and objectives of higher education. Of the many recommendations emanating from these commissions, a repeated theme was the desirability of making the experiences of higher education available in a non-sequential way, offering the prospect of lifetime learning to a broad spectrum of citizens within a broad and flexible set of institutional arrangements. There is still a clear and important place for the academic specialization required to produce highly qualified human resources for specific fields of endeavour. But, increasingly, important emphasis has come to be placed on the goal of social and cultural development with, however, a most significant difference: in the post-1960s world of higher education in Canada this objective is directed toward the many, not the few.

NOTES

1. *The Atkinson Study of Utilization of Student Resources*, Report submitted to the National Conference of Canadian Universities, June 5, 1958 (Toronto: Department of Educational Research, Ontario College of Education, University of Toronto,

1958); *Educational Research in Canada: Today and Tomorrow*, Quance Lecture in Canadian Education, 1961 (Toronto: W. J. Gage, 1962); "Supply of Teachers for Ontario Secondary Schools—15 Lean Years," *School Guidance Worker*, vol. 9 (May 1954): 32–33; (with W. G. Fleming), "Tomorrow's Leaders: A Search for Talent," *Canadian Education*, vol. 11 (March 1956): 3–16; "Critical Problems in Education in Ontario: Address to the Toronto Board of Education—May 21st, 1959," *The Argus* (June 1959): 217–25; and "A New Era: Its Implications and Challenges" (address to the Board of Christian Education, United Church of Canada, 1964).

2. Statistics Canada, *Education in Canada: A Statistical Review for the Period 1960–61 to 1970–71* (Ottawa: Information Canada, 1973), pp. 16–17.

3. Ibid., p. 57.

4. For an expanded discussion, see Edward B. Harvey, "Canadian Higher Education and the Seventies," *Interchange*, vol. 5, no. 2 (1974), pp. 42–43 especially.

5. Department of University Affairs, Research Branch, "Accessibility—1970" (unpublished paper, Oct. 1, 1970), reported by W. Johnson in "Gap between the Rich, Poor, in University May Be Closing," *Toronto Globe and Mail*, 15 October 1970.

6. For a summary of other criticisms and the author's own critique, see Lorna Marsden and Edward B. Harvey, "Equality of Educational Access Reconsidered: The Post-Secondary Case in Ontario," *Interchange*, vol. 2, no. 4 (1971): 11–26. Parts of this paper have been reproduced in the present article. See, in particular, Marsden and Harvey, pp. 15–19.

7. See, in particular, W. E. Kalbach and W. W. McVey, *The Demographic Bases of Canadian Society* (Toronto: McGraw-Hill, 1971), pp. 204–211.

8. See, for convenience, the bibliographies of the Council of Ontario Universities' *Accessibility and Student Aid* (Toronto: COU, 1971) and R. Pike's *Who Doesn't Get to University . . . And Why* (Ottawa: Association of Universities and Colleges of Canada, 1970), and the footnotes to "Social Class and Educational Opportunity," in John Porter, *The Vertical Mosaic: An Analysis of Social Class and Power in Canada* (Toronto: University of Toronto Press, 1965), ch. 6.

9. It should be pointed out that the policy of the Ontario government has been described as "universal accessibility, qualified by such concepts as academic achievement and a willingness to undertake at least partial personal financial responsibility." (COU, *Accessibility*, p. 9.)

10. P. Aucoin, "Theory and Research in the Study of Policy Making," in *The Structures of Policy Making in Canada*, ed. G. B. Doern and P. Aucoin (Toronto: Macmillan of Canada, 1971), p. 14.

11. See, for example, F. Bowles, *Access to Higher Education*, vol. 1 (Liège: Unesco and International Association of Universities, 1963); B. Fletcher, *Universities in the Modern World* (Toronto: Pergamon Press, 1968); C. A. Anderson, "Access to Higher Education and Economic Development," in *Education, Economy and Society*, ed. A. H. Halsey, J. Floud, and C. A. Anderson (New York: Free Press, 1961), pp. 252–68.

12. J. S. Coleman et al., *Equality of Educational Opportunity* (Washington, D.C.: U.S. Government Printing Office, 1966).

13. P. W. Musgrave, *The Sociology of Education* (London: Methuen, 1965).

14. For example, see Fletcher, *Universities*, and Coleman, *Equality*.

15. For example, Anderson, "Access to Higher Education"; N. Rogoff, "American Public Schools and Equality of Opportunity," in *Education, Economy and Society*,

pp. 140-47; C. Jencks and D. Riesman, *The Academic Revolution* (Garden City, N.Y.: Doubleday, 1968).

16. Musgrave, *Sociology of Education*.

17. Ibid., p. 76.

18. J. S. Coleman, "The Concept of Equality of Educational Opportunity," *Harvard Educational Review*, vol. 38 (1968): 7-22.

19. For a discussion of the process in the United States and United Kingdom, see R. Turner's famous article, "Modes of Ascent through Education: Sponsored and Contest Mobility," reprinted in *Education, Economy and Society*, pp. 121-39; for a description of the process in Canada, see Pike, *Who Doesn't Get*, part 1, and Porter, *Vertical Mosaic*.

20. See also J. Porter, "Social Class and Education," in *Social Purpose for Canada*, ed. M. Oliver (Toronto: University of Toronto Press, 1961).

21. See COU, *Accessibility*, pp. 6-9.

22. See, for example, Porter, "Social Class," and Pike, *Who Doesn't Get*.

23. See Porter, *Vertical Mosaic*, p. 155ff.

24. Sylvia Ostry is the chief author of studies of women in the labour force in Canada. For a summary, see "Labour Force Participation and Child-Bearing Status," in *Demography and Educational Planning*, ed. Betty MacLeod (Toronto: Ontario Institute for Studies in Education, 1970), pp. 143-56.

25. Whereas combined family income is likely to fluctuate over time (for example, females leave the labour force to raise children), units of education once earned remain constant. P. M. Blau and O. D. Duncan in their study *The American Occupational Structure* (New York: Wiley, 1967) find that 27 percent of the variance in college attendance is explained by father's education.

26. Eight bulletins by various authors (Toronto: Department of Educational Research, Ontario College of Education, University of Toronto, 1959-1964).

27. Report of the Royal Commission on Bilingualism and Biculturalism, vol. 2, *Education* (Ottawa: Queen's Printer, 1968).

28. G. Lesser and S. S. Stodolsky, "Learning Patterns in the Disadvantaged," *Harvard Educational Review*, vol. 37 (1967): 546-93.

29. Pike, *Who Doesn't Get*, ch. 7.

30. COU, *Accessibility*.

31. Porter, *Vertical Mosaic*, p. 160ff. See also C. Jencks, "Social Stratification and Higher Education," *Harvard Educational Review*, vol. 38 (1968): 277-316.

32. Porter, *Vertical Mosaic*, p. 174.

33. For further evidence, see Kalbach and McVey, *Demographic Bases*, p. 211.

34. See, for example, M. Sasnett and I. Sepmeyer, *Educational Systems of Africa* (Berkeley: University of California Press, 1966); it includes "interpretations for use in the evaluation of academic credentials." Those involved in evaluating incoming students to Canadian and American schools have means of measuring differences and, if required, these might be studied over time. The crucial question of what a certain degree of education means for the cultural climate of the home is much more complex—but not more so than evaluating how a certain family income will be distributed in a family with regard to higher education.

35. This question has been explicitly discussed by Porter in *Vertical Mosaic*, p. 19. Porter's cogent view—in favour of the use of intelligence as a criterion for educa-

tional opportunity—is that "what is required of democratic education is to treat equals equally by recognizing differences in intellectual capacity and to remove as far as possible social and psychological barriers that interfere with the sharing of educational experience by intellectual equals" (p. 1). He differentiates between political and intellectual equality in North America and makes the case for educational opportunity on the basis of the latter. Insofar as one foresees a measure of intellectual capacity that is absolute, we would agree with his argument. But we deem that highly unlikely. We are talking here about social equality of opportunity. This is a deliberate attempt to remove the discussion of access to higher education from the grip of those two beloved criteria—money and intelligence.

36. See Musgrave, *Sociology of Education*, p. 77ff; Porter, "Social Class and Education"; Halsey et al., eds., *Education, Economy and Society*, parts 3 and 4; R. J. Havighurst and B. L. Neugarten, *Society and Education*, 3rd ed. (Boston: Allyn & Bacon, 1967), chs. 2 and 3; Pike, *Who Doesn't Get*, p. 36ff.

37. For discussions of the student movement in the United States see, for example, Immanuel Wallerstein and Paul Starr, eds., *The University Crisis Reader*, 2 vols. (New York: Random House, 1971); John R. Searle, *The Campus War: A Sympathetic Look at the University in Agony* (New York: World Publishing Co., 1971); Seymour M. Lipset and Sheldon S. Walin, eds., *The Berkeley Student Revolt: Facts and Interpretations* (New York: Doubleday-Anchor, 1965); *The Report of the President's Commission on Campus Unrest* (September 1970); *Report of the American Bar Association Commission on Campus Government and Student Dissent* (Chicago, 1970); Daniel Bell, *Confrontation: The Student Rebellion and the Universities* (New York: Basic Books, 1973); Hal Draper, *The New Student Revolt* (New York: Grove Press, 1966); Phillip G. Altbach, *The Student Revolution: A Global Analysis* (Calcutta: Talvani Publishing House, 1970); Kenneth Keniston and Michael Turner, "The Unholy Alliance against the Campus," *New York Times Magazine*, 8 November 1970; Alan E. Bayer and Alexander W. Astin, "Violence and Disruption on the U.S. Campus, 1968–69," *Educational Record*, vol. 50, no. 4 (Fall 1969); and Stephen Spender, *The Year of the Young Rebels* (London: Weidenfield & Nicolson, 1969). For Canadian treatments of the subject see Norman Sheffe, ed., *Student Unrest* (Toronto: McGraw-Hill, 1970); Joel Loken, *Student Alienation and Dissent* (Scarborough, Ont.: Prentice-Hall of Canada, 1973); Timothy E. Reid, *Student Power and the Canadian Campus* (Toronto: Peter Martin Associates, 1969); Jack Quarter, *The Student Movement of the Sixties* (Toronto: Ontario Institute for Studies in Education, 1972); and Claude Bissell, *Halfway up Parnassus* (Toronto: University of Toronto Press, 1974), especially chs. 7–9.

38. See, for example, Theodore Roszak, *The Making of a Counter Culture: Reflections on the Technocratic Society and Its Youthful Opposition* (Garden City, N.Y.: Doubleday, 1969); *The New Student Left*, rev. ed., an anthology of counter-cultural interests, ed. Mitchell Cohen and Dennis Hale (Boston: Beacon Press, 1967); Paul Jacobs and Saul Landau, *The New Radicals: A Report with Documents* (New York: Vintage Books, 1966), a knowledgeable handbook, especially on historical background and the distinctions between many left-wing student groups; Timothy Leary, *The Politics of Ecstasy* (New York: Putnam, 1968); Norman Mailer, *The White Negro* (San Francisco: City Lights Pocket Poets Series, 1957); Theodore Roszak, *Where the Wasteland Ends: Politics and Transcendence in Post-Industrial Society* (Garden City, N.Y.: Doubleday, 1972); James S. Kliner, *The Strawberry Statement: Notes of a College Revolutionary* (New York: Random House, 1969); and William I. Thompson, *At the Edge of History* (New York: Harper Colophon Books, 1972).

39. Erik H. Erikson, "Identity and the Life Cycle," *Psychological Issues*, vol. 1, no. 1 (1959), Monograph 1.

40. Ruth Benedict, "Continuities and Discontinuities in Cultural Conditioning," *Psychiatry* (1938): 161–67.

41. See, for example, Lawrence Wylie, "Youth in France and the United States," in *The Challenge of Youth*, ed. Erik H. Erikson (Garden City, N.Y.: Doubleday, 1965), for a discussion of cultural variations in patterns of adolescence.

42. Lewis S. Feuer, *The Conflict of Generations: The Character and Significance of Student Movements* (New York: Basic Books, 1969); Dr. Barclay, "The Silent Generation Speaks Up," *New York Times Magazine*, 15 May 1960; Clark Kerr, "The Exaggerated Generation," *New York Times Magazine*, 4 June 1967; Seymour M. Lipset and Everett C. Todd, Jr., ". . . And What Professors Think: About Student Protest and Manners, Morals, Politics and Chaos on the Campus," reprinted from *Psychology Today*, November 1970; Jeff Greenfield, *No Place, No Place: Excavations along the Generational Fault* (Garden City, N.Y.: Doubleday, 1973); S. N. Eisenstadt, *From Generation to Generation: Age Groups and Social Structure* (Glencoe, Ill.: Free Press, 1956).

43. For an in-depth portrait of campus radicals, see Kenneth Keniston, *Young Radicals: Notes on Committed Youth* (New York: Harcourt, Brace & World, 1968), pp. 228–32.

44. For a statistical review of the great educational expansion in Canada during the sixties, see Statistics Canada, *Education in Canada*.

45. For a discussion of the "multiversity syndrome," see Clark Kerr, "New Challenges to the College and University," in *Agenda for the Nation*, ed. Kermit Gordon (Washington: Brookings Institute, 1968); and Clark Kerr, *The Uses of the University* (Cambridge, Mass.: Harvard University Press, 1963).

46. William Kornhauser, *The Politics of Mass Society* (New York: Free Press, 1959).

47. Carnegie Commission on Higher Education, *Dissent and Disruption* (New York: McGraw-Hill, 1971).

48. Bissell, *Halfway up Parnassus*, p. 142; also ch. 9.

49. For discussions of the expansion of Canadian education during the sixties, see Edward B. Harvey, *Educational Systems and the Labour Market* (Toronto: Longman Canada, 1974); also Edward B. Harvey, "Canadian Higher Education and the Seventies," *Interchange*, vol. 5, no. 2 (1974): 42–52.

50. Harvey, *Educational Systems*; and Edward B. Harvey and I. Charner, "Social Mobility and Occupational Attainments of University Graduates," forthcoming (1975) in *Canadian Review of Sociology and Anthopology*.

51. See, for example, James Park, "The Vanishing Graduate," *Macleans*, no. 85 (1972), pp. 29–31, 115, 117–19; Ministry of Colleges and Universities, Ontario, "A Survey Concerning the Short-Fall in Student Attendance at Ontario Colleges and Universities" (Toronto: Market Facts of Canada, 1972); and Erica Wright et al., "A Survey of 1971–72 Drop-Outs in a Secondary School" (Toronto: Department of Education for the Borough of North York, 1973).

52. R. Matthews and J. Steale, *The Struggle for Canadian Universities* (Don Mills Ont.: New Press, 1969).

53. Economic Council of Canada, Eighth Annual Review, *Design for Decision-Making* (Ottawa: Information Canada, 1971), pp. 205–213.

54. See, for example, J. S. Kirkaldy and D. M. Black, *Social Reporting and Educational Planning* (Toronto: Ministry of Government Services, 1972); and Edward B. Harvey and Jos L. Lennards, *Key Issues in Higher Education* (Toronto: Ontario Institute for Studies in Education, 1973), especially ch. 3.

55. For examples, see the Post-Censal Survey of Highly Qualified Manpower in Canada, soon to be available from Statistics Canada and the Ministry of State for Science and Technology.

56. Commission on Post-Secondary Education in Ontario, Report of the Commission, *The Learning Society* (Toronto: Ministry of Government Services, 1972).

57. Frank Kelly, *Prospects for Scientists and Engineers in Canada*, Science Council of Canada Special Study no. 20 (Ottawa: Information Canada, 1971).

Graduate Studies in Ontario Education at the Three-Quarter-Century Mark

George E. Flower

Nineteen seventy-five is, of course, the three-quarter mark of the twentieth century. As it happens, formal graduate work in education in Ontario is also about three-quarters of a century old. It was in 1898 that the University of Toronto conferred its first Doctor of Paedagogy degree, two years before its first Doctor of Philosophy degrees. This year—1974/75—Toronto will confer more than 40 doctoral degrees on candidates in education, and nearly 600 master's degrees. Ottawa will similarly confer 4 or 5 doctoral degrees and some 300 master's degrees in education. Queen's will graduate 75 or more from its relatively new education master's programs. The University of Western Ontario and Lakehead University have now also begun to offer master's work in education, and a specialized graduate program in extension education flourishes at the University of Guelph. Meanwhile four other Ontario universities—Brock, McMaster, Windsor, and York—are in the process of developing new master's programs in education.

After three-quarters of a century, education has come of age as a field of graduate study in Ontario.

What I propose to do in this paper is offer some frankly personal comments on this coming of age and raise a few questions about the future. I make no apology for dealing mainly with graduate studies at OISE. I do so not from any desire to overlook developments at other Ontario institutions, but because it seems fitting to concentrate largely on OISE. Not only is that the milieu I know best, it is Dr. R. W. B. Jackson's own milieu. In a very real sense (and here I write as one of those virtually prehistoric characters who were involved in the early planning for the Institute leading up to its establishment in 1965) there would be no OISE were it not for him. Graduate studies has been a central function of the Institute from the beginning, and the emergence of OISE as a major Canadian graduate school of education, in association with the University of Toronto, is something for which Bob Jackson deserves a good deal of credit.

THE DECADE OF DEVELOPMENT

The Establishment of OISE

One of the central objects of the Ontario Institute for Studies in Education, as expressed in the act which founded the Institute in 1965, is "to establish and conduct courses leading to certificates of standing and graduate degrees in education." In fact, the need for more and better graduate work in the field of education was one of the forces that gave rise to the establishment of the Institute.

Since World War II, an urgent problem in Ontario and elsewhere had been to prepare enough teachers to staff the schools. In our preoccupation with that problem, the important matter of advanced graduate preparation for specialized and leadership posts tended to be pushed aside. For many years the Ontario College of Education endeavored to supply staff and facilities for a relatively modest graduate department of educational theory within the University of Toronto's School of Graduate Studies. By 1960, graduates of its programs occupied senior posts in almost every provincial department of education, faculty of education, and major school system across Canada. Nevertheless, it had become increasingly clear that the need for persons in education with advanced qualifications greatly outran supply. Accordingly, when OISE was chartered as a new college under an independent board of governors in 1965, its mandate was to function not only as a research and development institute, but also as a graduate school of education. And by design, one of the first acts of the Institute was to set aside its own powers to grant graduate degrees in education in favor of an agreement of affiliation with the University of Toronto for purposes of graduate studies. Under this agreement (which may be reopened by either party on a year's notice), the Institute takes major responsibility for providing teaching staff and facilities for the University's Graduate Department of Educational Theory. Graduate programs lead to University of Toronto degrees, and the Graduate Department of Educational Theory at once possesses all the rights and privileges, and is subject to all the program responsibilities and controls, of any other department in the University's School of Graduate Studies. The Institute's Coordinator of Graduate Studies also acts as chairman of the University's Graduate Department of Educational Theory.

The Institute plan called for four years of "initial establishment," in which it would receive massive annual increases in budget and resources, followed by "years of stable growth." The immediate effects on graduate studies in education, then, were two. First, there was a dramatic infusion of new resources for graduate instruction; for example, full-time academic staff increased from sixteen in 1964/65 to twenty-six the following year, and to forty the year after that. (In 1974/75 the total was 143.)

The second immediate effect of the establishment of OISE on graduate studies was the rare opportunity it gave students and staff alike to share in what was at once a graduate school, a research and development institute, and a field development institute working with education practitioners where they are, to help them solve their problems as they see them. This uniting of three functions within a single institute was basic to the OISE design. The notion was that each function, which theoretically could proceed in isolation, in practice would be greatly strengthened by intimate and overlapping relationships with the others. While there are difficulties in obtaining the hoped for maximum interaction, after ten years I believe all concerned are more than ever convinced that the notion is a sound one, and indeed is the single factor that, more than any other, gives OISE its unique flavor and strength. Important as our graduate studies are, OISE is not just another graduate school of education. If the Institute did attempt to operate solely as a graduate school, it simply could not afford the full range of staff and facilities it has for graduate studies now, let alone provide the present breadth of experiences for students in terms of involvement in research and development or field development activities. Similarly, existing quality and quantity of staff would be an impossibility if the Institute were to try to operate as an R & D or field development facility alone, separated from graduate studies.

Ten Years of Graduate Studies at OISE
The agreement of affiliation with the University of Toronto meant that Toronto's preexisting graduate programs in education could be continued as a starting point; the Institute did not have to attempt the precarious feat of becoming an "instant" graduate school. The infusion of massive additional resources, however, and the promise of more, allowed for the early revamping and strengthening of those programs leading to the degrees of Master of Education, Doctor of Education, Master of Arts, and Doctor of Philosophy. This review and reorganizing of graduate studies became a priority for academic staff in 1964/65 (leading up to the Institute) and 1965/66 (the Institute's first year). Thus, by 1967 all of our current sub-fields of specialization had been established, with programs at master's and doctoral levels, though in some cases under names slightly different from those of today. This of course does not mean that OISE programs have stood still since 1966: quite the contrary. The process of continuing development and refinement goes on constantly. But programs were and are offered in the

following sub-fields of specialization within Educational Theory:

Adult Education	Educational Planning
Applied Psychology (including Educational Psychology, Counseling Psychology, and School Psychology)	History and Philosophy of Education
	Measurement and Evaluation
	Sociology in Education
Computer Applications	Special Education
Curriculum	Higher Education
Educational Administration	

Basic staff for the Higher Education Group has been provided directly by the University of Toronto.

At OISE education is regarded as a field of both theoretical and applied scholarship. The prime purpose of our graduate programs is to provide advanced study and preparation for individuals occupying, or preparing themselves to occupy, specialized leadership posts in local school systems, government, colleges and universities (including colleges of applied arts and technology), research institutes, and in business and industry and continuing education generally. The overall goal of OISE is to make a positive contribution to education, primarily in Ontario. We believe that in the long run one of the most effective ways of achieving this goal is through our graduates.

At the master's level, the M.Ed. is designed chiefly for the professional improvement of men and women already engaged in a career in education. As such it tends to be substantially a practitioner's degree, growing out of theory and research rather than contributing to theory and research. The M.A., on the other hand, includes a thesis and provides more opportunity for research work in some depth. Similarly, the Ed.D. typically falls somewhat closer to the applied end of a theoretical–applied continuum than does the Ph.D., though both are thesis programs. It is possible to proceed to the M.Ed. by part-time study, whereas the M.A. and other graduate degrees in education require varying periods of full-time study.

Graduate Enrollment at OISE

Demand for quality graduate programs in education in Ontario has remained high. In recent years, when graduate enrollment in many other fields has tended toward stabilization after the bulge of the 1960s, demand for graduate study in education, and enrollments at OISE, have continued to rise.

As shown in the accompanying table, in OISE's first decade enrollment in the regular academic year has increased five-fold, and in the summer session has more than tripled. More than half the full-time students are now doctoral candidates. Applied Psychology typically enrolls the largest number of full-time students, and Curriculum the largest number of part-time students; other heavily enrolled specializations are Educational Administration, History and Philosophy of Education, Adult Education, and Sociology in Education. Forty-five percent of the full-time students in 1974/75 were women, compared to 38 percent three years ago; the proportion of women in the part-time group this same year jumped to 34 percent from the 28 percent mark, where it had stood for several years. About six out of seven OISE students are Canadian citizens, and four-fifths of them list Ontario as their province of permanent residence.

Graduate Enrollment in OISE, Selected Academic Years 1965/66 to 1974/75

Regular Session	1965/66	1968/69	1972/73	1974/75
Full-time students	101	289	461	534
Part-time students	340	796	1,404	1,669
TOTAL	441	1,085	1,865	2,203
Summer Session	430	1,034	1,238	1,310

Graduate Degrees Conferred since 1965

As enrollment has climbed, so too have the numbers of graduates, as indicated in the following tabulation of degrees conferred over OISE's first decade:

	1965/66 (OISE's first year)	1974/75 (anticipated)	Ten-year total
Ph.D.	—	36	175
Ed.D.	1	2	49
M.Phil.	—	—	1
M.A.	1	62	354
M.Ed.	165	608	3,600
TOTAL	167	708	4,179

Our graduates in Educational Theory at present account for about one in four of the total number of graduate degrees conferred by the University of Toronto. In recent years graduate degrees in Educational Theory have exceeded the total number of graduate degrees in all fields conferred by any Ontario university except Toronto and Western Ontario. A recent survey indicates that just over half of our doctoral graduates go on to college or university appointments, and a further sixth go on to research positions. Nearly half of the Ed.D. graduates have gone on to administrative or other specialized positions in school systems, postsecondary education, or government. Of 105 recent doctoral graduates, 58 accepted positions in Ontario and 21 accepted positions elsewhere in Canada on graduation. About a third of these returned to their previous employer, though usually not in precisely the same position.

As Bob Jackson leaves the Institute—his Institute—he could be pardoned some justifiable pride in what has been accomplished in graduate studies at OISE in affiliation with the University of Toronto. In quantitative terms, over 4,000 degrees have been earned and conferred. As for quality, one could point to many very positive views of our efforts. The consultants to the recent Education Planning Assessment, in their report to the Advisory Committee on Academic Planning, refer to OISE in such phrases as "worldwide repuation," "faculty strength compares favorably with the best institutions of its type in the world," and "must, for the foreseeable future, be regarded as the pacesetter in the field."[1]

In summary, at this three-quarter-century mark graduate studies in education have indeed come of age in Ontario. OISE programs at both master's and doctoral levels are extensive and well established. They are supported by a large and capable staff, by highly desirable physical facilities in the 400,000-square-foot building opened in 1970, by an extensive library and other research tools, and by opportunities for meaningful involvement of staff and students in a wide range of research and development projects.

Lest that should sound as if "all is for the best in the best of possible worlds," it must be added that while graduate studies have come of age, a good many problems and issues surround their continuing development in Ontario. There are problems of program, of personnel, of procedures, of the purse.

THE FUTURE

Enrollment Trends

Graduate studies in education in Ontario have become big indeed, in relation to other fields of graduate study. Among the questions we now face are: Will that growth continue? How big should the effort be in Ontario? at OISE?

Mention was made above of the Advisory Committee on Academic Planning (ACAP). ACAP is a creature of the Ontario Council on Graduate Studies and the Council of Ontario Universities. At the risk of oversimplification, it seems fair to say that the establishment of ACAP in 1968 was a response of the universities of Ontario to pressures from the provincial government, which foots the bills, for more rational and cooperative planning of the continued development and operation of graduate work throughout the system. Graduate instruction is expensive to mount, but by the middle and late sixties graduate enrollments across the province were soaring. Under the enrollment-driven formula used as the basis for annual provincial grants to each university, there has been, as it were, every encouragement for each university to mount new graduate programs in more fields and to scramble for additional graduate students to bring in more revenue.

A major step was taken by Ontario universities, acting in concert through the Ontario Council on Graduate Studies (OCGS) and the Council of Ontario Universities (COU), when they introduced an appraisals procedure in 1967. Under these arrangements it was agreed that any new graduate program would have to undergo careful appraisal in some depth as to its academic quality and viability before it would receive the stamp of approval of the universities operating as a system. The teeth in the arrangement are that while any university is, of course, free to offer any new graduate program it wishes and that can be construed as permitted under its charter, student enrollment in the new program will not generate government grants unless that program has been appraised and approved. The intention was that eventually all graduate degree programs would be appraised, including those that existed before the procedure was set up in 1967. But appraisals are concerned, by definition, with the academic quality and viability of a program, not directly with whether the program is needed, given other programs elsewhere in the province. It was questions of this sort that the Advisory Committee on Academic Planning was meant to deal with.

ACAP's procedure was to mount a series of planning assessments, discipline by discipline. Each university was asked to report on its current activities and future plans for graduate work in the selected discipline (or "field," in the case of education); extensive data were collected and analyzed on present and past performance and future intentions for that discipline at each institution, and on staff and other resources available for it; efforts were also made to assess likely future manpower needs for graduates in that discipline. Teams of distinguished consultants were charged with visiting each institution and making recommendations to ACAP as to desirable parameters of development for graduate work in that particular discipline for the future, with special reference to the next five years. The effort was aimed at estimating provincial needs for graduate studies in the discipline, assessing existing and planned provincial resources throughout the university system, and matching the two. ACAP's report, after review and comment from the variety of sources appropriate in each case, was then discussed in detail by the Council of Ontario Universities itself. In each case the Council then produced its own report, including in it a series of expectations for action with respect to graduate programs in the discipline across the provincial university system as a whole and, indeed, for individual universities.

This process of planning assessments has been a difficult one. Some twenty-five disciplines have undergone assessment to date, and at the time of writing the two university councils previously referred to are reviewing the whole process in some detail with a view to suggesting possible revisions. Some of the difficulties are that major planning exercises are never simple matters in any case: to begin with, variables shift in unexpected ways. When ACAP was initiated, there appeared to be considerable necessity for giving attention to manpower needs: enrollments seemed to be climbing alarmingly in many fields. By the time the first ACAP reports were ready to be dealt with some years later, however, firm enrollment quotas based on manpower projections no longer seemed so desirable. In most disciplines the numbers of applicants had declined and enrollments were becoming more stable. But another and major source of difficulty remains, and that is the problem of the number of independent institutions seeking to act in concert as a system through COU, OCGS, ACAP, or whatever other acronymic or device may be possible. System-wide agreements inevitably affect individual member institutions within that system differentially: some will find their particular interests enhanced by some specific system-wide agreement, others will find their particular interests adversely affected. How far an individual institution can go in sacrificing some of its own legitimate interests in the greater interest of all the universities of the province combined is a key problem that arises month after month in "coordinating" council and committee meetings. It speaks well for the statesmanship of the executive heads of Ontario universities, and of their academic colleagues, that so much has been done in terms of action in concert over recent years through the Council of Ontario Universities and its associated groups.

All this, however, merely introduces the question of enrollment futures in education. A point of major difference between ACAP's Education Planning Assessment report and its reports on other graduate fields is the recognition that graduate enrollment in education can and should expand markedly. Indeed, the proposed rate of expansion at the master's level ultimately adopted by COU as a planning guideline—about a 50 percent enrollment increase over three years to a total of 3,500—seemed incredibly large to some, even after careful examination. After all, the school and teacher population in Ontario is projected to decline somewhat over the coming years.

Factors pointing to the necessity for expansion are many, however. First, education has been an underdeveloped field at the graduate level in Ontario universities; graduate work is simply not available to meet either the need or the demand. This is evidenced by inroads made by a number of American universities offering programs off-campus in Ontario. Second, specialties have developed within education requiring professional graduate preparation and upgrading. Third, the rise in standards over the years for initial entry to the teaching force (a university degree is now required for certification as an elementary school teacher) has resulted in an increase in the numbers of practitioners eligible for graduate study. Fourth, a higher proportion of teachers also go on to graduate work as the profession becomes more competitive. Above all, there is the fact of sheer numbers of individuals in the field of education in our "learning society": not only are there teachers and other officials in our schools and school systems, there are uncounted numbers engaged in education in business and industry and in other frameworks for continuing education. More than one person in four across Canada is now engaged full time in formal education, as student or instructor. When the need for expanded graduate opportunities was being explored in 1964 with a view to the establishment of OISE, it was pointed out that for every research worker in education in Canada there were about five research workers in fish and forty in agriculture.

The approved recommendations of the Education Planning Assessment, then, provide not only for enrollment expansion in existing graduate programs in education, but also for the development of additional master's programs, including new ones at Brock, McMaster, Windsor, and York universities.[2] All new programs, of course, whether at those four universities or at one of the six with currently approved programs (Guelph, Lakehead, Ottawa, Queen's, Toronto/OISE, and Western) are subject to standard appraisal procedures.

Enrollment will continue to grow at OISE, though much more modestly than in the first decade. A reasonable forecast would appear to be an increase of about 25 percent over the next five years, compared with 500 percent over the first ten. By 1979/80 full-time equivalent graduate students at OISE may well number about 1,250. It is to be hoped that among them will be some postdoctoral fellows: this was one of the recommendations of the Education Planning Assessment. A further recommendation was that new doctoral programs in education at other Ontario universities were probably not needed at the moment, beyond those to be continued at Ottawa and Toronto/OISE. In my opinion, the major determining factor in the extent of increase of enrollment at OISE will be not the numbers of qualified applicants—they will be there—but rather the numbers of qualified staff that the Institute may be able to devote to graduate studies. That will be, or ought to be, the chief limiting factor. Which leads to some problems of personnel.

Faculty Resources
For a member of faculty a particular attraction of work at the graduate level in education is the daily experience of sitting down with mature graduate students to attack together, as fellow scholars, some problem of scholarship. It tends to be a process of shared exploration, rather than of "laying down the word." In the field of education we are fortunate; our doctoral students are more likely to be experienced practitioners, returning to further formal study from responsible positions in education, than candidates fresh out of

undergraduate school. Good students make great institutions. But good staff are essential to a great institution, too; in fact, if one had to choose, I would argue that quality of staff is even more important than quality of student.

In the graduate schools of well-established Ontario universities, qualifications for appointment as a member of graduate faculty ordinarily include an appropriate earned doctorate, together with evidence of continuing scholarly productivity, often measured in terms of formal publications in books or refereed scholarly journals. These standard scholarly criteria have served well in many traditional academic disciplines, though increasingly in recent years demands have been heard (especially from students) to consider not only research productivity and publication, but also commitment to teaching, in making staffing decisions. Standard scholarly criteria can serve well for the selection of graduate staff in education, too: but surely they should not be the *exclusive* criteria. Education is a field that is concerned with both theory and its application. Ideally, then, we need members of faculty with a background in both theoretical and applied research. Some will be far more inclined to theory in their interests, orientation, and experience; and some—equally needed for strong programs in our professional field—will fall toward the applied and developmental end of the continuum. Since we are dealing with the process of education, we need—our programs and students need—some staff members with an intimate, firsthand knowledge and experience of educational systems in actual operation and with demonstrated competence in developmental work issuing from sound theory and research. Such persons are strongly recommended by their background and accomplishments in the field, and should be judged on that basis. Quality remains the criterion; but quality must be recognized in its varying forms. President John Evans of the University of Toronto puts the point well. In his comments on a report concerning recommended grounds for granting academic tenure, he is quoted as follows in the *Varsity* for November 5, 1973:

> Among the criteria listed . . . the task force stresses only teaching and research. Comments received from many divisions of the university have indicated a belief that university and community service should be taken into consideration. . . . The "works by which he shall be known" do not always, for professional faculty members, appear in the conventional scholarly literature. The evidence of accomplishment in this area may appear in steel and concrete, in codes of practice, in legislation, in cured patients, in policies adopted by public bodies.

In addition to quality of staff, however, the question of quantity inevitably arises. How many staff are needed for sound graduate programs? To phrase the question differently, what may be regarded as a reasonable and appropriate teaching load for a graduate faculty member?

It seems fiendishly difficult to obtain or develop any reliable and comparable indices of faculty load generally, either within or across institutions, much less definitive statements as to what a viable load should be in given situations. The Laskin report on graduate studies in the University of Toronto ten years ago merely suggests what a desirable load might be:

> If the ratio of full-time equivalent staff to full-time equivalent students is ten or twelve, a serious question arises whether the hypothetical staff member is not being overextended in his graduate studies responsibilities. Having regard to the individual character of graduate supervision, although not of graduate teaching to the same degree, it is of importance to the quality of graduate work that adequate staff in number as well as quality be available to minister to graduate students under a fair teaching load.[3]

One difficulty in making much sense out of staff–student ratios is the assumption that each student and each category of student in fact make equivalent demands upon faculty and constitute equivalent units of "load." In an effort to find a more comparable basis for quantifying load in Ontario universities, it has been suggested that the number of Basic Income Units generated by actual enrollment be used, rather than full-time equivalent enrollment itself. The BIU formula is weighted according to category of student and therefore does take into account, to some extent at least, the relative cost of providing the various programs to which differential BIU weightings are attached. Academic staff is only one item in that cost, of course, but it is typically the major one.

Rather interesting comparisons can be developed in this way. For example, the Council of Ontario Universities found that for 1972/73, across the provincial university system as a whole, the BIU/FTE (full-time equivalent) faculty ratio was slightly over 23 to 1; this had risen by 1974/75 to over 25 to 1: an increase of over 6 in load over the two years. Ratios for OISE for the same period show an increase of about 20 percent. This shift may be regarded as an improvement, if one believes (as one popular suggestion these days would have it) that what universities must do is produce "more scholar for the dollar." The same shift may also be regarded as a near disaster, unless one considers that academic load two years ago was far lower than it should have been. If it was too low, then it was too low for the entire university system, and not just for graduate work in education at OISE, since the OISE ratio and the system ratio two years ago were virtually the same. By the same token, the increase in load over the two years has been three times as great for OISE as for the system as a whole; for me that raises danger signals. There must soon come a point—if it has not already arrived —where further increases in enrollment without offsetting increases in academic complement can only have the effect of compromising the quality of the Institute's graduate work.

Graduate Programs for the Future
Assuming appropriate staff, what will be the likely shape and thrust of graduate study in education at OISE over the next decade? The consultants

to the Education Planning Assessment wrote as follows in discussing possible emphases and options for Ontario:

> The scale and type of graduate studies thought appropriate at any particular time will to some extent depend upon which mission is thought to be the most important. If emphasis is upon the training of practitioners, then a manpower approach is indicated. If stress is upon improvement of the competence of professionals, then an upgrading approach is indicated. If it is the advancement of knowledge that matters most, then graduate studies will be seen as part of an overall research and development thrust, and their scale and scope will be tailored to the apparent needs of the system for new knowledge and research skills. If the "educated man" ideal is dominant, then the scale of the operation will be determined by judgements about the pool of qualified aspirants to such status, and the numbers of scholars available to supervise and direct their induction.[4]

The consultants concluded that there are no simple black-and-white choices as to necessary and desirable emphases; they also agreed that continuing debate and dialogue are as essential as they are inevitable.

Personally, I believe that the Institute's specialized programs leading to graduate degrees have proven and continue to prove their worth. There is no need for dramatic reworking or drastic surgery. However, static and unchanging graduate programs in the field of education, which is itself changing so rapidly, would surely represent something of a dereliction of duty on the part of the institution concerned. The next decade will certainly see a great many changes in OISE's graduate programs. As new needs arise, both our own staff and practitioners in the field press for new arrangements toward meeting those needs. Just at the moment, for example, there are considerable stirrings toward more formalized programs in such fields as family life education and Canadian studies. The process of minor changes in existing programs and courses to reflect changing situations is of course constant.

My own convictions as to desirable directions for change, the better to meet the scholarly and professional needs of education in Ontario, cluster about increased flexibility in various aspects of graduate study. This includes flexibility in programs, as, for example, OISE's recent emphasis on revising and strengthening the Doctor of Education programs that parallel its Doctor of Philosophy programs. In the years immediately following the establishment of the Institute, with its rapidly growing staff and student body, considerable attention was devoted to making sure that the theoretical and scholarly basis of our programs was well developed. It was for this reason that, at the doctoral level, major attention was for a time devoted to Ph.D. programs and a temporary hold was placed on new applications for the Ed.D. With Ph.D. programs firmly developed, OISE then turned again to its Ed.D. programs. I welcome this dual emphasis. Program flexibility must embrace both the theoretical and the applied. In this regard OISE anticipated the recommendation of the Education Planning Assessment that programs for practitioners should be one of the major emphases in graduate study in Ontario education; the Ed.D. is designed primarily to meet the needs of the scholar/practitioner whose interests tend toward advanced study of the *application* of sound theory.

Another desirable type of program flexibility is one that gives the student and his advisor wide latitude in delineating the individual components in the student's study program. There is now considerably more freedom in this respect at OISE than there was at the beginning—always, of course, within the general requirements for the particular degree. I hope this trend can be continued and speeded up. While the detailed specification of compulsory program components may facilitate an institution's work in planning and administration, it can also result in a somewhat unsatisfactory program for an individual candidate because it "blocks him in" and does not take appropriate account of his particular background and study needs. One must subdivide the field of education in order to accommodate numbers of students and staff; but one must take great care that such subdivisions, by their sheer weight, do not become dysfunctional for individual students.

I also believe that a substantial degree of flexibility in admission requirements to graduate study in the field of education is both sensible and desirable. I hope more of this kind of flexibility will be evident in the years ahead. The great majority of our graduate students complete their undergraduate work some years before they come to us, and in some field other than education. In the interval most have been involved professionally in education. While undergraduate standing is of course not unimportant, under these circumstances it should scarcely be regarded as an overriding criterion in all admissions decisions. I welcome the position taken in the Education Planning Assessment that for admission purposes account should be taken not only of the applicant's university credits, but also of the length and quality of his professional contributions and experience. Taking the latter into account necessarily involves making a judgment on the individual case. That judgment—the admissions decision—cannot be relegated to a computer programmed to count the number of specified courses completed with given grades and to yield an automatic yes/no answer. Admission to graduate study in education should be something more than a kind of reward for an A record at the undergraduate level. In admitting applicant X to graduate study in education and rejecting Y, the university is making the judgment that X is more likely to complete the demanding graduate program satisfactorily than is Y, and that X—and through him the community that he will serve—is more likely to profit from that study than would Y. It would in my opinion be a travesty of the selection process and of what most of those concerned with the process of education have learned if the operative criteria for selection took in merely that which can be mechanically counted in mindless fashion—previous formal grades and numbers of individual courses in some named field.

A further aspect of flexibility, which is being increasingly accepted in many quarters, is the need for arrangements for part-time study and interrupted or recurrent study. On this point, in fact, those responsible for graduate study in education over the next decade are likely to meet with far less opposition than they may on the matter of "standards" for entry to graduate study. For many students in education, part-time and recurrent study make particularly good sense in terms of making formal graduate study possible for them and also in terms of fostering interaction between their graduate programs and their professional work experiences, to the benefit of both. Graduate schools of education in Canada and the United States typically offer extensive graduate programs in the summer, when many students employed in the school systems are free to make graduate study their first priority. It seems to me that the years ahead will see an increasing number of professionals making arrangements to combine systematic graduate study with their professional practice, rather than interrupting their professional career to pursue graduate work. This will certainly obtain in the field of education. Indeed, it is quite possible that recurrent lifelong education—continuing in-again-out-again systematic study—may well become the usual pattern for postsecondary education generally.

This may to some extent result in a blurring of what has so far been the rather clear-cut distinction between credit and non-credit offerings, between degree programs and non-degree programs. I trust the distinction will not become so blurred as virtually to disappear. Formal graduate study is only one route for continuing education in education; it is, and should be, limited to a highly selected and relatively small proportion of practitioners in the field. On the other hand, the explosion of knowledge at an exponential rate suggests that all practitioners—and not just the select few—need continuing education; but that does not mean that all continuing education should come under the rubric of graduate degree work at a university.

There appears to be demand on many sides for non-degree programs of continuing education, for special-purpose offerings for specialized client groups without reference to degree candidacy. Some of these activities may lead to a certificate of some sort, others not. Often the most desirable format may be a period of a week or two of concentrated study of a particular topic; alternatively, the best format may be a series of weekend activities, or of recurring seminars or clinics. The need for continuing education has recently been given considerable prominence in a number of studies, including the work of the Commission on Post-Secondary Education in Ontario.[5] In Unesco's language, the terms *post-experience higher education* and *lifelong education* are used.[6]

Activities of this sort are already extensive and can be expected to expand, but they do result in substantial demands on university staff and resources. The problem is, of course, that in this respect much of the effort of universities—including OISE—is necessarily made on an "overload" basis. With increasing credit loads not matched by staff expansion because of fiscal restrictions, the margin of overload available for non-revenue-producing activities necessarily diminishes. In view of the demand, it does seem important that the service role of universities, including the provision of non-credit offerings, be taken into account in establishing revenues for those universities, but so far this has not been done. Much is expected of OISE for education in Ontario now, and in the decade ahead there will be increasing demands for non-degree as well as degree programs. It will be exceedingly difficult to provide adequately for non-degree programs if a substantial part of their cost must be borne from revenues earned through the provision of degree programs.

Future Finances
It is difficult to discuss any major public enterprise without very soon being confronted with financial concerns. In these days of runaway inflation and increasing competition for the public dollar, this seems to be particularly true for universities. The sixties were dubbed the Decade of Education, when almost any expenditure for education was regarded as a Good Thing. The seventies will probably be dubbed the Decade of Pollution. The fact is that over the past ten years the Province of Ontario has invested very heavily in the development and operation of a wide-ranging provincial university system. In 1964/65 provincial operating grants to universities totaled $40.9 million; by 1974/75 that had grown to $447 million. Expressed as a share of provincial revenue, that meant an increase from 2.45 percent in 1964/65 to 5.79 percent ten years later. It would probably be unrealistic to expect such a rate of growth in the proportion of the public dollar devoted to universities to continue indefinitely. Certainly today there are signs of growing disillusionment with education, and perhaps even an erosion of public confidence.

One reason for this change in public attitudes is that Canadians may well have expected too much of education. For some years education was regarded, rightly or wrongly, as a talisman, a magic passport to anything, anywhere. Education was seen as the answer to all our problems, be they the personal problems of an individual, or the global problems of a world threatening to blow apart at the seams. Have we manpower problems? Education will solve them. Do we need more and better international understanding, or even national understanding in a multicultural setting? Clearly a matter for education. Inner-city problems of our cities? Rising rates of delinquency and crime? Increasing costs of social services? The gnawing fear that important moral and ethical and religious values are getting lost in the shuffle? Or the need for more positive and responsible citizen interest in government? Education is the answer, people said; turn to more and better education—that will do the job for us.

One would not wish to decry this faith in education. In fact, I share it. The difficulty is that we have expected too much too soon. In our impatience, we insist that everything should be done by Saturday night. I believe that, in the long run, education is indeed the servant of all our purposes, to use a memorable phrase of John W. Gardner's.[7]

The people of Ontario have much to be proud of in their universities. Every dollar devoted to universities is an investment in the future of this country; and university people—including those of us in graduate studies in education—have a heavy trust and responsibility to ensure that every such dollar invested is soundly invested. It is important to remember, however, that quality merchandise is only rarely found in the bargain basement; bargain basement graduate study may be, in fact, an unsound investment. Public support for graduate education on a "production unit basis" for four years running has not kept pace with the rate of inflation. Moreover, support for universities, including graduate studies in education, has not increased at anything like the rate of increase in support for elementary and secondary schools. The cumulative increase from 1971 to 1975 in permissible ceiling expenditure per elementary school pupil in Ontario works out to 69.9 percent, and to 35.9 percent for every secondary school pupil. Over the same period the value of the Basic Income Unit for universities has increased only 21.5 percent.

One can only express the fervent hope that graduate studies in education, having come of age in Ontario, will not have to continue to face such fiscal stringencies that the quality of graduate work is seriously eroded. Should that happen, the people of this province—and of future generations—will inevitably be the losers.

NOTES

1. Council of Ontario Universities, *Perspectives and Plans for Graduate Studies 2: Education 1973* (Toronto: COU, 1974), pp. A-38, A-39. The consultants were Professor Harold Baker, University of Alberta; Professor Roy Daniells, University of British Columbia; Dr. Lawrence Downey, L. W. Downey Research Associates; and Professor William Taylor, Director, University of London Institute of Education.

2. Ibid., pp. 4–7.

3. President's Committee on the School of Graduate Studies, 1964–65, Report of the Committee, *Graduate Studies in the University of Toronto*, Bora Laskin, chairman (Toronto: University of Toronto Press, 1965), pp. 57–58.

4. Council of Ontario Universities, *Perspectives and Plans*, p. A-8.

5. Commission on Post-Secondary Education in Ontario, *The Learning Society* (Toronto: Ministry of Government Services, 1972).

6. See "Lifelong Education," chapter 6 of *Education on the Move: Extracts from Background Papers Prepared for the Report of the International Commission on the Development of Education* (Paris: Unesco Press; Toronto: Ontario Institute for Studies in Education, 1975), pp. 107–117.

7. John W. Gardner, *Annual Report of the Carnegie Corporation of New York, 1958* (New York: Carnegie Corporation, 1958), pp. 11–18.

Policy Research and the Concept of Goal

William E. Alexander

THE IMPACT OF GOALS

In 1960 the President of the United States called upon the services of, among others, a general, a judge, several industrialists, and some university professors to "develop a broad outline of coordinated national policies and programs" and to "set up a series of goals in various areas of national activity." After considerable effort the commission produced its report, *Goals for Americans*. According to Alvin Toffler, "neither the commission nor its goals had the slightest impact on the public or on policy."[1]

But one need not draw on the United States for examples of impotence in setting goals. Ontario—even the Ontario educational sector—is replete with similar examples. The Hall-Dennis report, *Living and Learning*, summarizes the history of efforts at setting goals in Ontario education as follows:

> In its terms of reference the Committee was instructed "to set forth the aims of education for the educational system of the Province" and to propose means by which these aims might be achieved. The Committee found evidence that formal statements of aims have had little effect on educational practices in the past. Of four Royal Commissions that have reported on education in their respective provinces of Canada during the past eight years, only one published a separate chapter on aims.

The report then states that it will not attempt to deal explicitly with aims:

> This Report has been designed to communicate the Committee's view points, findings and recommendations in a manner which reflects the philosophy of the Committee. It contains a commentary on the aims of education, but it does not include a formal statement of aims.[2]

To the degree that this paper sheds any light on policy research, the light was illuminated by insightful comments and criticism from colleagues. In particular, I wish to thank Ross Hayball, Joseph Farrell, Edward Humphreys, Ross Traub, Muhammed Anwar, Terry Bunston, Cathy Marchand, Julie Alexander, Michael Skolnik, and Marion Bird.

Boards, too, have their problems. Recently I attended a meeting for several candidates who wished to become or remain trustees of the Toronto Board of Education. Each candidate gave a brief talk, and then members of the audience were invited to ask questions. One man from the audience asked an incumbent the following question: "I have noticed that, on a per pupil basis, the annual cost of educating a child is substantially higher in the Toronto public schools than in the Toronto separate schools. Yet, as far as I can tell there is no difference between these students in terms of what they learn. How, then, do you explain the difference?"

The trustee flushed a bit and then challenged his questioner: "What evidence do you have that there is no difference?" The man from the audience explained that he taught freshman courses at a university in Toronto and often played the game of trying to guess which students had been to separate schools and which had had all of their schooling in public schools. "I have never been able to guess with any degree of accuracy."

The trustee, obviously disgruntled, retorted that he too had experience with students who had been through both systems. But, unlike the professor, the trustee claimed that "students from the separate schools may be a little better in the three Rs, but students from our schools are much better when it comes to creativity." The implication of the trustee's statement was clear enough; compared to the separate schools, Toronto public schools put slightly less money into teaching the three Rs but substantially more into creativity programs (whatever those may be). This, implied the trustee, is how it is and how it should be.

On April 9, 1970, the Toronto Board adopted what was presumed to be a policy statement: "be it resolved that language development and reading skills development have top priority."[3] Although the trustee's remarks clearly contradicted the policy, not one of the candidates sharing the platform with him challenged his statement of priorities.

In the course of the next few weeks, I had the opportunity to talk with some other trustees as well as principals. When I asked them to comment on the episode, they all gave surprisingly similar responses. They did not argue that the trustee had misrepresented the goals of the Toronto Board. Rather, they suggested, his response was naive and he should have said that the extra money was spent on such programs as special education. None of the trustees with whom I spoke evidenced any intention of discussing the issue—or any other issue—in terms of the Board's goals, the cost of pursuing each goal, and the relationship of goal attainment to expenditures. In fact, the very idea of discussing goals seemed anathema.

WHAT ARE GOALS?

In spite of the fact that some trustees will, for the sake of argument, insist that the Board has established goals for schools, and that these goals do have an impact, there is little evidence to support such a contention. In the Toronto Board of Education's 150-page book, *Policy Decisions of Board*, there is only one policy that specifically uses the word "goal." The Board, in 1972, adopted "a goal of providing for all of the educational needs of all of the people in the City of Toronto."[4] Taxpayers, not to mention university and college presidents, can only hope that little effort will be made to achieve this one goal stated.

Still, parents continue to ask what the goals of schools are, and in some cases principals have responded. One teacher I know told me that, at the insistence of her principal, she and many of her colleagues spent several hours producing statements of the school's aims. Some examples are:
– to foster a zest for learning and satisfaction in accomplishment;
– to provide equal opportunity for living and learning for all of our students;
– to encourage adaptability to a changing world.
This same teacher said that during one meeting she asked for time to be set aside to discuss possible means of implementing each aim. The administrator in charge of the meeting facetiously told her that she should come right up to the front of the room and tell the staff exactly how such aims should be implemented. The teacher explained that she could not. That was approximately a year ago and was the last she has heard about either the aims or their implementation.

It would seem then that, in general, official statements of educational goals, as the Hall-Dennis Commission tells us, have little effect on educational practices or for that matter on policy formation or decision making.

Are Goals Real?
According to James March, "few organization theories escape the need for postulating a concept either labelled as, or analogous to, organizational goals."[5] Not only is the concept a critical one in theoretical discussions of organizational behavior, but for Talcott Parsons, among others, goal attainment takes precedence over all other organizational activities.[6]

Etzioni defines an organizational goal as "a desired state of affairs which the organization attempts to realize."[7] For a number of reasons, some of which were pointed out previously, many theorists distinguish between the "official" and the "real" goals of an organization, for, it is argued, although official goals may not truly reflect "desired states of affairs," the real goals do.

But this raises a serious methodological question; how can we come to know (and agree) what are the "real" goals of an organization? It seems clear that asking the chief policy makers—the principal of a school, the director of education, the chairman of the board, or the Minister—does not suffice. Skeptics can always respond by saying, "that's just a bunch of talk."

In order to determine whether or not the concept of a "real" goal is useful, it is necessary to agree on a criterion of meaningfulness. I think that most social scientists would agree that in order for a proposition to be accepted as meaningful, it is necessary that one's belief in the truth or falsity of a proposition be subject to change as a result of empirical evidence. This criterion is applicable to all scientific propositions. In fact, it extends to much of ordinary discourse although it is often difficult to tell when a person is willing to accept this criterion. We do, however, make a commitment to accept this criterion when we serve on juries. The juror is supposed to begin with an open mind and permit the accumulation of evidence to alter his belief in the innocence or guilt of the accused. If he votes "guilty," the evidence must have persuaded him that the probability of guilt is extraordinarily high—"beyond reasonable doubt." It is more difficult to tell if an individual accepts this criterion when talking, for example, of the greatness of his country, or about the goals of his country or an organization, but in the social sciences there is, I believe, general agreement that this criterion will apply.[8]

If one accepts this criterion, then it is incumbent upon the theorist who develops propositions concerning organizational goals to inform the rest of us what we must observe in order to confirm that proposition. If a colleague tells us that an organization has goals A, B, and C, then we may legitimately ask how this was determined and *what* procedure must be followed if we are to reach similar (or contrary) results. If we accept the procedure as a valid means of collecting evidence, execute the procedure, and find evidence that tallies with our colleagues' conclusions, then the chances are that we will have a greater degree of belief in the truth of his proposition.

But here is the difficulty with the concept of organizational goals. There is no agreed upon procedure for determining what the goals of an organization are. There is not even agreement in principle on how to define the characteristics of goals, much less on the procedures one might use to identify them. As a result, during the past few years many social scientists have begun to question the utility of the concept of organizational goals.

Simon points out that "in the classical economic theory of the firm, where no distinction is made between an organization and a single entrepreneur, the organization's goal—the goal of the firm—is simply identical with the goal of the real or hypothetical entrepreneur."[9] But who, in education, is the entrepreneur, the individual whose personal goals represent the organization's goals? The educational system is simply too complex, decision making too pluralistic and too fluid, and the structure too poorly defined to permit the identification of one individual as the entrepreneur. Furthermore, as noted earlier, official statements of organizational goals are often viewed as irrelevant, and officials tend to present unreal goals.

It is also interesting to note that while principals, trustees, and other officials comfortably use such expressions as, "the first thing we must do is examine our goal priorities," or, "we must constantly strive to meet our goals," rarely does one observe them actually examining their goal priorities or organizing to systematically assess what should be done to meet the goals decided on. Agendas of meetings seldom include such items as, "The consideration of strategies to better achieve goal A." Nor do minutes of meetings record the goals that decisions are meant to achieve. Statements about specific goals are simply not part of the lexicon of most education organizations that are going about their everyday business, or, for that matter, even about their most serious business, policy formation.

One easy way of making an education official very nervous is to ask him to tell you exactly what are the goals of his program, department, school, or board. The official who does respond will often provide different answers to the same question at different times. A principal, for example, may tell you that his school's goals are A, B, and C during a fall meeting, then later, at a spring meeting, may offer what is, to the policy researcher at least, a totally different set. Yet, when questioned further, the same official may insist that the goals have not changed. It would seem, then, that asking officials to indicate the goals of their organization is not a very fruitful approach.

Another approach is to argue that the organization has a life of its own, regardless of who the leaders are at a given time. This implies that organizational goals exist over and above individuals, but it gives no suggestion as to how one might identify these reified goals.

An approach that some analysts favor is to identify the goals on the basis of decisions that have been made. But this raises even more issues. How, for example, does one go about determining which decisions should be analyzed?

In 1970, Joseph Farrell and I conducted a study of OISE.[10] As part of this study we listed thirteen decisions that were perceived as most significant by fifty individuals. They included all formal authorities (department chairmen, senior administrators, and unit heads), all association heads (chairmen of the Association of Research Officers, the Academic Council, etc.), and a handful of others (faculty, students, and support staff) who were reported to be influential or knowledgeable about OISE.

Certainly one can quarrel with our choice of individuals. However, even if one accepts our choice of who should identify decisions, there remains the problem of determining what goals these decisions reflect. Thirteen decisions were most frequently mentioned in the OISE study:

1. *Appointment and Promotion*—The decision by Academic Council to recommend "that the sole criterion for appointment and promotion to and within academic ranks be scholarly achievement" and "that ordinarily such achievement will be evidenced by suitable publication." (Nov. 9, 1966)
2. *Department Chairman's Tenure*—The decision by Academic Council to

recommend that a department chairman's tenure of office be limited to four years, renewable. (Jan. 11, 1967)
3. *Sociology in Education*—The decision by Academic Council to approve and recommend the establishment of a Department of Sociology in Education. (Feb. 22, 1967)
4. *Research Review Board*—The decision by Academic Council to recommend the establishment of a Research Review Board. (Mar. 8, 1967)
5. *Program Budget*—The decision by Academic Council to broaden participation in internal budgeting procedures through the use of a program budget format. (Oct. 11, 1967)
6. *New Building*—The decision by the Board of Governors to construct a new OISE building. (Oct. 12, 1967)
7. *Development Review Board*—The decision by Academic Council to recommend the establishment of a Development Review Board. (Feb. 14, 1968)
8. *Task Force*—The decision to establish a task force to recommend an alternative organizational structure. (Fall, 1968)
9. *Assistant Director*—The decision by the Director to recommend the appointment of a department chairman to the post of Assistant Director. (Sept. 26, 1968)
10. *Field Centers*—The decision by Academic Council to approve in principle and recommend the establishment of field centers throughout the province. (Nov. 27, 1968)
11. *Department of Special Education*—The decision by Academic Council to approve and recommend the establishment of a Department of Special Education. (Jan. 15, 1969)
12. *Merger of Research and Development Co-ordinatorships*—The decision by Academic Council to approve and recommend the merging of the offices of the Co-ordinators of Research and Development into a single Office of Research and Development. (Apr. 9, 1969)
13. *Departmental Guidelines*—The decision by Academic Council to approve and recommend acceptance of the Guidelines for Departmental Decision-Making. (Nov. 12, 1969)

While we recognized that these thirteen decisions might be classified in a variety of ways, we viewed each decision as falling into one of five categories: democratization, centralization of decision making on funding research and development projects, legitimation of development projects and the implementation of research findings, growth, and entrenchment. Although some respondents referred to these categories as "goals" (the democratization goal, the growth goal, etc.), we preferred to refer to them as "patterns," arguing that the decisions identified as significant by the same individuals might be different at a different point in time.

The problem with using decisions as the unit of analysis for determining organizational goals is that one must use the process of induction. And, as George Homans has pointed out, induction is a creative act "which has no rules of procedure that will ensure you success." Only deduction has definite rules, the rules of logic.[11]

There are, then, three problems entailed in using decisions as the unit of analysis for identifying organizational goals. First, organizations make too many decisions for them all to be of use as the units of analysis. The list needs to be reduced, but how? Second, if one identifies significant decisions by interviewing selected individuals in an organization, then the decisions named are, to some extent, dependent on what the current organizational issues are. In other words, the selected decisions may be a better index of current concerns than of historical goals. Third, even if respondents agree that a specific decision is significant, they may disagree on the ends that the decision was meant to achieve. There is, therefore, no guarantee that any two individuals will reach the same conclusions concerning goals, even if they do happen to agree on the same list of decisions to be analyzed.

Another argument for the existence of goals that is sometimes heard is that everyone agrees that organizations have goals so they must have goals. However, people in the same organization often fail to agree on what those goals are. Some even deny that their organization has goals. This, at least, was the stance taken by Ronald Jones, the former director of education for the Toronto Board of Education, who was quoted in the *Toronto Star* as stating that "the Toronto public school system is being run without any aims and objectives."[12]

Finally, of course, some individuals use precisely the same argument for the existence of organizational goals that have been used to defend the existence of God (the ontological and teleological positions). One could, of course, counter these arguments with precisely the same logical arguments that philosophers have used to *deny* the existence of God, but this would serve no particular function because the identification of goals is an empirical issue as well as a logical one.

These, then, are some of the current views on organizational goals. While many theorists have not yet abandoned the concept, some have sufficiently altered it to a point where it is virtually useless as a construct for policy researchers. In fact, Lawrence Mohr begins his article "The Concept of Organizational Goal" with the following statement: "Much has been written in recent years about the concept of organizational goal, some of it rather discouraging; the most frequently cited papers offer little hope that the concept will have any real utility for social scientists."[13]

The Policy Researcher's Concept of Goals
It has been argued that, in general, goals have no effect on decision making or policy formation. It has also been argued that real goals cannot be identi-

fied. Nonetheless, the policy researcher informs us that his first task is the identification of goals. He would have us believe that once he has identified official organizational goals, he translates them into more concrete terms and devises or borrows some instrument to measure these concrete terms; however, the outcomes that the researcher measures generally cannot be deduced from official statements of goals or policies. The vagueness and ambiguity of most official statements make such deductions impossible. Instead, the researcher tends to use official goals and policy statements as general guidelines for deciding which class of outcomes will be measured.

These guidelines restrict the selection of specific measurable goals or outcomes, but they do not determine them. The choice of the specific outcomes is generally left to the researcher and reflects *his* personal values. Thus, at some point in the research procedure, there will appear a written list of prescriptive sentences that are operationally defined and are therefore measurable. I choose to call these linguistic entities, which can be broadly referred to as outcomes as distinct from inputs, policy researcher's goals (or, simply, PR goals).

In his book *Diffusion of Innovation*, Everett Rogers notes that

an innovation is an idea perceived as new by the individual. It really matters little, as far as human behaviour is concerned, whether or not an idea is "objectively" new as measured by the amount of time elapsed since its first use or discovery. It is the newness of the idea to the individual that determines his reaction to it.[14]

A potential problem is that PR goals will be seen as innovations by the administrative officials concerned. The problem can be compounded if the administrative officials see the PR goals as ones that are highly innovative, since they are more likely to resist accepting research findings if they see the goals as major departures in form, function, and structure from currently accepted ideas or practices within the organization.

If one compares the sentences that principals and other education officials call goals with the sentences offered by researchers and also called goals, it becomes apparent that they differ in very basic ways. PR goals are explicit, concrete, and measurable. Many researchers view PR goals as dependent or "effect" variables and suggest that the logic of evaluative research is equivalent to the logic of basic research; that is, both are concerned with hypothesis testing. In evaluative research, the dependent variable becomes "the goal to be achieved." On the other hand, administrative officials' "goal-like" sentences are vague, ambiguous, and rich in connotative terms, but lacking in denotation. The function (or perceived functions) of goals can also be very different. The goal-like sentences of the researcher (PR goals) are intended to serve as basic elements in formal and explicit planning, evaluation, and decision-making exercises.[15] The goal-like sentences of administrative officials may be used for a number of purposes, but they are generally not perceived as basic elements in planning, evaluation, and decision making.

PR goals can be viewed as an innovation, but that is not to say they are not useful. Double-entry bookkeeping, after all, was an innovation developed largely in the fourteenth century. The father of modern accounting is said to be a Franciscan monk, Fra Luca Pacioli. Goethe viewed Pacioli's work as one of the finest discoveries of the human intellect. Oswald Spengler claimed that Pacioli's work ranked in importance with the discovery of the New World and the theory of the rotation of the earth around the sun. And, according to the nineteenth-century economic historian Werner Sombart:

> One can scarcely conceive of capitalism without double-entry bookkeeping; they are related as are form and content. It is difficult to decide, however, whether in double-entry bookkeeping capitalism provided itself with a tool to make it more effective, or whether capitalism derives from the "spirit" of double-entry bookkeeping.[16]

Accounting, like PR goals, provides a method for abstracting one part of an organization's reality. From double-entry bookkeeping one constructs balance sheets and profit-and-loss statements—the two most popular abstractions of a modern profit-making firm. These two documents constitute an important part of the economic history of the organization and, with other accounting information, provide input for decision making, data for policy evaluation, and a linguistic style for formulating and evaluating some of the important goals of a firm.

PR goals, then, can be viewed as innovations. This is also the perspective taken by Gail Stewart with respect to social indicators. She writes, "since every social indicator, no matter how apparently isolated, represents a way of viewing reality and hence represents a value judgement on the part of its creator, shouldn't every social indicator be signed by its creator as an artist might sign his work?"[17]

SOME NEGATIVE CONSEQUENCES OF PR GOALS

While many individuals who engage in policy research are loath to admit it, those who have scrutinized the field generally reach conclusions similar to those of Reginald Carter: "Although there are a number of examples within the industrial and educational settings that demonstrate the effects of social science research on implementing successful organizational change, they are exceptions rather than the rule."[18]

It is quite true that the number of policy research studies has increased rapidly over the past decade; however, the function of these studies is not always what it seems to be. Francis Caro believes that "a number of covert motives of actionists for engaging social scientists to 'evaluate' programs [are] (1) for arbitration to settle an internal dispute; (2) to justify decisions already made; (3) to support a bid for power; (4) to postpone action." And Carter claims that "one of the primary latent functions of many evaluation studies [is] a legitimization process for predetermined policies."[19]

Viewing PR goals as innovations provides a frame of reference for examining the manifest and latent functions of policy research and the resistance to negative findings. The framework is provided by scholars in the field of diffusion of innovations.

Katz, Levin, and Hamilton have defined the diffusion process as "(1) acceptance (2) over time (3) of some specific item—an idea or practice (4) by individuals, groups or other adopting units, linked to (5) specific channels of communication, (6) to a social structure and (7) to a given system of values, or culture."[20] It is not at all clear what "acceptance" means with respect to PR goals, but what does seem clear is that resistance to policy-research findings—negative findings at least—is an area receiving increasing attention. Donald T. Campbell writes that "in the U.S.A., one of the pervasive reasons why interpretable program evaluations are so rare is the widespread resistance of institutions and administrators to having their programs evaluated. The methodology of evaluation research should include the reasons for this resistance and ways of overcoming it."[21]

Carter presents three propositions concerning resistance, one of which reads: "The greater the difference between the client's or manager's concept of the social reality being studied and the research findings, the greater will be his resistance to negative research findings."[22]

There are deficiencies in the most commonly used design or process of "inventing" PR goals that may account for some of this resistance; the process may lead to a concept of social reality that differs from that of the client or manager, and that is incompatible with certain social or cultural values. More specifically, this common approach to design tends to—

1. usurp the authority of legitimate policy makers by permitting researchers to choose the goal criteria;
2. deny individuals their legitimate right to participate in the goal specification process;
3. culminate in a single set of values—in the form of instrumental or ultimate PR goals, which are imposed on units that have a legitimate claim to diverse sets of values.

To illustrate each of these points, I shall use examples from both my own work and the work of others. I trust that the authors of the studies I cite will accept my criticisms in the spirit in which they are intended, as criticisms of a pervasive and conventional *style* of research and not of the conclusions per se.

Usurpation of Authority
Social accounting and evaluation studies typically begin by analyzing statements of aims and purposes made by legitimate policy makers, constructing or selecting a list of measurable outcomes that more or less reflect these statements, applying these measures to all units being evaluated, and either

rank ordering units according to the outcome measures or treating all units as components of a single system and arriving at generalizations about the system as a whole. Sometimes the measures are aggregated into a single index and sometimes they are not. Depending on the nature of the study, and whether or not an aggregated index is used, the measures are referred to by such terms as goal measures, social indicators, performance measures, measures of the quality of life, and welfare aggregates.

In view of the consequences, the critical point in the research process is the first step, the selection of measurable outcomes, that is, PR goals. The social scientist will ordinarily try to select PR goals that fall within the context of vague statements of purposes as they appear in formal documents or speeches. However, translating these statements of purpose into measurable goals is an activity requiring the exercise of substantial discretionary power. Goals, objectives, and aims are usually presented in vague and ambiguous terms and only rarely do they denote measurable goals. For many and perhaps most programs in the public sector, it is impossible to compile a list of statements from policy makers that indicates they have reached a consensus on even the general aims of a program, much less on the specific PR goals that best reflect the aims.

The researcher often generates a long list of PR goals that are "in the ball-park" and then, owing to time or cost constraints, proceeds to eliminate a large number of these goal measures. Rarely are policy makers consulted on which PR goals to exclude and which to include. This is tantamount to giving the researcher broad powers to interpret the aims of the program and decide which slice of reality is most important for assessing its effectiveness. To cite an example, one research project in which I participated attempted to assess the credit system in terms of its effect on the postsecondary experiences and attitudes of secondary school graduates.[23] Credit system aims, as they are reflected in formal documents, are embraced in more general statements on the goal of the school:

The primary purpose of a school is to help students develop to the maximum their potential as individuals and as members of society. This purpose can be achieved by facilitating the intellectual, social, physical, and emotional growth of young people and by developing more fully the knowledge, skills, and aptitudes that they bring with them to the secondary school.[24]

Our research team originally selected sixteen measures that we believed reflected these general aims. However, we also felt that collecting data on all of these measures would require respondents to answer a questionnaire that was too lengthy to result in a high response rate. It was decided, therefore, to eliminate several of these measures. Among the measures eliminated were those dealing with the need for achievement, self-concepts, and feelings about others. The research team made this decision, as is typical in such studies, without consulting either the Ministry personnel who contracted the study or the principals whose graduates were being assessed. The research team, not the policy makers, decided that an outcome such as changes in one's feelings of efficacy is a more important criterion of credit system effectiveness than is an outcome such as changes in one's feelings about others.

There are researchers involved in evaluation studies who may disagree with the above thesis, namely, that the selection of PR goals—and goal measures—is the responsibility of the policy maker. Susan Kaufman, for example, notes that "the choice of what will be measured by an evaluative study often reflects the values of the researchers who designed the study." She does not argue that the values of the policy maker should be reflected; instead, she suggests that the group whose values should be reflected are those who participate in the study. Koopman holds a similar view and argues that involvement in evaluation should be community-wide.[25]

Neither Kaufman nor Koopman indicates exactly how participants or the community should be involved, what information they should provide, or how the information they provide should be used. However, Kaufman's monograph is a prelude to an evaluation study of occupational programs, and she notes that her monograph should be read before the research report itself because "the information and references it contains will help the reader to understand the evaluation process and approach the research study with greater ease and insight."[26]

The report to which Kaufman refers is "A Follow-Up Study of Special Vocational and Special High School Students" by Reich and Zeigler, a study of ten special schools in Toronto and the Borough of York requested by the Toronto Board of Education (Board Minutes, July 15, 1970).[27] Some of the "success" criteria, or, as Kaufman phrases it, "the choices of what will be measured," were the number of students who transferred to other, more academically demanding, schools; their employment rate; employment stability; salary levels; male–female salary disparities; the relationship between vocational specialization and occupational placement; and student judgments of the school program. These, and the other criteria used in the study, are but a small sampling of possible criteria. Further, there is no evidence in the report to suggest that individuals other than researchers selected the measures. The acknowledgments tell us that directors of research and heads of guidance from the various boroughs "made major contributions to details of design and development of the interview schedule." Apparently neither the principals responsible for operating programs within the special schools nor members of the boards of education responsible for funding the special schools even contributed, much less chose what would be measured.

It could, of course, be argued that if policy makers are permitted to choose the criteria they will simply choose the PR goals and measures that will make their programs look successful. But social science research is—or should be—open and explicit, and such tactics would become visible to the decision makers' superiors and to interest groups who disagree with the criteria.

Unrepresentative Participation

Citizens, as well as decision makers, are often excluded from participating in choosing the PR goals that are of direct concern to them. For example, a 1969 paper by Thoman reports on a study that was to be conducted by the Regional Development Branch of Ontario's Department of Treasury and Economics. This study was part of an attempt to meet the general aims of regional development, as expressed in the white paper "Design for Development" (Phases 1 and 2) and in subsequent speeches by the Premier and other members of the Cabinet. The three objectives cited by the report are—

1. The encouragement of each region of the Province to achieve its socio-economic potential, insofar as such encouragement is in harmony with overall provincial interest and development.
2. The encouragement of careful use of the natural environment.
3. The improvement of both efficiency and effectiveness of provincial departmental services by encouraging a coordinated rather than a unilateral or piecemeal approach to (*a*) regional problems of interest to more than one department, and (*b*) general administrative matters, especially those involving administrative regions.[28]

Thoman's paper goes on to describe a study designed to assess the performance of geographical units within the province. This assessment was accomplished by using sixty-three indicators of population and economic change and classifying the performance of the units or communities into five levels, ranging from high to low.

These sixty-three indices and their weights represent a value system that was used to judge the performance of communities. The author of the report stresses such concepts as "human values" and "the optimization of the quality of life"; however, one cannot help but wonder to what degree the researchers' own values are defining what will constitute a community in which "the quality of life" has been optimized, for, as far as I have been able to determine, community members were excluded from the process of influencing the selection of indices or the weight an indicator would carry.

Failure to Recognize Individual Differences

The aforementioned studies can also be used to illustrate a third negative effect, the evaluation of similar social units using one, and only one, set of values.

At all levels of government one finds increasing concern for preserving and perpetuating individual, organizational, and cultural variation. The general principle was expressed during the Speech from the Throne in the autumn of 1970:

The Canada of the seventies must continue to be a land for people; a country in which freedom and individualism are cherished and nurtured; a society in which the Government lends its strength to withstand, rather than support, the pressures for conformity ... with foresight and stamina and enterprise ours may be, if we wish it ... a society in which human differences are regarded as assets, not liabilities.

In our society there are a number of similar social units that can legitimately claim the right to pursue different goals, even though their general aims may be much the same. Universities, for example, traditionally have diverse goals and priorities. In Ontario the same is true for colleges of applied arts and technology and for school boards. Cities and smaller jurisdictions also have a claim to diverse goals, as is evidenced by the degree of financial autonomy granted to municipal governments. These governments have considerable power to decide what kinds of services will be given high priority and what kind of land development will take place within municipal boundaries. The current debate concerning the mix of high rises and single-family dwellings is one that is being settled in the cities, one by one, and the outcome of this debate may differ with each community.

The previously mentioned study by Thoman evaluated the performance of all geographical units within the province. It was claimed that this study was concerned with optimizing the quality of life. The position of the government, as reflected in the Speech from the Throne and other documents, is to encourage differences in values and to acknowledge that what is best for one person or one community may not be best for some other person or community. The Thoman proposal, however, judges the performance of all communities by only one set of values. Here, then, a premium is placed on homogeneous rather than heterogeneous values. Communities were not permitted to add new indicators—ones that they believed best reflected their goals and aspirations. Nor were communities permitted to tamper with the weighting system, which meant that a specific indicator carried identical weight in all communities. Could it not be that one community values x more than y, while another community values y more than x?

The case is much the same in the study of the credit system. The Ministry informs parents that individual schools are to remain flexible: "Flexibility is the keyword of the Credit System, and this carries through to the program of each school. Schools are being encouraged to offer the types and levels of courses that best fit their students."[29]

Many evaluation studies of the credit system apply the same outcome measures to every school in their study. A principal who views his implementation of the credit system as a major vehicle to improve students' understanding of other students, and who, for example, creates a house system to further this goal, may simply not receive information relevant to his goal.[30] If his school ranks poorly on the outcome measures that are used, he may feel pressed to shift his policies in an effort to show up well on the goals that are measured.

Imposing a single set of indicators on social units is a strategy that can lead to a complete homogenization of goals. This could then reduce innovations and, if carried far enough, threaten the very survival of our social system. In Donald C. Campbell's essay on social evolution, he argues as follows:

> . . . variations provide adequate raw materials for selective systems to operate on, whether the variations are deliberate or haphazard. The more numerous and the greater the heterogeneity among variations, the richer the opportunities for an advantageous innovation. Note, however, that at many levels of cultural development, and for organic evolution, variation is at the expense of jeopardizing the already achieved adaptive system. Too high a mutation rate threatens the preservations of the complexly adapted animal form. Nonetheless, other things being equal, those social-environmental settings providing the greatest range of variations, are the most likely to produce cultural advances.[31]

Imposing the same set of PR goals on all schools could reduce efforts at individualization and inhibit the development of innovative policies and practices.

It would be paradoxical if social scientists, in the name of optimizing the quality of life, inadvertently used their technical expertise to destroy rather than renew and protect the freedom and values central to the individual and social pursuit of the good life. Clearly needed are planning, evaluative, and social accounting procedures that are capable of reflecting and working with differences in individual and institutional values.

TOWARD A NEW DESIGN

In this concluding section, I describe a design that was consciously constructed to avoid the kinds of problems outlined in the preceding sections of this paper.[32]

The study, a component in a large project dealing with student participation in decision making, required that we evaluate the effectiveness of student governments in thirty-six Ontario secondary schools. The purpose of the study was, first, to provide a measure of student government effectiveness that could be used as a variable for testing a series of hypotheses, and second, to provide information to principals that would stimulate them to act if confronted with negative findings.

A conventional design approach might have begun with a request that the schools provide official statements of the goals of the student government. If statements were available, then a list of measures or criteria would be constructed that more or less mapped to the official aims. If they were unavailable, then principals would be interviewed and asked what the goals of the student government were. From these statements, measures would be constructed.

But asking principals to report the goals of their student governments evokes those typical uninterpretable, unmeasurable, vague statements that were discussed earlier—for example, "to promote good citizenship."

The second approach we considered was simply to use a design constructed by other researchers. In one such study, James McPartland and his colleagues examined fourteen urban high schools in the Baltimore area. The study defined a student government as perfectly effective if (and only if) 100 percent of the student body in a school agreed that—

1. student government can change school rules even if teachers or principals are against the changes;
2. student government does not worry only about social activities in the school;
3. teachers and principals do let students who really disagree with them get elected to student government;
4. students who are interested in making changes will go to the student government;
5. the people elected to student government usually do not simply say what will make the teachers and principals happy.[33]

We rejected this design on the grounds that to use this index for Ontario secondary schools would, like the first design, (1) usurp the authority of the chief policy maker—in this case, the school principal, (2) exclude the possibility of participation by others in the school, and (3) impose the same criteria on all thirty-six schools. In addition, it seemed less likely that a principal would accept negative findings and act upon them if he had no commitment to the evaluation criteria.

Our new design approach began with a perspective provided by T. H. Huxley in his essay "We Are All Scientists":

Scientific investigation is not, as many people seem to suppose, some kind of modern black art. You might easily gather this impression from the manner in which many persons speak of scientific inquiry, or talk about inductive and deductive philosophy, or the principles of the "Baconian philosophy."

The method of scientific investigation is nothing but the expression of the necessary mode of working of the human mind. It is simply the mode at which all phenomena are reasoned about, rendered precise and exact.[34]

Huxley's argument is that the social science methods used by policy researchers are not unique, but extend, make more precise, and deal more systematically with those thought processes already used by principals. This process is delightfully expressed in A. A. Milne's *Winnie The Pooh*. Winnie, in search of Piglet, goes to Piglet's house. But, writes Milne, "To his surprise he saw that the door was open and the more he looked inside, the more Piglet wasn't there." This humorous statement is an accurate description of the process of testing a hypothesis and arriving at a conclusion. A person may begin by hypothesizing that a friend is at home. As the person accumulates more and more evidence, his belief in the truth of the proposition diminishes. He may ring the bell, enter the house, search every room, and, if he believes something sinister might have taken place, even check the closets and the basement. Each additional observation added to the evidence already accumulated serves to change his opinion and lead him to reject the initial hypothesis.

Our first task was to determine what kind of empirical evidence principals use in order to infer whether or not student governments are effective. We began by interviewing principals not included in our sample, asking them, "If you were to enter a secondary school and wanted to determine the effectiveness of the student government, what questions would you ask and of whom would you ask them?" One principal told us he would ask the student government members if they trusted their principal. Another told us that he would ask teachers if the members of the student government represented the best political skills among the students in the school. A third told us that he would want to make certain that students understood that the principal has the major responsibility for decision making.

By listing the principals' questions and adding questions from other research studies, we compiled a list of 49 items that were, like the McPartland items, stated in an agree–disagree format. However, while McPartland used students as the only relevant opinion group, our list had 16 items with students as the opinion group, 26 with student government members as the opinion group, and 7 with teachers as the opinion group.

Our list of 49 items was then sent to each of the 50 principals participating in the study, with the request that they select the six they believed to be the most important for assessing the effectiveness of their schools' student governments. Each principal was also given an opportunity to list additional criteria, but only a couple did so.

To motivate principals to take the selection task seriously, we told them that because of financial constraints we would only be able to provide them with data on their school for the six items they selected. Thus, their choice of criteria was based on the information they most wanted to receive. While some criteria were more popular than others, no two principals selected the same six items.[35]

Finally, to prevent the possibility of a principal choosing the items that he believed would reflect most favorably on him, we stressed that the results for his particular school would be made known only to him. Each principal could, of course, choose to distribute the findings to others in the school, and some principals later informed us that they did discuss the results with their student government or their staff.

By avoiding any discussion of "goals" and focusing on "evidence," we were able to add other features to the research design that helped to overcome several problems. There is a tendency for clients to refuse to acknowledge the validity of research findings that show a problem may exist.[36] There is also a tendency for clients, and sometimes researchers as well, to change their terms of reference after the fact when they are confronted with research findings that could be construed as inconclusive or negative. As Peter Rossi observes, "without commitment to the bet, one or both of the gamblers usually welch."[37] But if evaluative research cannot act as a stimulus to decision making, it is probably useless.

In an effort to reduce the tendency to "welch," we asked each principal to record his "critical decision range" prior to his being given any actual data on his goal measures. The critical decision range was defined as the values that a measure must assume in order for the decision maker to feel that a problem exists. For example, a principal's first item might deal with the percentage of student government members who report that they "trust the principal." If 100 percent of the members report that they trust the principal, then the principal would feel the evidence supports his conception of an effective student government. In this situation no problem could be said to exist (unless it was a problem of measurement). If 90, 80, or even 70 percent of the student government members say they trust the principal, then the principal may also deny the existence of a problem. However, at some point, 60, 40, or 20 percent, the principal will say, "Wait a minute. If only n percent of the members say that they trust me, then something is wrong and something must be done to correct the situation." All points that evoke this "wait a minute" response are said to constitute the critical decision range.

In an effort to reduce the possibility that a principal, on receiving a negative finding, would rationalize it away by saying to himself, "I knew that I had a problem here all along," we asked each principal to give us, for each item, his prediction as to how the opinion group would respond to the item he selected. By comparing this estimate with the principal's critical decision range, we knew whether or not he was predicting the existence of a problem. Interestingly enough, more than 50 percent of the principals predicted that they had one or more problems, leading us to conclude that our format was successful in encouraging principals to acknowledge the existence of problems.

This design attempted to avoid the problems raised earlier. The policy maker was given the responsibility for selecting his own criteria. He was also given the opportunity to be influenced by others in the school, not only with respect to the selection of effectiveness criteria but also with respect to defining the critical decision range.

C. West Churchman offers the following comments on educational goals:

I realize that the attempt to define the goals of education was at one time very popular and has since entered into a period of disillusionment as we discovered how difficult it is to define these educational goals in a manner which would make any difference in the educational process. I think the disillusionment itself was mistaken, just as a disillusionment in the attempt to define national goals would be a mistake. Obviously, an area so rich and difficult as the definition of human goals demands, like any life form, a growth through immaturity to some kind of mature status; and the maturation period may be very long, indeed, as I am convinced it will be in the case of educational goals. Simply to be disappointed because in a relatively short period of time we have not been able to reach a reasonable consensus on educational goals is certainly no reason to give up the enterprise.[38]

The study we conducted gave the principal complete authority for selecting PR goals and, in the short run at least, also gave him complete responsibility for considering the relationship of his PR goals to the general aims of the student government program. This same design could be used to determine the PR goals of students, teachers, and members of the student government. If that were done in future studies, principals might then be stimulated to initiate a more general discussion concerning the most appropriate PR goals as well as a dialogue dealing with the relationship of PR goals both to the more general aims of the student government and to the more general objectives of the school.

There are many problems with our design. It is more time-consuming and expensive; it restricts the type and form of evidence to be collected; there is not yet evidence that it has a greater effect in stimulating organizational change or increasing participation than do other types of research design. However, as one colleague is fond of saying, anything worth doing is worth doing poorly. We felt the risk of doing the new design poorly was one worth taking. At least it lays the groundwork on which improvements can be based. But most important, policy researchers must begin to deal with the possible implications of their designs and the possible negative consequences that occur if their findings are taken seriously. Failure to do so may well stimulate Tom Lehrer to provide a verse for policy researchers similar to the one he provided for a famous physical scientist:

> Once the Rockets go up
> who cares where they come down
> That's not my department
> says Werner Von Braun

NOTES

1. Alvin Toffler, *Future Shock* (Toronto: Bantam Books of Canada, 1971), p. 472.
2. Provincial Committee on Aims and Objectives of Education in the Schools of Ontario, Report of the Committee, *Living and Learning* (Toronto: Ontario Department of Education, 1968), p. 3.
3. The Board of Education for the City of Toronto, *Policy Decisions of Board 1969 to 1973, Inclusive* (Toronto: Board of Education, Administrative Services Department, 1974), p. 33.
4. Ibid., p. 88.
5. James G. March, "Theory of Organizational Decision-Making," in *Small Groups, Studies in Social Interaction*, ed. A. Paul Hare, Edgar F. Borgatta, and Robert F. Bales (New York: Alfred A. Knopf, 1965), p. 146.
6. Talcott Parsons, "A Sociological Approach to the Theory of Formal Organizations," in *Structure and Process in Modern Societies* (New York: Free Press of Glencoe, 1960), pp. 38–41.
7. Amitai Etzioni, *Modern Organizations* (Englewood Cliffs, N.J.: Prentice-Hall, 1964), p. 6.

8. For a more detailed and precise discussion of this topic see Alfred J. Ayer, *Language, Truth and Logic* (New York: Dover Publications, 1946); and Rudolf Carnap, "Testability and Meaning," in *Readings in the Philosophy of Science*, ed. Herbert Feigl and May Brodbeck (New York: Appleton-Century-Crofts, 1953), pp. 47–92.

9. Herbert Simon, "On the Concept of Organizational Goal," *Administrative Science Quarterly*, vol. 9 (June 1964): 2.

10. William E. Alexander and Joseph P. Farrell, "Who Are We and Where Are We Going? An Analysis of Patterns of Development in a New Academic Institution," *Research in Higher Education*, vol. 2, no. 4 (1974): 341–60.

11. George C. Homans, *Social Behaviour: Its Elementary Forms* (New York: Harcourt, Brace & World, 1961), p. 10.

12. "Ex-City Schools Chief: Trustees Bow to 'Mob Rule,'" *Toronto Star*, 19 November 1973, p. A4.

13. Lawrence B. Mohr, "The Concept of Organizational Goal," *American Political Science Review*, vol. 67 (June 1973): 470.

14. Everett M. Rogers, *Diffusion of Innovations* (New York: Free Press of Glencoe, 1962), p. 13.

15. Caro indicates three "stated objectives" of evaluation research: (1) providing accounting information for funding sources, (2) feedback to administrators to aid in refining and improving the program, and (3) dissemination of program information to the general public. Rarely are official goals constructed with these objectives in mind. (Francis G. Caro, "Approaches to Evaluative Research: A Review," *Human Organization*, vol. 28, no. 2 [1969]: 89.)

16. Goethe and Spengler, cited in T. A. Wise, "The Auditors Have Arrived," in *The Accounting Sampler*, ed. Thomas J. Burns and Harvey S. Handrickson (New York: McGraw-Hill, 1972), p. 18; and W. Sombart, *Der Moderne Kapitalismus*, as quoted in Myron J. Gordon and Gordon Shillinglaw, *Accounting: A Management Approach* (Homewood, Ill.: Richard D. Irwin, 1974), p. 6.

17. Gail Stewart, "On Looking Before Leaping," in *Social Indicators, Proceedings of a Seminar*, Novia A. M. Carter, coordinator (Ottawa: Canadian Council on Social Development, 1972), p. 30.

18. Reginald K. Carter, "Clients' Resistance to Negative Findings and the Latent Conservative Function of Evaluation Studies," *The American Sociologist*, vol. 6 (May 1971): 123.

19. Caro, "Approaches to Evaluative Research," p. 89 (the motives were originally identified by Anthony Downs in "Some Thoughts on Giving People Economic Advice," *American Behavioral Scientist*, vol. 9 [September 1965]: 30–32); Carter, "Clients' Resistance," p. 118.

20. Elihu L. Katz, Martin L. Levin, and Herbert Hamilton, "Traditions of Research on the Diffusion of Innovation," *American Sociological Review*, vol. 28, no. 2 (April 1963): 237.

21. Donald T. Campbell, "Assessing the Impact of Planned Social Change" (background paper presented at the OECD seminar, Social Research and Public Policies, Dartmouth, N.H., Sept. 13–15, 1974), p. 28.

22. Carter, "Clients' Resistance," p. 118.

23. V. R. D'Oyley et al., "Comparative Study of Post-Secondary Achievements and Attitudes of Students from Traditional and Credit System High Schools" (unpublished report submitted to the Ministry of Education, Ontario, 1973).

24. Ontario Department of Education, *Recommendations and Information for Secondary School Organization Leading to Certificates and Diplomas*, Circular H.S. 1 (1972/73), p. 3.

25. Susan Kaufman, "Issues in Evaluating Occupational Programmes," no. 101, mimeographed (Toronto: Board of Education, Research Service, 1971), p. 6; and P. Koopman, "What Do We Mean by Evaluation Research?," *Education Canada* (March 1971), pp. 48–51.

26. Kaufman, "Issues," p. 2.

27. Carol M. Reich and Suzanne Zeigler, "A Follow-Up Study of Special Vocational and Special High School Students," no. 102, mimeographed (Toronto: Board of Education, Research Service, 1972).

28. Richard S. Thoman, "Regional Development in Ontario," mimeographed (Province of Ontario, Department of Treasury and Economics, Sept. 8, 1969), pp. 10 and 11.

29. *Response to Change, Information Guide for Parents* (Toronto: Ministry of Education, Ontario, October 1972).

30. William E. Alexander and Joseph P. Farrell, *The Individualized System: Student Patricipation in Decision-Making* (Toronto: Ontario Institute for Studies in Education, 1975).

31. Donald T. Campbell, "Variation and Selective Retention in Socio-Cultural Evolution," in *Social Change in Developing Areas*, ed. Herbert R. Barringer, George I. Blanksten, and Raymond W. Mack (Cambridge, Mass.: Schenkman Publishing, 1965), p. 28.

32. A complete description of the design and the major findings of the evaluation study is currently in preparation.

33. James McPartland et al., *Student Participation in High School Decisions: A Study of 14 Urban High Schools* (U.S., Department of Health, Education and Welfare, 1971), pp. 13–14.

34. T. H. Huxley, "We Are All Scientists," in *Basic Problems of Philosophy*, ed. D. J. Bronstein, Y. H. Krikorian, and P. P. Wiener (Englewood Cliffs, N.J.: Prentice-Hall, 1956), p. 233.

35. For a discussion of those problems, see John W. Holland, " 'Priorities,' the Most Important Nonsense Word in Public Finance and Policy Making," mimeographed (Toronto: Ontario Institute for Studies in Education, Department of Educational Planning, March 1973).

36. Carter, "Clients' Resistance," p. 120.

37. Peter Rossi, "Boobytraps and Pitfalls in the Evaluation of Social Action Programs," in *Proceedings of the Social Statistics Section of the Annual Meeting of the American Statistical Association* (Washington, D.C.: American Statistical Association, 1966), p. 129.

38. C. West Churchman, "R^2 on E: Some Suggestions for Research on the Role of Research in Higher Education," in *The Outputs of Higher Education: Their Identification, Measurement and Evaluation*, ed. Ben Lawrence, George Weathersby, and Virginia W. Patterson (Boulder, Colo.: Western Interstate Commission for Higher Education, 1970), p. 41.

Education, Public Policy, and Personal Choice

John W. Holland

THE IMPORTANT OCCASION

Having an important occasion for writing an essay is the next best thing to having a theme. In this case, the occasion invites the theme, and I welcome the opportunity to respond.

The occasion is the joint occurrence of Professor R. W. B. Jackson's retirement from the directorship of OISE and the tenth anniversary of the founding of this institution. Since Professor Jackson is the only director this institution has had, and because his influence has determined to such an important extent what the organization is and is not, I consider the occasion at hand to be more the joint observation of the tenth anniversary of the Institute and of his directorship than of his retirement.

As he has gone about his job as director, Professor Jackson has always had my admiration for the competence, generosity, and patience he has demonstrated, and even my gratitude for subjecting himself to the dangers and rigors of the job. As a researcher, spokesman for educational expansion, and administrator of an educational research organization during the 1960s, Professor Jackson made the case for public policy appropriate to the educational demands and demographic realities of the time—convincingly, and with a candor and sobriety almost unmatched among education lobbyists. As we get further into the 1970s, the more convinced I become that this province benefited materially from his style of restraint.

The other part of the occasion, the tenth anniversary of OISE, is to me an exciting event—perhaps for what some people will consider the wrong reasons. I have been a part of OISE for eight and a half of its ten years. From my first days here I have listened to observations as to how what was happening differed from what "was supposed to be happening." Those observations became more frequent in about 1968, and I found it strange that, as often as not, they came from people who had not been here as long as I had. Even today I am sometimes overcome by a strange feeling that there circulates among my colleagues the original detailed plan for all that OISE was to be and do. As it moves from hand to hand, they remind one another that everybody can look at it but I.

Though I have listened respectfully and patiently for hours and hours while the real old-timers, those who put the Institute together, talked about what they thought they had been up to, I must confess that I don't see clearly the difference between what was supposed to be and what has been. With due respect to my seniors and with much gratitude for interesting stories well told, I must say that, for me, the only common theme of all their tales is that the world and Ontario have evolved quite differently from the ways they anticipated back in 1965.

No doubt I might have a different attitude about what has happened to us these ten years had I been a founding member of the Institute. As one of the innocent, lucky foreigners sucked into the professorial vacuum that Ontario declared to exist when OISE and a half-dozen new universities were created, I cannot claim to have arrived in these halls with any picture in mind of what this institution should have been. The excitement of circumventing one of the world's great inland seas, and the surprise of learning that there was civilization of a sort even beyond Buffalo, caused me to disassociate what I saw here from any prejudice I may have had about what a new university, a new graduate department of education, or a new social research center should be or look like. It certainly did not occur to me that what I saw was in any way different from what should have been. I had to be told that some things had gone awry before I got here. (It has sometimes been my function to serve as evidence that they did.) But to me it has generally seemed that OISE has been unfolding pretty nearly as it should, considering that Ontario and Canada have unfolded as they have.

Matthew Arnold described his university as that "home of lost causes, and forsaken beliefs, and unpopular names, and impossible loyalties." I've made it a point never to check the context in which he said it, because that might damage my happy conviction that he was telling us what every academic institution is likely to be. Certainly he describes every one of them that I have ever known, this one being no exception. And I don't think I could ever grow fond of one that didn't meet that description. Even less do I suppose that I could muster much enthusiasm for an institution that worked out the way its founders had in mind that it should.

Academic institutions are very much like love children. They exist in one period of time as the products of what has turned out to have been an overly enthusiastic relationship in another period of time. They usually grow up in a climate quite different from the one in which they were conceived. In the early 1960s, Ontario became incautiously enamored of the academic community. Her ardor has cooled, but she now has OISE, indeed a sizeable litter of new institutions, to care for or neglect as she can and will. There may be some reconciliations between policy makers and the academic community of Ontario in the future, but they shouldn't be expected to last, and this institution like many another will have to find affection where it can, and a place in the sun if it can.

Love, whatever else it may be, is one of our inventions for handling conflict. Founding new institutions is another way. It was to deal with the conflicts of 1965 that OISE was created. The conflicts of 1965 are not the conflicts of today, and consequently OISE, like all institutions do at some time, faces a trial—a test of its "institutionality."

The word "institution" is commonly used in several ways. When we are not being careful with our language, we apply it to practically any organization. We are seldom reluctant to apply the term to a large, not-for-profit, chartered establishment with some claim to autonomy. Autonomy comes in all degrees, however; and when such an establishment is vitally dependent upon short-term, recurring subsidies from the state or another institution, it is very difficult to distinguish between agency and institution.

How will we know when OISE has passed or failed the test of institutionality? We might appeal to authority and use the test implicit in Parsons and Smelser's definition of institutions as the "ways in which the value patterns of the common culture of a social system are integrated in the concrete actions of its units in their interaction with each other through the definition of role expectations and the organization of motivation."[1] The rigorous test implied here suggests that the Institute will unquestionably be an institution when we can say that the roles of certain occupational groups, organizations, or agencies are commonly accepted as legitimate—or are not—because OISE says they are. Or, just as unquestionably, OISE will be an institution when large numbers of people, organizations, or agencies choose to do something or refrain from doing it because OISE tells them it is a good thing to do it or not to do it.

As an institution watcher, I shall apply a less demanding test to this organization. In 1964, the members of the Inter-University Research Program in Institution Building, in "The Guiding Concepts," offered a triple test to apply when determining whether an organization has become an institution. The first test involved survival. The second, autonomy and influence. The third pertained to evidence that "specific relationship and action patterns embodied in the organization have become normative for other social units."[2] It is a variation on these tests that I am applying as I watch—and live through—what I now expect to be the successful institutionalization of OISE.

"The Guiding Concepts" did not make clear what degree of longevity constitutes survival. My own minimum criterion of survival for an institution is outliving success or failure a few times (the former is frequently more fatal to an organization than the latter). When an organization has done that, and outlived the conflicts associated with its origin, I have no doubt that it has passed the survival test of institutionalization.

It is just plain sentimentality, plus the kind of interest in institutions that I have, that causes me to wax excited over the occasion of this tenth anniversary, and to listen with curiosity, but not much regret, when people tell me about what OISE was supposed to be and what it is. I listen mainly because I am concerned with the differences between the conflicts the people in OISE were dealing with, or thought they were dealing with, ten years ago, and the conflicts OISE has to deal with now. I am even more concerned with the difference between conflicts that this society had to deal with in 1965 and the ones it must deal with now.

The conflicts a society must deal with at a particular juncture in its history are not necessarily new, or even newly discovered. More often they are long-standing conflicts that in earlier periods were regarded as acceptable ironies or were tolerated in accordance with some well-established compromises. But for ironies to be palatable and for compromises to stand, it is usually necessary that they accommodate some consensual, almost universal, notion of a societal imperative. If that consensual notion erodes, old conflicts emerge to be dealt with. For practical purposes, they are new conflicts.

The theme to which this decennial occasion has steered me, then, is the importance of a long-standing consensus on progress—its importance to modern public education in particular and to modern public policy in general. That consensus, in our society, has been to the effect that progress is to be served, and that we all pretty well know what progress is and what decisions it demands of us.

I am not among those overly impressed by claims that we are living in a time of unprecedented technological change. Indeed, I suspect that the physical environment and technological style changed people's lives more dramatically during every decade from 1870 (at least) to 1960 than they did during the 1960s or the first part of the 1970s. I am not even convinced that our pace of reworking social arrangements or reshuffling values is unprecedented. But I am convinced, or almost convinced, that these past ten years have bracketed a period of rapid erosion of consensual notions on progress. Consequently, an important century-old compromise is threatened. That compromise has been crucial to public policy and public education styles. It is possible that prevailing ideas about progress, public policy, and personal choice in 1985 will be more similar to those of 1965 than to those of 1975. But the fact remains that shifting notions about progress (which represent an exciting phenomenon, but one which I choose not to call a crisis) are rapidly changing the context in which we make public policy. They are also presenting OISE (and, for that matter, the whole educational establishment) with a set of popularly perceived and politically important conflicts that are different from the ones it was created to cope with.

STARTING OUT IN THE SIXTIES

OISE has, from its very first days, been recognized by all parties as a product of its time. Hackneyed as this cliché is—since, after all, the challenge is not to find institutions that reflect the peculiarities of the time that produced them, but rather to find some that don't—it is helpful to many people attempting to explain OISE and other vestiges of our shifting collective mood in the 1960s. It acknowledges that styles of thinking about public policy have changed with unusual rapidity since about 1960, and, perhaps more importantly, that the feelings associated with these style changes have been uncommonly intense. We have, during these years, demonstrated a remarkable propensity to act on new and often short-lived convictions.

Notions of good public policy succeeded one another with such rapidity in the 1960s that to explain any product of that decade as a creature of its time demands that we be specific about which point in the decade we refer to. The decade contained many critical points and what in retrospect emerge as possible watersheds of long-run significance. So far as the style of thinking related to public policy for education on this continent is concerned, 1965 appears in retrospect as one of those critical points. If the shift in people's approach to thinking about education and public policy (or public policy for education) was not yet discernible in popular media or in political rhetoric, it was noticeable, if only as a minority approach, among researchers and students of public policy with a special interest in education. Within two years the minority approach of 1965 would vie with the "orthodox" approaches of the early years of the 1960s. Concerned parties would soon align themselves on this issue as perceptions, ideologies, and vested interests dictated; and what had seemed for a few years to have been an established consensus regarding education's contribution to the commonweal became a historical oddity before the decade ended.

In the early 1960s, ebullience was the hallmark of successful politicians everywhere. It was particularly noticeable in politicians with education portfolios or even with some indirect attachment to educational activities. Most of all it characterized education lobbyists, people who for a variety of reasons carried a brief for expanded educational opportunities and for expansive education policies, in any or all of the ways that term is construed. The early years of the decade were a time of positive thinking in, for, and about education.

There is more to positive thinking, however, than optimism—even unwarranted or dangerous optimism—and high expectations. Positive thinking is dependent upon a view of the world in which bad is only the absence of good, evil the absence of virtue, and sin the absence of grace. Most of us appear to have this orientation at least some of the time. It is a respectable and long-standing view of the world, which without it might be a very dull place full of very unadventurous people. It is an inordinately simple view of the world, however.

Sympathy with the notion that anything "wrong" is only an invitation to add something or do something is a matter of attitude or mood. An important aspect of character, however, is the attitudes customarily assumed in connection with specific roles and functions. An important aspect of societal character is the prevailing views on what are appropriate and legitimate attitudes to assume in connection with governing and policy making. The propensity to combine positive thinking with statecraft is a relatively new component of the character of Western states, one with important consequences for public policy. Not the least of these is that once all major factions concede the existence of some deplorable condition, whether it be depression, recession, inflation, social malaise, or underdevelopment anywhere in the world, the burden of justification for activist policies is minimized. It is the advocate of caution, nonintervention, noninvolvement, and passivism who must make the stronger case.

The 1960s, at least something more than half of them, were very good years for activists and positive thinkers in many lands. In very recent years we have come to think of the particular styles of activism and positive thinking that characterized the greater part of the 1960s as having been peculiarly American, essentially American, or predominantly American. Such was not really the case, however. It is true that much of the American propensity for viewing the problems of the world, particularly the world beyond its borders, as an invitation to furnish whatever was lacking was an aspect of American celebration of a generation of American world leadership. But the conviction that the dominant role of the Americans in world politics and economics meant that the Americans were doing something right was often better established among people other than Americans.

The appeal of activist, positive-thinking politicians, and their consequent success, affected many aspects of public policy in the 1960s. No aspect of public policy was so much affected, however, as public education policy. The immediate impact upon education as an industry in many countries, notably and particularly Canada, was remarkable. In addition, the education industry was to be the ultimate "beneficiary" of public policies with immediate expansionary effects on other industries. The Kennedy Administration's policy decision to send volunteers to aid the development of poor and benighted peoples on a scale dwarfing any international volunteer or missionary efforts the world had ever seen, and the subsequent decisions in other countries to mount more or less comparable operations, need not have become, first and foremost, exercises in the international mobilization of teachers—

but in most cases they did. The United States policy decision to put people on the moon had its primary impact on the aerospace industry, the spoilt child of the sixties and the unloved orphan of the seventies, but the derived demand for products of the education industry was very great.

The go-to-the-moon policy may be passed off as serious business only for the Americans and Russians, and as entertainment for the rest of the world. But it is worth noting that, on the American side of the story at least, it was a paradigm of positive, activist policy. Consciously and deliberately, even candidly, the United States government identified an eroding sense of national mission as a problem of the time. The problem, in the spirit of the times, was articulated as *something lacking*. A trip to the moon was to take the place of whatever was lacking.

The moon-business was also a component of a serious, sustained competition between the communist states of Eastern Europe and the other industrialized states of the world. Sometimes that contest focused only upon the two main protagonists, the United States and the Soviet Union. The happiest phases of the contest were probably those that were most ritualized. Certainly the most colorful and harmless, as well as ritualized, aspect of the competition, and the one that focused most on the two super-powers, was the race to the moon. However, the notion that international competition involves the design and production of elaborate hardware, the effective mobilization and organization of large numbers of highly skilled, expensively educated people, and being first to get a complex capital-intensive procedure into effective operation was well established everywhere in the 1960s and had important consequences for public policy.

Certainly Canada was not going to excuse herself from that competition. Moreover Canada, like the United States, had a history that had sharpened the skills and insights of her citizens for this particular competition. As rich, democratic, industrializing societies without the "fixed" cultural and population centers of the older industrial states of Europe, both Canada and the United States have exciting histories of regional economic competitions. They also have well-developed systems for accommodating these competitions. To an important degree, domestic politics in the two countries has meant lobbying, organizing, propagandizing, and maneuvering to determine the geographical distribution of industry. Politicians have long known that their constituents hold them responsible for the shares of high wage paying and high tax paying industry that locate in and stay in their constituencies. Canadian politicians are very adept at the kind of positive thinking suggested by statements like: "All this town needs to be a metropolis is a national railroad going through"; "All this province needs is a fair system of freight rates"; "This city needs more contracts for its Canadian Forces shipyards"; or "This region needs a low tariff on machinery and a high tariff on wood products." It is no great challenge for them to apply the what-is-needed approach to formulating strategy for the international competitions to get what are perceived to be the most desirable industries. One strategic question raised in the 1960s was "How can Canada get and hold the highly skilled, expensively educated workers those industries need?" One of the answers was "Expanded educational opportunities, from kindergarten through graduate school, for its citizens." Interestingly, for Ontario politicians that answer applied whether the competition for attracting industries was viewed as Ontario versus California or Ontario versus Alberta.

Ebullience thrives on competition. Political ebullience in Ontario in the 1960s thrived on global, national, and provincial competition. On the global level, Ontario, like the rest of Canada and much of the world, enjoyed the vicarious thrill of beating the Russians to the moon. As a nation, Canada was attracting and nurturing a growing and satisfying proportion of the new, sophisticated, capital-intensive industries associated with national prestige and prosperity. In addition, by all the usual indexes of national economic progress, Canada was faring well, with one exception. Canada, as was apparent by the early 1960s, was not doing well in comparison with the industrial nations of Europe or with Japan in combating unemployment. Frequently, she did not even do well in comparison with the United States by this index. But it seemed only appropriate to discount that unhappy differential in light of the facts that Canada was not only mobilizing the highest proportion of domestically produced new members of the labor force, but was also accepting large numbers of immigrants from the very states that could boast low unemployment rates. And not only was Ontario enjoying low unemployment rates by Canadian standards, she was absorbing many of the new labor force members from other provinces and receiving a disproportionately large share of immigrants. In terms of provincial competition, Ontario was doing as well in attracting and holding the lion's share of the complex new industries as she had done in earlier generations with conventional manufacturing industries.

Competition, when it is cheerfully acknowledged, is also a wonderful goad to positive thinking. A jurisdiction that rises to the challenge of competition is resolving, or at least putting aside, irksome questions of what to do and what is worth doing. It is free to concentrate its resources. Free to simplify policy making and focus on questions of *how*—how to do what the competition demands.

But in the complex forms of competition in which modern states engage, nothing is really simple. There are no substantial rewards, no substantive winnings or accomplishments to measure. What would seem the simple business of keeping score is not merely a demanding chore for a great many clerks, it is a very challenging and arcane aspect of policy research. For example, most Canadians are aware—or convinced—that the value of the Canadian dollar vis-à-vis the United States dollar is important to our "international economic competitive position"; few, however, are certain whether they should be worried or comforted when the Canadian dollar goes down. Even the experts on international trade and finance are hard put to tell us how we are better or worse off when the Canadian dollar goes from $0.90 U.S. to $1.10 U.S., and just who among us will experience most of that benefit —or cost.

The benefits and rewards of effectively competing for new industries or of successfully serving such "tangible" objectives of economic policy as a favorable balance of trade are neither obvious nor certain, and must be taken on faith. Such faith was more abundant through most of the 1960s than it is in 1975. It is now becoming increasingly obvious that popular support for the competitions that are intended to promote domestic cooperation and cohesion is related to the credibility of measures of policy achievements. The ephemeral and remote qualities of the benefits attendant upon the achievement of policy objectives, and the associated difficulties in keeping score, present serious problems in reinforcing will and commitment. In political terms, there are serious problems to maintaining social discipline.

Making policy for big, rich, industrial, democratic societies would be very different from what we have known it to be if there were no social indicators such as gross national product, consumer price indexes, work-force measures, unemployment rates, housing starts, box-car loadings, and capital expenditures forecasts, and if we had not had the sustained social-sciences research efforts that have made these indicators understandable and feasible. Just as certainly, the modern social sciences would be very different from what they are if they were not harnessed to the service of what we often call policy related research. Without their relationship with government, those sciences would amount to a very modest-scale industry, and quite likely their practitioners would be more modest than we know them to be.

No doubt, policy related social-sciences research performs several different functions in modern political systems. Keeping score, or more correctly, keeping score and thus reinforcing interest and commitment, is one of those functions. Another function, and in a society where policy making is characterized by positive thinking, an equally important function, is to determine the missing elements that will close the gap between the existing state of things and the desired state.

In the climate of positive thinking that prevailed in the early 1960s, policy related research was characterized by positive results. The results were positive in several interestingly interrelated ways. They identified determinants of productivity and progress in the past. They also identified the investment strategies appropriate to the achievement of policy objectives for the future. The two types of results are interdependent, in that the first class of results provides assumptions upon which the research activities leading to the second class are based.

Of most interest to us here is the importance that education assumed in the positive results of public policy research in the early 1960s. In simplified terms, the positive policy-research results of those years may be summed up this way:

1. Yes, we can identify the "extra" factors (i.e., other than constant-quality labor and capital) that have allowed continuing progress in the past, even in the face of declining per capita natural resources. Whether progress is taken to mean only an increase in per capita (or per worker) product, or that increase plus a decrease in the proportion of the population living in poverty, the extra factors are the same: improvement in the quality of labor and technology (advances in the state of the productive arts and improving organization). A behavioral variable related to these improvements, a variable perceived as particularly amenable to influence in the form of public policy, is investment in education, or more correctly, the propensity to invest more—in absolute and relative terms—in education over time.
2. Yes, we can assume that per capita product and the erosion of poverty can still be served through public policy that promotes increasing educational investment and, indirectly, improvement of labor quality and technology. The high correlation between progress and educational investment across nations attests to this. So does the obvious relationship (over time) between productivity and educational investment in the United States.

The most influential policy research supportive of expansionary education policies came from economists, of whom Edward Denison has been the most influential. His book *The Sources of Economic Growth in the United States and the Alternatives before Us,* published in 1962,[3] became the model for many good, indifferent, and poor studies to follow. Denison and his disciples proceeded on the assumption that to understand or to ensure progress, we must identify the factors that, as complements of a growing population and accruing capital, assure increasing productivity, even under conditions of diminishing per capita resources. The facts that increasing productivity (of labor) has accompanied growing populations in the past and that the increasing productivity was often in excess of that presumed to be due to incremental capital accumulation offer apparent justification for the assumption that such complementary factors exist. Using equations that they regarded as acceptable mathematical expressions of the relationships of the total product of an economy to the several factors committed to the processes involved, these researchers identified a residual factor—that is, something other than labor and capital. Careful definition of terms can make plausible the explanation that the residual factor represents changing technology and labor value. Still more assumptions and some faith are required to connect that residual to education, however. Research of this genre is quite uniformly associated with such assumptions, some researchers attributing most or nearly all of that residual to education, others attributing only some substantial part of it to education.

In Canada, probably the most influential and certainly the best-known study relating public policy to progress through educational investment is Gordon Bertram's *The Contribution of Education to Economic Growth*, published in 1966.[4] As an Economic Council of Canada study, it was doubtlessly intended to have relevance for public policy making. Because Bertram concluded that the residual component in Canada's production function for the half century ending in 1961 was substantial (though he did not actually produce such a coefficient) and because he attributed a considerable portion of it to education, but more importantly because he attributed much of the per capita income differential between Canada and the United States to educational investment differentials,[5] Bertram and the Economic Council may be described as having contributed a great deal to the enthusiasm for expanding education that characterized the mid-sixties in Canada. They also furnished an impressive source of legitimacy for the ebullience of those proposing public education policy in Ontario, and even for the claim that OISE, the new universities, the colleges of applied arts and technology, and a lot more education all round was necessary for us to compete with the Americans.

The facts that the Economic Council of Canada published its most influential pro-educational expansion background policy study in 1966 and that expansion of all kinds was a popular Canadian theme throughout the sixties might lead one to suppose that OISE existed for half a decade in a pro-expansion climate—for everything, but for education in particular. Such was not the case, however. From about 1965 on it can be said that there was a counter-trend to expansion in the literature and thinking bearing upon public policy.

In 1975, when unqualified enthusiasm for expansion has come to be regarded as a crass component of Americanism, an attitude that we in Canada will do well to shun, it is rather difficult to re-create the climate of the late 1960s. It was a time of flux and reorientation. On the one hand, it was a time when more than one immigrant professor who suggested that having larger numbers of Canadians might not be conducive to attaining a higher standard of living for Canadians or to maintaining some valued qualities of Canadian life was forcefully reminded of his unfamiliarity with Canadian reality. A time when a famous Canadian nationalist, one destined to be a best-selling author, captured the imagination of many with a plan for populating "the mid-Canada Corridor" and a proposed goal of 100,000,000 Canadians. And a time when, with some pride, Canada claimed first place among the nations of the world as a spender on education (i.e., education expenditures as a percentage of GNP). On the other hand, it was a time of growing disenchantment with industrialization, urbanization, and rising expenditures for public services—for education in particular.

Indeed, a more careful review of the 1960s demands an acknowledgment that throughout the decade there had been a counter-trend to the ebullient politics of growth and public policy for expansion. It was at the beginning of that decade that the lifelong proselytizing and organizing of Margaret Sanger and the research work of Dr. John Rock provided a new contraceptive technology that became the rallying point of the anti-natal forces in society. In the seventies, with a veritable arsenal of contraceptive means available, it is obvious that low birth rates are more a function of will than of technology. But the fact remains that the appearance in the early sixties of one new technique helped many people overcome theological, esthetic, psychological, and political inhibitions to effective contraception. And it was in the sixties, not the seventies, that sustained, serious population-policy discussions began on this continent.

The prime ingredient required for the serious discussion of population policy is acceptance of resource constraints, of a finite continent and planet. It may have been discussion of the economics and sociology of conception, more than the theology and politics of it, that made us aware of the limited resources this world offers us. Perhaps it was TV, Telstar, and McLuhan's essays. It may have been both, or neither. In any case, this awareness invites concern for conservation. Ecology may not have concerned many of us until the late sixties or replaced conservation in our vocabularies until the seventies, but it was a product of the early sixties and of a wave of intuition that swept the continent. When it became obvious that the separate save-a-tree, save-a-park, save-an-estuary movements and population policy had something in common, ecology became a movement, dampened the ebullience of politics, presented a near crisis for positive thinking, raised questions about some positive research results, and painfully complicated the rationalization of public policy.

Throughout the sixties, then, there were counter-trends to those of exuberance, growth, and positive thinking applied to public policy, and before the decade was spent they characterized the climate of public policy in general and education policy in particular. A more interesting and more fundamental contest, however, was that between two very different orientations toward public policy and the environment. One orientation was to this effect: the needs of society are readily discernible; we can generalize about them in aggregate; those generalizations are the source from which policy imperatives are derived; good government demands that those policy imperatives be the immediate determinants of public policy; and the institutions through which policy is implemented must not be inhibited, by history or by their autonomous objectives, in serving public policy. The other orientation was to this effect: barring a few notable exceptions such as mobilization for all-out war, inertia is the main determinant of public policy; policies and the institutions through which they operate must ordinarily be made to accommodate changing physical and political conditions by means of sequential adjustments; and the function of policy research is to relate particular social conditions or trends to corresponding policy issues. By 1965 it had become appropriate to add: the political process with the most immediate and predictable effects on policy and institutional adjustment in a modern democratic state is the budgetary process; and, given the considerable lead time required to make policies and institutions accommodate ambient conditions, the best hope for good government is the systematic preparation of data on existing and forecasted conditions in forms amenable to specific, sequential budget decisions. According to the latter orientation, the "political climate" or the immediate social–attitudinal environment is only one determinant of public policy and institutional development, and an indirect one at that.

It would be difficult to put OISE into perspective without acknowledging the importance of these two counter-trends in thinking about public policy of the last decade. Without the first trend, it is unlikely that OISE would have begun as a large, expensive institution. Without the second, Professor Jackson would have presided over a very different type of institution these ten years.

To an important degree, apparently, it was determined even before the Institute was chartered that the second trend would characterize its approach to policy study and policy planning. If the evidence in our library is to be accepted, much of the credit for this goes to Professor Jackson.

The style and content, but in particular the chronological sequence, of the items behind R. W. B. Jackson's name in the card catalogue are evidence that a demographer and statistician working in educational research became, some time in the 1950s, something of an education policy lobbyist. Bob Jackson the education lobbyist did not write exactly like Professor Jackson the statistician. He became easier to read, and developed a rather folksy prose style. But he continued to deal from strength, and that strength was numbers —carefully compiled, competently processed, soberly interpreted numbers. It is my impression that Bob Jackson's best-known and most influential piece of work is *The Problem of Numbers in University Enrolment* (1963).[6] It is an easy-to-read, carefully organized, and nearly irrefutable brief for a mobilization of political and financial resources to accommodate predictable social, demographic, and economic realities.

As Bob Jackson wrote (and spoke) more directly to influence policy, he demanded less of his readers by way of expertise or insight. In general, the linkage was obvious between the information he offered, the case he made, and appropriate policy. He offered information of a specific type that was appropriate to the fashioning of "finite" policy decisions. Alternatively, we can say that the same information that indicated direction could be used to answer the question of "how far?" However, it must not be supposed that Canadian education policy style has been overly influenced by the invitation to carefully programmed expansion that Jackson's work contained. Certainly nothing in his writings calls for the "open-ended" expansion that prevailed for a while in the mid-sixties.

No attempt will be made here to estimate the degree to which policy research affects public policy. Let us only assume that it does have some influence, and that policy makers do not respond perversely to research results. Since the general purport of research reports bearing upon education policy in the 1960s was to the effect that society (presumably any and every society) had not spent enough on education, and that the rewards to spending more would be high and certain, it must be conceded that research was contributing to the pro-expansion arguments and climate. It is important, though, to distinguish between the research that dealt with the most general relationships between education and society and the research that confined itself in the main to relationships between particular social conditions or trends and corresponding problems in the education system.

Several significant points can be made about research of the first (general) type: (1) it is a long-established tradition to introduce policy related educational research results with a few contextual generalities about the benefits of education to society: (2) only in the 1950s and 1960s did the most general educational and social relationships become a "researchable" topic for a considerable number of scholars of the applied social sciences; (3) among the very general educational and social relationships that applied social scientists purported to have specified and measured, economic ones predominated, and it was these that were most often and most convincingly offered as guides to public policy in the 1950s and 1960s; (4) in Ontario, as in Canada generally, research of this type, or at least well-publicized reports of it, did not precede the period of remarkable expansion in the early and mid-sixties (if such research did influence policy, it must have been American research); (5) in Canada, research of this type, or at least well-publicized reports of it, appeared almost coincidentally with the "corrective reactions" to the "open-ended" policies of expansion—that is, very shortly before some research reports in both the United States and Canada began to cast doubts on the high probability of very satisfying returns to increasing education expenditures, and after such trends as program budgeting and "accountability" had begun to pose questions about the policy relevance of research dealing with very general educational/social relationships.

The public policy that corresponded to the implications of research dealing with general educational/social relationships (and in some cases to the explicit policy recommendations of the researchers) was the general expansion of educational establishments. Not surprisingly, lack of discrimination in that expansion, with the resulting inability to spend successive large increments gracefully, became a point of vulnerabilty for the policy. It appeared to many people that the limits to satisfying results obtainable from educational expansion might be just as Fritz Machlup had indicated in *The Production and Distribution of Knowledge in the United States* in 1962.[7]

At a time when many, notably American, economists were producing research favoring educational expansion and rising education expenditures, Machlup was claiming that a major expansion in a nation's educational institutions results in most of the expected marginal product being lost to "inflation." For example, the expansion associated with the changing of the normal duration of education from eight years to twelve years results in a rising price in years of students' time (and taxpayers' money) needed to acquire a given amount of knowledge, with marginal returns to the incremental years being nearly nil.[8] Needless to say, Machlup's book is a great joy to read for anyone in a temporary or permanent mood of skepticism about the blessings of public education to the taxpayer.

It is of interest to me that very little of the research intended to influence Ontario education policy in the 1950s and 1960s was of the type relating education in a general way to social conditions. Bob Jackson produced a large part of that work, and his mode of research was the dominant one in Ontario. Because policy research at OISE has been in considerable measure a continuation, in style and purpose, of the work done by Bob Jackson and the Department of Educational Research that he headed, it can be said that the initial policy research at OISE was predestined to be of the type that relates specific social conditions and trends to corresponding policy problems. It is also interesting, but ironic, that the first years of the Institute's operations were those when public policy was most influenced by notions—whether derived from research or not—on very general educational/social relationships—indeed, by very generous interpretations of the policy implications of such notions. Furthermore, the early history and growth rate of OISE itself, as well as of many other institutions, could only be explained in the context of a prevailing policy mood sympathetic to expansion and only minimally concerned with graceful accommodation to large budget increments.

But the early years of OISE represent one phase of a public expenditure cycle; the later years, since 1970 at least, represent the other. It has been Bob Jackson's lot, in this decade of transition, first to preside over an institution absorbing such great annual budget increments as to make graceful expansion impossible, and then to preside over an institution accommodating itself to expenditure policy made in a mood of reaction to that period of expansion.

No doubt the 1960s and early 1970s would have been less innervating for those of us in the education industry had all the jurisdictions on this continent increased education budgets by smaller increments before 1968, and handled any corrections since then through small adjustments, carefully spaced. It is doubtful, however, that policy makers, students of public policy, or any other group could have done more than marginally influence collective behavior in this respect. The first part of the 1960s were years of remarkable faith in progress and in our ability to discern the requisites of progress. In consequence, policy imperatives were inescapable. The late sixties and early seventies have been years remarkable for the erosion of faith in our ability to discern the requisites of progress and even of consensus on what progress is. Policy imperatives, particularly those with some tenuous connection by way of educational or social-sciences research to progress, now seem a quaint fad of a bygone era.

A HUNDRED YEARS OF PROGRESS

Progress is the hallmark of the modern, secular, industrial society, but it can hardly be discussed apart from another, older, more essential characteristic of modern society—the nation state. The clever Italian invention of a single, bureaucratized, secular authority, with perfect sovereignty over a fixed population and specified boundaries, is the ultimate human accomplishment in institution building. As the supreme source of legitimacy within its boundaries, even for sacred establishments, the state is a necessary precondition for progress as most of us think of it today. At the very least, the state is indispensable to our styles of conceptualizing and measuring progress.

The state was a new and still emerging phenomenon in Machiavelli's time. Indeed, since he was the first to write about it, speculate on it, and design policy for it, it might be said that Machiavelli discovered it. Machiavelli gave us the concept of the state as man's creation and, as such, subject to improvement by man. Among other things the state, fashioned by mortals but itself potentially immortal, is the best basis for long-term data collection that the human race could ever have. How could we deal with gross product, unemployment rates, and income distribution without it? Could we even make much sense out of birth rates and censuses without it?

Though Machiavelli gave us the notion that the state is subject to perfection by us, he did not give us an orientation for that process. Apparently, he had no strong opinion that we, too, are perfectible. He had no ideas to the effect that as we perfect the state, the test of that perfection is our own perfection—and that as we are perfected we can further perfect the state. He was a perfectionist and reformer, but he was no progressive. Eighteenth-century Anglo-Saxon political philosophers on both sides of the Atlantic were progressives—at least some of them were. They believed in, indeed were committed to, human perfectibility. Their notion of human perfectibility, when superimposed upon the Machiavellian concept of the state, evoked corollaries of personal choice, capitalism, and economic growth (but also of state intervention in the development of institutions and personalities). That notion about human nature, plus that view of the state, are the prerequisites of progress in any modern sense.

It was to improve our conceptualization of progress, of the state, and of public policy as the link between progress and the state that Adam Smith and the political economists that followed him wrote. The philosophers we conventionally refer to as the Anglo-Saxon classical economists wrote with a specific purpose: to educate. Their teaching was not an end in itself, however. They taught in order to affect policy. The perennial theme in these writings—from approximately 1775 to 1875—was economic individualism and its relation to the commonweal. They dealt with the normative, political, analytical, and technical aspects of individualism. Ultimately, they prepared us not only to define the commonweal in terms of individual choice and well-being, but also to measure it in such terms. The style they imposed upon us leaves us with some ethical dilemmas, of course. Indeed, it is not uncommon for us to indict them as philosophers with underdeveloped ethical sensitivities. This is unfair, however, as in fact they were much concerned with the character of the individuals whose personal choices would determine the commonweal. For this reason a recurring minor theme in their writings is education. They were particularly attracted by the potentialities of public (and compulsory) education as a control device available to the state, even as the state turned over the major role in determining social well-being to individual choice.

Rudolph Blitz, in his 1961 essay "Some Classical Economists and Their Views on Education,"[9] reviewed the works of Adam Smith, Thomas Malthus, Nassau Senior, John McCulloch, and John Stuart Mill, scholars whose writings, beginning with Smith's *Wealth of Nations* and concluding with Mill's late works, spanned the first century of the Industrial Revolution and take us to the first decade of the century now ending. In his conclusion, Blitz said that "Smith was the most reluctant advocate of public education, but all the others . . . advocated education with increasing zeal." Blitz's theme is that the value placed upon an intelligent and properly oriented populace frequently caused the classical economists to advocate state education systems and something approaching universal education, and the tendency to advocate these things was increasing over the century between 1775 and 1875. To this I add my view that advocacy of public and compulsory education, though it contradicts the principles and policy of individualism, was a concomitant development of the intellectual foundations of individualism and capitalism. To advocate public education and individualism at the same time is, of course, to reserve for the state a strong position from which to control the development of institutions, values, and orientations. It is to compromise. And it is precisely that compromise that was fixed about 1870 and gave us the century of public education and progress.

Not everyone shares my conviction that 1870 (or the decade of the 1870s) constitutes a starting point for the modern phenomenon of public education. Students with an intellectual and emotional commitment to the work and times of Egerton Ryerson in Canada, or to the contributions of Horace Mann and Henry Barnard in New England, object with vigor to such a late beginning. Those more oriented to British educational developments register fewer objections.

I could, but will not, list about a dozen legislative and organizational occurrences in the United Kingdom, United States, and Canada of the early 1870s and a few years just preceding that I personally find to be strong indicators that public education had not previously been, but would thenceforth be, an important aspect of statecraft. I will, however, refer to a few pieces of evidence—from the literature in which and by which we rationalize public policy—supporting the claim that about 1870 the modern notions on which public education is based became "settled" components of accepted wisdom and right thinking.

An important point to be made about the classical economists is that contemporary politicians of the Anglo-Saxon (English-speaking and white) societies, educational politicians at least as much as any others, all exploit the writings of those scholars, albeit selectively, to rationalize their own behavior. Of course, as is always the way with political philosophy, the literature operated in two directions at once. Retroactively, it legitimated policy developments that, when initiated, had not been in accord with established (i.e., written and respected) norms. But it also served as the legitimate and rational frame of reference for future policy making. I readily concede that what the political economists and a few political philosophers of a different genre had written by 1870, and which provided a rationale for relating education and public policy, did not go beyond putting a seal of approval on reforms for which a number of activist education reformers in the Anglo-Saxon societies (Mann, Barnard, and Ryerson included) had been working for two generations at least. However, before public education could become an integral component of modern society rather than a reform movement or a social experiment, the social and political problems to which those reformers addressed themselves had to be recognized as intrinsic aspects of modern society, and reform through education had to be provided with "rational" support in the evolving scholarly literature of economics and politics. It is my claim that this process of "rationalization" and legitimation of public education was completed about 1870. It was accomplished by the establishing or fixing of a few eclectic notions about education that have survived as the salient features of policy for public education in Anglo-Saxon societies.

The notions on which public education has operated for a century are the social–psychological bases of modern public education systems in democratic societies with free or partially free markets. There are only two—or perhaps three—of these notions. They are so fundamental to a public education system and so universally accepted that they are rarely questioned. Indeed, they are seldom mentioned. The first is, quite simply, that the principle of the identity of self-interest and the common good is not applicable to the field of education. The second is the moral argument that the state should interfere by way of public education in the affairs of its citizens when there exist sociological reasons to suppose that the improvement in their lot resulting from economic reform and industrial progress might be missed, or might come much later, without that interference. The third notion, the candidate for possible elimination, is that of the assumed contraceptive effects of education. This notion is a candidate for exclusion because of the possibility that it can be subsumed by the second one, and because the first and second provide an adequate conceptual foundation. Whether two or three in number, these notions are the social–psychological bases of public education because they are a rationale for compulsion.

The essential ingredient of public education is, of course, compulsion. Interestingly, or ironically, the business of educating citizens became a matter of public policy and a sphere of activity where the most direct forms of state intervention are acceptable at the very juncture in our history when individualism triumphed over statism, when the concept that efficiency in promoting the commonweal depended upon freedom of choice made all abstractions of the organic state seem "foreign," when the process of dismantling all the institutions that deny liberty to some people in our societies became an established component of partisan politics, and when the movement toward a universal franchise achieved such momentum as to be irreversible.

It can be said, of course, that public education is only a component of the myriad activities that make up the public sector. After all, publicly provided schools need not be very different, in public finance terms, from public libraries and public clinics. One might make too much of what seems the irony of the final establishment of the state's role in education at the same moment in history that saw the political, economic, and intellectual triumph of individualism. That was also the point in our history when the remarkable growth of public expenditures began. Indeed, very early in the hundred years referred to here, Adolph Wagner gave us what we sometimes call his "law of growing public expenditures." Wagner's observation in 1883 that the public sector's share in a modern economy will increase with economic growth remains one of the few well-established "theories" we have about public spending.[10] Wagner's theme was that the opportunities and conditions of modern life invite ever-increasing communal consumption. Such communal consumption need not be the product of compulsion—though, of course, the attendant taxes are compulsory.

A benevolent and protective government might be expected, from time to time, to decide that its citizens, out of ignorance, spend less on libraries, clinics, and schools than their own best interest dictates. We would expect such a government to impose taxes adequate to provide the scale of operations for these establishments that it believes its citizens should want, or would want if they were as enlightened as they should be.

A government more oriented to efficiency in promoting the commonweal than to benevolence and protection might observe that some of the benefits of expenditures by individuals on schools, libraries, and clinics accrue not to the persons making those expenditures but to other citizens, or that some of those benefits accrue jointly to the spending party and to others. It might also be observable that individuals spending on those operations spend less than they would if those external benefits were included among the considerations affecting individual expenditure behavior. The efficiency-oriented government would be compelled either to cause individuals to spend on those operations at the level they would if all the benefits were accruing to the spenders, or to assume direct responsibility for those expenditures and maintain them at the level determined by the value of benefits being received by all citizens. Such interference to determine expenditure levels is a function of government that has been emphasized by modern states. As a public finance development it is in accord with a more general expression of the first of the notions mentioned above as basic to public education, and it suggests a context in which to view the rise of public education. There is reason to suppose, then, that what we have done in the name of public education is explained in some measure by what we have done in the field of public finance.

Nevertheless, the second of the notions basic to public education makes it a very special part of the public sector. Compulsion is, of course, the factor introduced into the environment to cause individuals to supply the quantity of education that is in the best interest of society. When, however—out of a concern for symmetry that we do not show when the business at hand is public parks, clinics, or libraries—compulsion is used to ensure that individuals demand the quantity of education that is supplied, we call the resulting phenomenon, quite straightforwardly, public and compulsory education. More often than not, though, we simply say public education, but expect others to know that we are referring to the situation in which coercion determines both the supply and the demand.

For us who have lived all our lives in the twentieth century, there is nothing strange about the coexistence of enthusiasm for freedom, personal choice, even capitalism, and an unquestioning faith in the virtue and wisdom of public education. If we are appreciative of the social–political order we have known, we usually assume that a recognition of the value of public education was part of the cumulative genius that designed the system as we received it. If we are critical of that social–political order, we usually assume that our ancestors' recognition of the importance of public education was a saving grace that has contributed to the amelioration of an imperfect system. But more understanding of the compromises our forefathers had to make may evoke a more appreciative interest in the contradictions or ironies in the social system bequeathed to us.

No doubt those compromises were difficult, painful, and challenging for the Victorian men of affairs in all the Anglo-Saxon states who reformed and reorganized their world into the societies we know today, but for the men who wrote the books containing the rationales for the main themes in that reorganization, those compromises must have been more difficult still.

In addition to the fact that compromise bearing upon issues of conscience and conviction is never easy, two inhibitors had to be overcome before the philosophers of freedom, individualism, and capitalism could accept the particular compromise represented by public education in a free society. First, problems of inefficiency would be invited by excluding the education industry from market determination of its demand and supply, its style and content. Second, there was an absence of faith in schools and what schools do. As the political philosophers looked at what went on in schools, whether village primary schools, the endowed secondary schools, or Oxford and Cambridge, they were, more often than not, appalled. Moreover, as they speculated about what schools might be, they found no psychological basis for faith in formal education, no learning or teaching theories on which to base a rationale for public education.

Unequivocal endorsement of public education, when it came, was based upon educational sociology, not psychology. Fertility was to be the initial link between education and policy objectives, a causal link between schooling and more rational individual behavior. Malthus and Ricardo, among others, attempted to relate schooling to rational attitudes toward procreation by identifying something that happened to people in schools that affected their reproductive propensities. Either psychology failed them, or they failed as educational psychologists. Nassau Senior, writing in the 1850s, was more successful. He didn't claim for schools any contraceptive powers related to the prudence schooling would engender in youths, but he did find a direct link, a causal relationship, between education and economically rational fertility rates.

As we would expect of an economist, he regarded long-run labor supply (fertility rates) as being determined by wages. Because he considered it to be the family wage and not the individual worker's wage that determines the supply of labor, he reasoned that compulsory education would keep children out of the labor market longer, turn children into short-run liabilities rather than assets, and increase the price of labor.[11] The higher market price of labor he reasoned to be in the interest of society and the child. The longer economic dependency of children would make it in the parents' interest to have fewer children and slow down the growth of the labor supply.

The consequence of this would be a reconciliation of the long-run interests of society and the child with the shorter run interests of the parents. Of course, that long-run interest of the child apparently presumed that something beneficial would happen to the child in school, but it was the counter-progenitive effects on parents that Senior offered as the basis for public policy.

John Stuart Mill, a strong advocate of state education but also a philosopher dedicated to the significance of the individual, provided the "definitive rationalization" (i.e., one that could last a hundred years) for the coexistence of individualism and public education. A reformer calling for a thorough social reorganization dependent upon education, he too based his arguments for public education policies on sociological rather than psychological grounds.[12] He had the practical insight to advocate—cautiously—mechanical contraceptives as the means to population limitation, but he also had a view similar to Senior's on education's role in fertility control. More importantly, he recognized the occupational selection function performed by education. His enthusiasm for the education of females as the means to equal opportunities for both sexes reflected an appreciation of education for women more as a route to occupations other than wife and mother than as a learning experience valuable in itself.[13]

J. S. Mill's writings, in my view the culmination of the classical Anglo-Saxon political–economic literature and capstone of the philosophical basis for economic and political developments of the last hundred years, are adequate rationalization for the compromise represented by public education in democratic and capitalistic societies. Mill's writings seem all the more appropriate as our intellectual frame of reference for public policy in general, and for public education policy in particular, in view of the facts that he seemed all his life to have been a troubled man, that he never completely reconciled his concerns for individualism and for social justice, and that W. S. Jevons, his contemporary and probably his superior as a theoretical economist, could say of him that he was "essentially illogical" and that his philosophy was notable for its "intricate sophistry."

Educational sociology, or at any rate the kind of educational sociology that Mill wrote when he addressed himself to education, offered a logical basis for state education policies (interestingly, not dependent upon the quality of education schools offer). It still remained, however, for someone to complete the moral argument that the state should interfere in the affairs of its citizens, by way of public education, when there were sociological reasons to suppose that improvement in their lot (as a result of economic reform and progress) might be missed or come much later without such interference. Not an economist, but a philosopher, poet, and education reformer, Matthew Arnold offered the most convincing case for state education based on this argument. Arnold's social status, professional reputation, and literary ability assured a respectful hearing for his views. In *Culture and Anarchy*, which came out in 1869, he prepared the way intellectually for direct intervention by the state in ensuring the economic and cultural improvement of the population through state education. His eloquent arguments on the futility of liberal economic reform (notably elimination of the Corn Laws)[14] as an automatic means of improving the lot of the laboring classes forced the issue of relating public policy to problems raised by the questions: What sort of life for individuals ought we to encourage in modern society? What can we do, collectively, to enhance the quality of life in mass industrial society?

By the eighth decade of the nineteenth century there existed in the mainstream of our political–economic and political–philosophical literature about the same rationalization for a state education system, and for education policies to serve specific social objectives, as we have today. That rationalization contained the compromises and contradictions we have lived with for a century. That rationalization did not exist before—or very very long before—that decade.

Not until about the same time did a consensus appear in the literature of political economy that corresponded even roughly to modern notions of progress. That consensus was to the effect that progress is an improving standard of living for an increasing proportion of a growing population.

Probably the first economist of influence to speak with enthusiasm, and without caveats, of population growth, increased productivity, and equitable distribution as simultaneous—even complementary—policy objectives was Henry George in 1879.[15] For George, general prosperity waited only upon policy to free up the laboring classes, in particular to free them from the debilitating institution of rent.

George's proposed disestablishment of rent identifies him as a radical economist. His view that the potential of ordinary men to cope with and benefit from freedom did not depend upon a period of education, socialization, or gradual emancipation indicates that his psychology and sociology were as radical as his economics. It is possible, however, to overemphasize the degree to which George's philosophy was a new departure in the literature of political economy. Mill had already conceded the inevitability and, in cautious terms, the desirability of the complete enfranchisement of workers and their complete emancipation from the paternalistic control of governments and superior classes.[16] Mill's continuing concern for population limitation may raise some questions about his faith in the ability of even a "freed-up" labor force to provide an improving standard of living for an increasing population indefinitely. On the other hand, his willingness to depend primarily upon civic and economic equality for women as the means to population control suggests that he did not see population growth as a barrier to progress in the short run.[17] Finally, Mill's conviction that effective reform depended in the long run on cooperative reorganization of society suggests that, like George, he recognized the need for redefining the institution of private property in the interests of efficiency and equity.

Henry George's *Progress and Poverty* is perhaps the most exciting, virile, and impudent essay on radical reform ever written by an original and creative scholar. Of the political–economic treatises of the nineteenth century, only Marx's *Das Kapital* had a comparable impact upon reformers across the world. Before 1917 it would have been difficult to say for certain that the influence of Marx would eclipse that of George. In the Anglo-Saxon societies, until the 1930s at least, there was not much of a contest. George, not Marx, was the philosopher of radical reform, his works the literary blueprint for social reorganization, and his optimistic economics the antidote to the melancholy engendered by the teachings of Malthus and Ricardo, a melancholy only somewhat alleviated by the precepts of such later disciples as Nassau Senior, John McCulloch, and John Stuart Mill.

It is possible, even probable, that some of the optimism for democratically oriented social reform and the faith in progress found in writings of the late classical economists has been "read into" their work in order to foil the crusades of social and economic reformers inspired by the radical philosophy of George. George, with his message that universal prosperity depended upon a new dimension of freedom for the laboring classes, in particular freedom from the burden of rent, was more of a danger to established social philosophy and to capitalism as it was then being fashioned than any anarchist out of a Latin quarter or industrial slum. George offered no indictment of capitalism and was a champion of lower-middle-class virtues. He was dangerous because he "defined" progress in such a way as to put it out of the realm of public policy at a time when political philosophers were helping liberal politicians and the entrepreneurial classes to articulate progress as a viable public policy objective. He almost succeeded in making progress a pejorative term ninety years ago.

In *Progress and Poverty* an important semantic maneuver is performed. Progress is not defined as a process dependent upon the right public policies and as the only hope for ameliorating poverty. Rather, progress is presented as a *cause* of poverty.[18] Progress is the simultaneous growth of population and per capita product (or wealth).[19] Progress and the institution of landed property produce poverty—and, of course, great fortunes. Prosperity, for the greater part of a population, characteristically erodes with progress.[20]

George was different from other late classical economists in several ways. While they never ceased reminding us that in the long run population growth is a threat to progress, George was enthusiastically pro-progenitive. While they identified formal education as an important component of public policy and a contribution to economic growth, George dismissed it, in scathing terms, as very nearly useless and contributing little to the economy or any other aspect of the commonweal.[21]

George's view of progress and prosperity came closer to becoming the established political philosophy of this century than we usually acknowledge. Had his views carried the day, we would be having very different policy discussions now than we are having, and a decade of policy like that of the 1960s would have been very unlikely.

George was enthusiastic, hopeful, even optimistic. But he was not a positive thinker—particularly not from the point of view of politicians, bureaucrats, professional social scientists, and the politically influential classes. As he assessed the deplorable aspects of the world he knew, he was not moved to assume that more of something was needed, not even more study or more research. Something was wrong. It was necessary to take a decisive negative action: to disestablish one very important component of our social structure. Whether or not the disestablishment of property in land (more accurately, unearned profits from land) could have taken place without constituting a threat to property in general is now only a matter for speculation.

George certainly viewed the state as a phenomenon subject to our improvement, and, without question, he regarded mankind as a perfectible species. The important difference between him and the late classical philosophers, between him and the neoclassical philosophers of his time and of a generation or so to come, and between him and most of us who have made, proposed, or studied public policy in the twentieth century is that he is not associated with the intellectual compromises required if we subscribe to the principle that public policy should promote individualism and personal choice except when progress calls for state intervention and coercion. To George, progress was the natural result of free men exploiting the resources around them. Progress meant general prosperity only when rent did not transfer incomes from workers to *rentiers*. Progress and prosperity depended upon institutional arrangements determined by public policy, but progress (either as he defined it or as other economists were coming to define it) was not something to be reduced to objectives of positive or activist public policies.

George is not given a place in that pantheon of economic philosophers that starts with Adam Smith and concludes (at least for the nonce) with John Maynard Keynes. This is appropriate, since George is not one of those who provided us with an abstraction of our economies that has served as a major frame of reference for rationalizing public policy. He is, after all, a defunct, passed-over, and rejected philosopher. Political historians usually make little of his influence on the Fabians and the emerging Labour Party in the United Kingdom. Students of urbanology and municipal government are not impressed by his contribution to the rationalization of real-estate taxation.

In the years from 1880 to 1910, approximately, George's philosophy was tried in the balance of democratic politics and found wanting. There is really not much reason to bring him up in discussion—except when the questions at issue are "How did we come to have the notions about progress that we do?" or "Why do we make the distinctions that we do as to which decisions are matters for public policy and which are matters for personal choice?"

Those economists who wrote during the latter part of the nineteenth century and the first three decades of the twentieth and who are sound, memorable, conventional, and not so specialized as to be out of touch with major themes in their discipline are usually referred to as neoclassicists. A technical but fundamental difference between the neoclassicists and the classicists was that the former shifted the focus of economic logic away from the concept of diminishing returns to labor, capital, or both, to the concept of declining marginal utility. This reordering of the content of economics was probably necessary if the science was to be of immediate relevance to progress, and thus to public policy. Of more significance to us right now, however, is the attitudinal difference between the neoclassicists and the classicists. A late classicist like Mill could work up some faith in progress and some enthusiasm for the role of public policy in serving reasonably specific policy objectives related to progress in an increasingly free society, even though he had to repress his doubts about progress as a long-run phenomenon. The neoclassicists had much less trouble repressing misgivings about the long run. In many cases this simply meant they ceased to think as demographers. They had faith in progress, and they had faith in their ability to formulate public policy to serve progress. In particular, they accepted the elimination or abatement of poverty as a special aspect of progress and a special objective of public policy.[22] There were differences among them concerning which aspects of personal choice should be curtailed in the interest of which aspects of progress, and what forms intervention should take, but they were not troubled by the compromises on which the public policies they proposed depended, compromises that gave us the styles of public policy we have lived and labored under in the twentieth century. They were not discomfited by the idea that the imperatives of progress, no less than the imperatives of national defense, demand the reservation of certain residual totalitarian powers to the state: the power to deny the liberty of personal choice when progress—or defense—demands it, and the power to decide when progress—or defense—demands such denial.

A particular statement of the general imperative of intervention pertains to education: any form and amount of public and compulsory education may be justified in the interest of progress. This particularization of the general public policy imperative is clearly the one that has most influenced modern politicians and the social scientists who propose or rationalize policy for them. But it is also the one that political philosophers—political economists in particular—have for a hundred years most often singled out for special mention. They, in turn, were only building upon the argument of the classical economists that education is the sector of the economy where arguments for the priority of public policy over personal choice are most convincing.

It is only in the years since about 1870 that the germ theory, and subsequent abstractions bearing upon health as a social phenomenon, began to have relevance for public policy. Beginning about that time, knowledge about public health plus advances in transportation and communication—in particular those dependent upon the electric dynamo—offered unusual opportunities to ameliorate the consequences of population concentration in large cities. It became possible to postpone the point at which urban growth would be associated with intolerable erosion of health, congestion, chaos, and declining productivity—provided that appropriate positive public policies were adopted. Had such possibilities been presented to political economists of the hundred years before 1870, arguments for the precedence of public policy over personal choice would certainly have been presented in more general terms than they were.

George's views on progress and the elimination of poverty failed to become the foundation for public policy at the end of the nineteenth and the beginning of the twentieth century in part because they were not germane to the technical and organizational problems of the time. There was, however, an important consequence to our styles of public administration in rejecting George's idea that general prosperity depends, in an otherwise free society, only upon the disestablishment of rent. The consequence was that progress (including redistribution) became an administrative responsibility both in practice and in almost all conceptualizations of government and administration. It can be argued, of course, that the rise of the public administrator was inevitable in the process of urbanization and industrialization that has characterized the last hundred years. No one denies that public health and effective communication in urban society demand the centralization of decision making if we are to exploit the present state of the sciences of biology and physics. Students of public policy and public administration have all found the logic of an increasing scale of activities in the public sector compelling, philosophical orientations notwithstanding. Arguments for public control or ownership of monopolies in the interest of efficiency need not be related to a particular ideology. Efficiency, and perhaps justice, dictate the public provision of goods to satisfy social wants—that is, wants that cannot be provided for one citizen without providing them also for his neighbors. And any notion of the commonweal demands state intervention of some kind in the management of industrial processes notable for external costs—for example, processes destructive of their environment. But all of this only refers to the minimal responsibilities of public policy and administration in modern society. The administration of progress implies more.

Progress is connotative of harmony, enthusiasm, hope, and sometimes absurd amounts of optimism, particularly in the rhetoric of positive-thinking politicians and social planners. Actually, however, progress pertains to developments in a grim biological contest. It pertains to how many years of life we may expect for ourselves and our children, how hard we must labor to stay alive, and how many of us will have the leisure to reflect on the nature and worth of those years and that labor. When it is assumed that personal choice is not necessarily the surest means to progress, public policy and public administration must assume responsibility for more than a well-run public sector. Public policy and public administration must then cause individual behavior to conform to policy whenever the dictates of personal choice and public policy are not identical. In the longer run, they must intervene in the development of personalities in order to encourage identity between personal choice and public policy.

If it is true that in the last hundred years a public policy that was sometimes the instrument and facilitator of personal choice and sometimes a substitute for personal choice has led to biological success and some cultural advance for the majority of the population, it is not so regrettable that our political philosophers did not fix personal choice as the only criterion of good public policy. The imperatives of progress would seem to have been a not intolerable guide to policy, and it is doubtless to our good that a consensual definition of progress was forthcoming. But it should be of concern to us today that this consensual definition of progress reflects some intellectual and political compromises of the last century.

From the perspective of 1975, we can see that the enthusiasm for population growth in George's explanation of progress and the de-emphasis of the population challenge in the neoclassical commitment to progress reflect the special conditions of the late nineteenth century, in particular the opening of the North American prairies. Those special conditions made it possible to ignore—for some period of time—the absurdity of progress as a long-run policy objective, when progress is understood to mean an improving standard of living for an increasing proportion of *an expanding population.*

In the short run, progress can be served by better organization of resources, by improved entrepreneurship. In the longer run, progress depends upon the establishment of an identity of personal and communal interest. Ultimately, in this world of limited resources, progress depends upon a special case of that identity, one pertaining to population. At some point that identity must affect the definition of the progress it serves, it must make "an expanding population" a superfluous phrase in the definition of progress.

Only recently—indeed, in the years since OISE was founded—has emphasis shifted in political rhetoric and in the applied social sciences from the short-run and longer run imperatives of progress to the longer run and ultimate imperatives. In the early 1960s, the salient theme in the literature of political economy and in public policy was progress, meaning an improving standard of living for an increasing proportion of a growing population. Nowhere was this concern more evident than in the economics-of-education literature and in public education policy.

The prevailing conceptualizations of education and public policy in the early sixties were very much a continuation of the best-established notions on education and public policy of a century ago, and almost a celebration of the ideas on public policy, education, and progress that were so well established early in the twentieth century, namely:

— Progress, in the longer run, is beyond question a matter for public administration and depends on the establishment of an identity of personal and communal interest.
— Educational sociology can guide public policy on education, whether or not learning theory or psychology is capable of producing congruent research results.
— The quantity of education produced and consumed in a society is an important (perhaps the major) determinant of social product per capita.
— In the interest of longer run progress, the policy imperative is the provision of more public education.

Those were conceptualizations conducive to positive thinking, particularly on the part of politicians, policy makers, and social scientists concerned with public education. They were ideas that depended upon a consensual definition of progress, or at least a consensual assumption that we all recognize the imperatives of progress when they are presented to us. They depended upon unquestioning acceptance of the notion that the imperfect identity of interest of individuals and society is legitimation for any amount of intervention by the state. And they depended upon the moral argument that the state should interfere by way of education in the affairs of its citizens when sociological evidence indicates that the benefits of reform and new technology will accrue to the citizens later or less certainly without such intervention.

Those conceptualizations reflected concern for the short-run and longer run imperatives of progress, but minimal concern for the very long-run or ultimate imperatives of progress. More importantly, they reflected no concern at all for the fact that the consensual definition of progress breaks down in discussion of the very long-run requisites of the commonweal.

COMING TO GRIPS WITH FREEDOM AND SUCCESS

We are a hundred years into the era of progress and public education. Almost everyone now alive who has grown up in this country, or in at least a half dozen other countries similarly blessed, has been conditioned to accept the existence of personal choice, freely registered, as the prime criterion of good government. He has absorbed the lessons that people produce the most wealth where they are most free, and that the distribution of that wealth is most equitable where people are most free to choose among the possible uses of their labor and capital. He has learned too that freedom is an exciting prospect only when it pertains to the use of one's surplus energy and product, but that it is a cruel hoax upon those so poor as to have as options only degrading dependence or relentless, debilitating labor.

Some of these lessons are taught in the schools to which parents are required by law to send their children. Some are taught in educational institutions which the law does not require students to attend, indeed where attendance is a privilege related to competition and selection, but where non-attendance means exclusion from the employment to which some aspire. Our citizens are products of governments that have steadfastly adhered to the imperatives of progress, and of public policies that have artfully preserved the compromises between the general rule of personal choice and the unblushing application of compulsion in the interest of progress.

Along the way, quietly and without warning, success has stolen up on our policy makers. We have produced a generation, perhaps several of them, so productive that policies for the redistribution of wealth can be taken seriously—they need not result in universal poverty. We have produced a literate population and a veritable flood of literature, popular and technical, related to the science of government. Will is the only requirement for any citizen to become a modest expert on good government. Indeed, sound critics of government abound in every community. If Thomas Malthus were alive today he would have no occasion to register this hope for education's contribution to the civic peace:

> The poor are by no means inclined to be visionary. Their distresses are always real, though they are not attributed to the real causes. If these causes were properly explained to them, and they were taught to know what part of their present distress was attributable to government, and what part to causes totally unconnected with it, discontent and irritation among the lower classes of people would show themselves much less frequently than at present; and when they did show themselves would be much less dreaded. The efforts of turbulent and discontented men in the middle classes of society might safely be disregarded if the poor were so far enlightened respecting the real nature of their situation as to be aware that by aiding them in their schemes of renovation they would probably be promoting the ambitious view of others without in any respect benefiting themselves.[23]

Nor would he have occasion to register this regret:

> We have lavished immense sums on the poor, which we have every reason to think have constantly tended to aggravate their misery. But in their education and in the circulation of those important political truths that most nearly concern them, which are perhaps the only means in our power of really raising their condition, and of making them happier men and more peaceable subjects, we have been miserably deficient.[24]

In addition, there is no reason to assume that ordinary citizens are less aware than Malthus would have them be concerning the relationship of prudence regarding reproduction to their own prosperity and the commonweal.

As we receive the rewards of a century of positive public policies serving the imperatives of progress, rewards for which a high price was paid in liberties forgone, positive public policy is proving singularly inadequate to the problems of governing a free and prosperous society. Perhaps the most outstanding failure of public policy pertains to wages. As governments struggle to administer a wages system, it is becoming painfully evident that we are incapable of producing a wages policy. More depressing still, no philosophers have provided a rationale for such a policy that is appropriate to our institutions and traditions.

There is a cheering aspect to our problems regarding a wages policy, however. They are, after all, the problems of prosperity; more specifically, they are the problems of administering the distribution of prosperity. They are, presumably, the problems to which we have long aspired, and the problems to which people in most countries still aspire. They are the problems we had hoped to have in the future during the long century of sacrificing personal choice to the dictates of public policy for progress. It is not surprising that political philosophers have no rationale for policies appropriate to our present problems. Their specialty, after all, has always been policy as a means to the end that is prosperity. They have had much less to say about how we should deal with prosperity after we got it.

Some people may attempt to rationalize wages policies, and any attendant interventions in the affairs of individuals and institutions, as an imperative of progress. They are not likely to be very effective, however, because they will be arguing for progress as the answer to the problems of progress. It remains to be seen how wage conflicts will be dealt with, but given the lack of a rationale or consensus favoring any positive measures, it is not surprising that the problem of a wages policy is associated with a rather general erosion of faith in public policy.

This is not to imply that the absence of a rational wages policy invites the dismantling of the public sector, or even a reversal in the long trend toward more public consumption in relation to private consumption. It is only to draw attention to a waning enthusiasm for public policy as the certain instrument for promoting the commonweal. In the most cautious of terms, the popular mood is one of low tolerance for public policies requiring the sacrifice of personal choice for any but the most specific and certain of objectives.

It seems certain that the near future will see an increase in public policies that noticeably limit personal choice in the interest of very specific objectives. In particular, it is hard to imagine that pollution abatement and traffic control will not cause some definite constraints to be placed on personal choice. Such policies represent the use of centralized authority to better exploit the present state of technology in dealing with physical problems of the day. It seems much less likely that the near future will see bold new policies introduced to influence the character and personality of citizens.

Most modern rationalizations for coercive and restrictive policies, in Marxist societies no less than in capitalist societies, are offered as intermediate measures. They are intended to facilitate a period of socialization preparatory for greater freedom. In Anglo-Saxon societies, public education policies have depended very much upon the idea that order, stability, and prosperity will only be assured when the general population has achieved a higher state of development. That claim can hardly be made today. Some disestablishment of compulsion in education—both its most overt and its more subtle forms—seems inevitable. Indeed, the process is already well begun, and some awkward stages of transition are now evident. In our secondary schools we offer students under sixteen internal freedom, but not the freedom to leave. In effect, the law now requires attendance at a place, but does not stipulate what sort of experience is intended. In our universities, the choice of experiences requisite for degrees is being expanded, but very little corresponding latitude in professorial employment qualifications or in degree credits for external experiences is noticeable. The situation is one in which it is not the nature of the experience that determines whether or not it can be part of a degree program; rather it is in what place and under whose supervision the experience takes place.

Institutional adjustments at all levels will undoubtedly follow upon the certain reassessment of compulsion's role in education. To date the adjustments have been mainly internal. Ultimately, there will be fundamental adjustments in the external relationships of all educational institutions—for example, with the law, the public treasury, the professions, and the family.

The great expansion in the 1960s of the educational establishment of this province, in particular of higher education, provided new institutions not particularly different from the older ones they complemented. They were designed in accordance with the assumptions that compulsion at the lower levels would play its traditional role, and that higher education would continue the authoritative roles then associated with it. OISE itself was fashioned as an institution to complement a set of school systems and other institutions that were products of a century of public policy that assumed an important role in public education for compulsion and direct intervention in the affairs of individuals.

OISE is perhaps unusual, at least in its capacity as a policy-study center, in that it has a tradition of focusing upon specific conditions and trends in society and the problems they pose for the education system. This focus may render the Institute marginally better prepared to make sustained sequential adjustments, in internal policies and in external relationships, than if its commitment were to deriving grand policy propositions from presumed general relationships between society and education. But like every other educational institution, OISE faces the challenge of accommodating to a remarkable environmental change attendant upon the virtual collapse of a century-old consensus on the imperatives of progress.

NOTES

1. Talcott Parsons and Neil J. Smelser, *Economy and Society: A Study in the Integration of Economic and Social Theory* (Glencoe, Ill.: Free Press, 1956), p. 102.

2. The Inter-University Research Program in Institution Building, "The Guiding Concepts" (an unpublished plan for the coordination of basic research on the role of innovative institutions in nation building, prepared at the Maxwell School, Syracuse University, Syracuse, N.Y., 1964), pp. 6–7.

3. Edward F. Denison, *The Sources of Economic Growth in the United States and the Alternatives Before Us*, Supplementary Paper no. 13 (New York: Committee for Economic Development, 1962).

4. Gordon W. Bertram, *The Contribution of Education to Economic Growth*, Staff Study no. 12, Economic Council of Canada (Ottawa: Queen's Printer, 1966).

5. Ibid., pp. 56, 57.

6. R. W. B. Jackson, *The Problem of Numbers in University Enrolment*, Bulletin no. 18 (Toronto: Canadian Education Association and the Department of Educational Research, Ontario College of Education, 1963).

7. Fritz Machlup, *The Production and Distribution of Knowledge in the United States* (Princeton, N.J.: Princeton University Press, 1962).

8. Ibid., pp. 128, 139.

9. Rudolph C. Blitz, "Some Classical Economists and Their Views on Education," *Economia* (Santiago, Chile), vol. 72 (1961): 34–60. Several somewhat revised reprintings have appeared in English-language publications.

10. Adolph Wagner, *Finanzwissenschaft* (Leipzig: C. F. Winter, 1883). Wagner is familiar to English-speaking students of public finance, in large measure through excerpts of his work in R. A. Musgrave and A. T. Peacock, *Classics in the Theory of Public Finance* (London: Macmillan & Co., 1958).

11. Nassau Senior, *Industrial Efficiency and Social Economy*, ed. S. Leon Levy (New York: Henry Holt & Co., 1928), part 5, ch. 8.

12. For a most interesting comment on Mill's passionate dedication to the significance of the individual, see Michael S. Parke, *The Life of John Stuart Mill* (New York: Macmillan Co., 1954), particularly p. 269. For a demonstration of Mill's views on reform through education, one could not do better than to use Blitz's essay as a guide to selective reading in John S. Mill, *Principles of Political Economy*, ed. W. J. Ashly (London: Longmans Green, 1920).

13. Mill, *Principles*, p. 760.

14. Matthew Arnold, *Culture and Anarchy* (Cambridge: Cambridge University Press, 1963), pp. 184–88.

15. Henry George, *Progress and Poverty* (New York: Robert Scholkenbach Foundation, 1966).

16. Mill, *Principles*, p. 756.

17. Ibid., p. 760.

18. George, *Progress*, p. 10.

19. Ibid., p. xv.

20. Ibid., pp. 7–8.

21. Ibid., pp. 307–310.

22. Appropriately, chapter 1 of Alfred Marshall's *Principles of Economics* (1890) is a short essay on poverty. It is a hopeful essay, giving much credit to the blessings of economic freedom but claiming for the science of economics considerable credit

for bringing free enterprise "somewhat under control." He concludes with a confident statement on the contribution of economists to our ability to relate policy to "the quality and tone of man's life." Eighth edition (London: Macmillan & Co., 1956), pp. 1–11.

23. Thomas Malthus, *An Essay on the Principles of Population* (London: Ward, Lock & Co., 1890), p. 477.

24. Ibid., p. 496.

Funny Things Happen on the Way to Parnassus

Alan M. Thomas

Within this century, Canada's educational system has been constantly assaulted by conflicting demands for change; by the sixties, it was obvious that a compass bearing, a balance point, must be found or the elementary/secondary system would continue to flounder aimlessly. R. W. B. Jackson's work provided such a balance point and indicated the direction in which the educational system should move. Unfortunately, the winds of change continue to blow; and at present the elementary/secondary system of education in all of Canada seems hopelessly adrift. The relentless decline of numbers is only part of the problem. The real difficulty is the school system's loss of its centrality, its unity, and its sense of purpose. An understanding of this loss and a formulation of possible alternatives requires an examination of the historical factors reflected in the present situation.

At the turn of the century, social needs for stability, socialization, equality, and preparation of the labor force were translated into learning needs and educational needs provided for almost exclusively by schools for the young. Similarly, individuals translated their needs for upward mobility into learning and educational needs for their children. Recruitment and enrollment met in the simple decision to compel participation by law, in terms of both attendance and financial support. The system operated largely on principles of growth; and once the compulsory period was past, participants were eliminated progressively on the basis of academic competition.

The secondary school served fundamentally as preparation for those lucky few who continued on to the university. As the century progressed, however, more and more social needs were translated into recruitment of the young for further education. The larger and increasingly varied secondary school population, encouraged to remain for longer and longer periods in school by the Family Allowance and the growing complexity of employment preparation and certification, was demanding a much greater variety of programs, courses, teachers, and resources. These factors, combined with the "last chance for education" philosophy that prevailed until well into the sixties (and still does among some teachers and administrators, in contrast with many of their students), served to break up the secondary school's former single academic purpose of preparing students for university. This break-up was first signaled by Hilda Neatby.[1] While apparently attacking the loss of intellectual rigor and formal unity in secondary schools riddled with "progressive education," Neatby was in fact firing the first round in a continuing battle over the failure of secondary schools to provide automatically and exclusively for university entrance requirements.

This failure was also an unanticipated consequence of compulsory attendance, which during the first part of the century was pushed steadily upwards to the age of sixteen, with hopes and promises of even further advancement. Compulsory attendance makes the elementary and secondary system more a social system than an educational one, since participation does not rest on educational grounds. A major non-educational need—for simple custody and supervision of children—became associated with the school. This need increased as wars were fought, houses grew smaller, and both parents joined the labor force. The conflict between the custodial function and educational purposes of the elementary/secondary system had reached serious proportions by the sixties and was an important factor in the dawning realization that an accurate interpretation of existing educational realities and future educational needs was crucial.

One of R. W. B. Jackson's most notable and significant contributions was to bring the two elements of the educational enterprise—social needs and individual needs—into balance, or, one might even say, to harry, shove, and wrestle them into position. The mixture of hard data, gentle reproof, and goading in his now famous address to the 40th Convention of the Canadian Education Association in Quebec City, in September 1963,[2] suggests how delicate and fragile the balance was, and how difficult to hold in place while at the same time persuading others to accept it. That he succeeded is supported by any analysis of the recent history of education in Ontario and elsewhere in Canada.

Working with the complementary projections of Edward Sheffield, Jackson was able to assume certain constants about the nature of educational participation. "We have not finished the elementary school expansion, the secondary school expansion has just nicely begun, and in a few years we will start the *real* expansion of post-secondary education! How much more will it cost? Can we afford it? Since the children are here and must be educated, the questions are of more academic than practical interest, surely."[3] Jackson was obviously confident that uniform participation in successive grades would increase predictably, that the institutions were identifiable, and that the patterns of participation in them would remain and predominate in terms of duration, programs, and processes of certification. In short, it was assumed that the recognizable stars and planets of the educational universe would remain moving immutably about the "formal" sun, at least for as long as mattered.

Jackson did, indeed, refer to growing demands for adult education in the province; but the spirit of his time is reflected perhaps in a parenthetical remark, "Ontario has more [population than Quebec] at each year of age from 21 onwards, and nearly twice as many of the very old—fortunately, the old do not need education as much as care."[4]

In the introduction to his paper Jackson argued that the final choice is one of value.

> In many cases, as we have learned in our discussions and planning in Ontario, a choice must be made on the basis, not of logic or of fact, but of philosophy, beliefs, or sets of values. Some of the decisions which must be reached are crucial, with very far-reaching implications for society in general as well as for individual universities and students. For the most part, fortunately, the facts are clear, possibly too clear for comfort and certainly too clear to permit continued complacency or inaction on the part of any of us. The decisions are difficult to make, unfortunately; most of them call for sacrifice, and some of them for a radical departure from hallowed traditions.[5]

One cannot help but wonder exactly what sort of sacrifice (and by whom) Jackson had in mind, since one consequence of his work was the largest provision of resources for educational purposes and the creation of the largest and wealthiest educational establishment in our history. His position was valid for the period in which he elaborated it. Or we made it valid by accepting his argument and creating the means to fulfill his predictions, which meant assuming the value of concentrating primarily on the education of the young, and the efficacy of graded schooling. These practices were maximized, and we live now with the consequences of putting so many young through formal educational processes and neglecting the education, formal and otherwise, of other groups in our society. What was sacrificed was the growth of continuity in the educational system, the articulation of school and work, and the educational needs of older groups in the population who were facing an increasing rate of technical change.

Jackson could not have foreseen that by the end of the decade students, parents, numbers of adults, and various minority groups by confrontation and relentless pressure for access would call into question the fixed nature of the educational universe itself, and insist on using it in all manner of unpredictable ways.

One way to get a grip on the events of the past two decades is by analyzing the relationship between the learning needs of the individual and those of society.

All individuals in a society have needs. Some of these needs are translated into, or find expression as, learning needs. These needs may be satisfied by consciously learning something, such as a skill, an attitude, a set of facts. Some are translated or transformed into educational needs, which then express themselves as *demands* for enrollment in a formal educational system. Two points should be noted here. One is that to the individual the act of formulating a need as a need for "education" may not in itself be a purely individual decision; the student may be persuaded by parents, employer, or others that the need is a learning or educational one. The other point is that not all individual needs are educational ones, nor are all needs that are educational identified as such.

Not only do all individuals have needs, but so do all societies. These are collectively identified and expressed through political and administrative processes and structures. Some are learning needs which can be satisfied—or the problems reduced—if some individuals or collections of individuals acquire through learning new skills or knowledge or attitudes. Some of these learning needs are seen as needs for education and through the provision of facilities are translated into efforts at recruitment by educational agencies.

The means of effecting such a translation are complex and subject to varying degrees of efficiency. The dramatic increase in the number of groups and individuals participating in the translation process is one example of the alteration in educational activities in the past five years. The "community school" movement, for example, represents an attempt to make the process of translation more direct and immediate. Its success has been limited, perhaps because the movement has so far concentrated on the young rather than dealing with a broad range of needs.

When the processes reflecting individual needs resulting in demands for enrollment precisely match the processes involving collective needs (with their interest in recruitment), the educational activities of any society reach a state of reasonable tranquility. That such a state rarely, if ever, occurs scarcely needs mentioning. The number of variables present suggest the pressures to which such a balance can be subjected. Further analysis suggests that perhaps this state is not desirable, since a great deal of the society's validity appears to stem from the constant effort at adjustment of the various factors or processes involved. Learning, it appears, not only requires energy for its accomplishment, it also generates it. The active learner has more energy for everything around him. There is a curious two-level characteristic about learning. Just as individuals repeatedly must learn how to learn, so a society must continually "learn" how to manage learning. The continual effort to produce the equilibrium implied by the "needs" metaphor, an unlikely achievement in any society which encourages change, creates its own energy.

We can now, using the individual/collective perspective, attempt further analysis of the period of the fifties and sixties. On the collective side, Jackson's data supported the then fashionable economic argument that a very much larger segment of social need could be interpreted as learning needs and, with only a brief pause at that step, could be translated into educational needs and efforts at recruitment. Recruitment took the form of the provision of particular facilities, universities, colleges, schools, professional teachers, scholarships—all those symbolic and substantive resources and activities that in the absence of outright compulsion serve the engines of persuasion. Simultaneously, both substantively and symbolically, employment opportunity was being adjusted to synchronize with prolonged preparation and academic achievement. That is, other collective endeavors in the society—industry, the professions, the armed services, and so forth—were expressing more and more of their problems in terms of educational needs of a relatively conventional nature, and thus supporting the provision of conventional educational resources. On the individual side, sufficient stability existed to allow some balance, at least until the middle of the period. There was a continuing tendency to identify needs as the educational needs of a specific group of individuals, namely the young, who in fact until much later played little or no role in the interpretation themselves. Numbers, the basis of Jackson's argument, were obviously increasing. Hindsight now suggests that "more of the same" was not what was required. For a brief period the balance was maintained, but even in that period, events occurred that disturbed the regular operation of the system, and at approximately the end of the decade the balance was seen to have deteriorated.

Canada, in common with many other countries, had accepted the existence of a simple relationship between the education of the young and economic development. Spawned perhaps in North America, few ideas have become so pervasive in so short a time. The assumed relationship was understandably prominent in Jackson's work and also, presumably, in the minds of those he influenced. By the early sixties, however, the results of Canadian and American poverty studies began to indicate that the assumption was unfounded that a child-centered school system could intervene successfully between a child and the economic and cultural circumstances of his family. Educators were slow to take notice of these results, and even slower to realize that the segregation of children for educational purposes was the main cause of the problem.

At the same time, in the face of the drying up of supplies of skilled immigrants, observers of the Canadian labor force began to see that there were large numbers of adults with increasingly redundant skills and little skill in learning new ones. There was pressure to translate needs of groups in society other than the young into learning needs, and to translate those needs into such educational variants as new programs, living allowances, counseling resources, and, in time, differently trained teachers and differently designed facilities.

By the end of the sixties the flowering of postsecondary commissions, province by province, gave evidence of the extent of the disarray in educational systems. More individuals were translating more needs into learning needs, and then pausing to consider, often with vehemence, whether these could be satisfied at all by conventional "educational" means. Enrollment dropped, temporarily but unexpectedly, while educational agencies scrambled to make themselves more flexible. More individuals and groups indicated a wish to participate in various ways in decisions on the collective side—decisions determining which needs were to be viewed as learning needs, and which of those as educational needs. "Openness" became a byword, "free schools" and "alternative schools," some of them bankrolled by public money, flourished, and the number of part-time registrants at every level began its slow increase. The orderly process, on which so much of Jackson's predictions had depended, of expressing all the learning needs of the society as the educational needs of one group, namely the young, had to be abandoned. But there was reluctance apparent in the change. The participation of the young was compulsory, and it remains so, for nothing is more deceptively simple than solving social problems by making others attend to them. Examples of such a view still abound.

An example of the decline of this view can be found in the mixture of surprise and vigor with which the report of the Select Committee on the Utilization of Educational Facilities argued that education takes place in more places and forms than we had thought and that forms previously relegated to positions of minor importance, however difficult they may be to define or predict, must now be given equal stature with already established patterns.

There are, in fact, two educational systems in Ontario: the formal system offering full-time educational programs to young people through schools, universities and colleges, and the informal system which encompasses a wide spectrum of activities for young and old. These range from continuing education courses offered by the various publicly supported educational institutions to the personal interest and recreation programs offered by such volunteer agencies as the YMCA or YWCA, to the upgrading and retraining opportunities provided by business and industry, to the activities of a large number of cultural institutions, and groups, and further. We thus define "educational facilities" in terms of all the places where education is being, and can be, pursued.[6]

The report of the Select Committee is one of many attempts in the seventies to provide us with a balanced vision comparable to the one Jackson provided in the sixties. It is obvious that the terrain over which such a vision must range has changed radically. What must be done now is to identify and assess the changes. Examining the balance between individual and collective needs provides a vantage point for this assessment and may perhaps serve as a basis for valid and useful prediction.

One obvious pressure for change in the educational structure is the growing introduction of day care centers for children below school entry age. Clearly custodial at present, they cannot exist for long before some eager educators pounce on the opportunity to educate provided by the existence of substantial groups of younger children gathered in identifiable places at identifiable times on a regular basis. In some respects the same forces that combined seventy years ago to bring compulsory schooling into existence are now joined to bring about voluntary but publicly provided day care centers. The fact that they are voluntary, publicly supported, collective in nature —and more important, basically custodial—may provide a new mix of practices and events that will generate innovations in the elementary/secondary school system.

A more subtle but more pervasive and significant change is that of the reduction of the need for socialization as an exclusive function of the elementary/secondary school system. The principal purpose of the "common school," compulsorily attended and financed, was that of "socializing" the young. In societies subject to slow rates of change, socialization occurs simply in the early stages of life and over a relatively short period of time. Roles, attitudes, hopes, and aspirations, familiar in and acceptable to the society, are learned mostly by example and can be counted on to persist, reinforced relentlessly by the normal processes and procedures of ongoing social life. It is easy to see how in societies wedded to technical and social change, and based on large successive cycles of immigration, much responsibility for socialization was likely to fall on the common school. Hence, in both Canada and the United States, the impressive concern for such schooling, and the growth of huge, uniform, highly centralized school systems. Hence also the persistent conflict in both societies over public and sectarian schools.

Recently it has become apparent that in societies characterized by both rapid change and heterogeneous populations, the expectation of socialization by the schools can no longer be fulfilled. Socialization must take place throughout life. The elementary/secondary system is no longer the sole place or only time to accomplish it. What is occurring in this case is the translation of what has been characterized as an exclusive educational need of the young into learning needs that cannot be concentrated on that group only, or on conventional schools. Although the circumstances of the transfer are not yet clearly understood, it is already clear that to a degree the socialization function is now the province of the all-pervasive mass media.

The inability of the elementary/secondary system to act as sole socializing agent has led to several developments with interesting implications. There are growing demands for increased private learning for the children and youth involved in the elementary/secondary system. Internationally, the present interest in "non-formal education"[7] suggests that translation from the learning-need stage to the educational-need stage has been somewhat hasty, and that some learning needs can be met—indeed can only be met— outside the formal educational system. Such learning needs can, it is argued, be accommodated through the family and other private endeavors, where more direct individual and private-group determination can be maintained. The movement is associated with new public concern for the revitalization of the family, and it is interesting to speculate on cause and effect. A danger lies in the fact that the strength of such movements may be determined by financial resources, and when families with enough money pull their children out of the public sphere, the public sphere is left with diminishing resources to provide for those families that must remain. This is occurring in the adult education sector and can only be prevented by maintaining general financial participation in the public sphere and by encouraging the public education sector to include characteristics of imagination and flexibility associated with private and individual learning. (Alternative schools are examples of such attempts.)

There are at present large numbers of people, however, for whom most learning has taken place in the public sphere, and who are accustomed to identifying private learning needs with public educational resources. Despite this fact, it seems clear that here too there is a balance that by the mid-fifties had been seriously disturbed. In particular, compulsory attendance laws may have to be debated. The new forces supporting wide educational participation are likely to be more functional than are laws compelling mere attendance.

The problem of where to place the responsibility for socialization, in addition to such factors as increasing specialization, employment trends, and increasing longevity, help explain the evolution of a "postsecondary system," and a number of events now taking place in adult education.

A massive system of adult education already exists in this society, in the sense that large numbers of adults participate in public and private, open and closed, educational endeavors. Societies as a whole and large systems or organizations within societies have increasingly translated their needs into learning and educational needs, and they have done so for increasing numbers of adults. The armed services, with immense resources committed to training and education in both war and peacetime, are an obvious example. The extent to which such participation in learning is imbedded now in military life is indicated by Baum.[8] Industrial systems of training (and more recently management development) began to appear in the late twenties, notably among the oil companies, as their research and its application, for which specific training was needed, began to outstrip the resources and flexibility of public educational institutions. Almost every organization of any size has introduced educational programs designed originally to further the organization's technical and economic interests, but that increasingly reflect the fact that for both public and private social reasons the organization must provide educational opportunities of various kinds because it has direct access to substantial numbers of individuals. A recent law in France, for example, compels all large commercial organizations to make available a certain percentage of their revenues for educational opportunities for their employees. Similarly, educational opportunity appears with greater and greater frequency in the results of labor negotiations.

In the face of the so-called knowledge or information explosion, all professions, through their professional associations and their associated schools, have moved to institute elaborate systems of adult education for their members.

Many of these developments, which have occurred throughout the society without much public notice, followed the still prevalent tendency to move past the learning-need stage and directly to the provision of educational resources. Increasingly familiar, however, is a tendency to resist the swift passage over the learning-need stage, and, in combination with the public interest in openness, to concentrate on the provision of learning resources in less formal, more individually centered and presumably less expensive circumstances. In the eighth report of the Economic Council of Canada the argument was advanced that too great a proportion of the Manpower Training Program was being conducted in formal educational institutions and too little in factories or places of work.[9] It is evident that the federal government accepted that argument since, as a result, programs in work places have been vigorously encouraged.

Work by Allen Tough and others indicates that the abundance of information and expertise to be found outside the educational system makes possible the flowering of entirely private, individually determined learning programs.[10] At the same time, the exact nature of this system (if it can be called one)—its purposes and functions, and its susceptibility to planning and manipulation—remains obscure.

The system of adult education which now exists represents a substantial deployment of financial and, more important, human resources. Accurate descriptions of its scope do not exist, however, perhaps because of our prior conditioning by educational systems that were and are highly visible, perhaps because it has arrived so swiftly and so variously, and perhaps because it has largely remained in the hands of individuals who characteristically have their eyes fixed on the future rather than the present. But if we are to work with the adult education system so that it may serve both social and individual ends and provide for both institutional education and private learning, then it is important to understand it as it is.

There have been encouraging indications that Statistics Canada is preparing to develop and carry out regular surveys of adult educational activities. However, the most recent attempts to acknowledge, describe, and rationalize the new developments in adult education can be found in the postsecondary reports of recent years.

The vast expansion of colleges and universities, supported by previously unimagined proportions of the public treasury, provoked growing restlessness and criticism and led inevitably to the establishment of postsecondary commissions. Unfortunately, the inability of these commissions to break away from the traditional model has led to their formulation of additional formal educational systems which in at least two cases have new and separate government bureaucracies to administer them. By creating or insisting on "parallelism"—the right to admission independent of performance or achievements in the elementary/secondary system—they have shattered the original purpose of that system. The result for the elementary/secondary system has been to increase the conflict between educational purposes and custodial functions. In Ontario, the elementary/secondary system recently retaliated in order to reestablish its own integrity. It now insists that if admission to the postsecondary system is not dependent on a secondary school diploma, then such admission, based on outside criteria, shall not be taken as an equivalent of the secondary diploma. Thus the segregation between the two systems is maintained and furthered, and they now proceed as ocean liners on parallel courses with little reference to each other, seemingly unaware that a host of individuals are attempting to cross between them for reasons of either age or need. One cannot doubt that the sea claims many.

Only the Province of Alberta has attempted to deal with the entire educational system and with the problem of continuity on a large scale. While somewhat amorphous in style and content, the Alberta report[11] deserves more national attention than it has received. In Ontario, the report of the Commission on Post-Secondary Education[12] has been followed swiftly by a small-scale attempt at rationality under the unlikely guise of a consideration of the use of material facilities already available for education. Both the pressure of events and the imagination of the committee members made it impossible for that investigation to remain restricted to such matters as unused buildings and twenty-four-hour schedules, and the result is the first major attempt in Ontario to develop a blueprint for continuing education.

The necessity for continuity in the educational system is focused at present in the demands for private and self-directed learning expressed not only by adults but by upper-level secondary school students. Emphasis on "learning needs" stresses the right of the learner to make use of educational and other resources in a manner determined by him. Students in "alternative" secondary schools have used a great variety of sources, including universities, other cultural institutions, individuals in the community, and private agencies, on grounds acceptable to the agencies for the most part, without regard for the traditional concept of educational "level." Freedom to use such private and public resources must be assured not only to full-time students in the elementary/secondary system, but also to any part-time and intermittent students who wish to adapt such resources to programs of their own. While willing to admit the legitimacy of wider learning needs, the public authorities and investigating commissions—again with the exception of Alberta, and Ontario's Select Committee—have shown little concern for the provision of continuity, and in effect have reduced it.

While rejecting any need to rationalize vertically (partly because of the presumed contrast between the basically compulsory elementary/secondary system and voluntary postsecondary system), the various commissions, with the noted exception of Alberta, attempted to rationalize horizontally and to provide some intellectual and administrative order for the myriad kinds of adult and continuing education which take place after childhood. Uniformly they acknowledged the immense past translation of learning needs into educational needs and resources, and the likelihood that the tendency would continue. But just as uniformly and solemnly they assured the public that no comparable financial "binge" could be anticipated, no new temples to education contemplated. Properly, they stressed relationships, techniques, skills, and novel deployment of existing resources.

Nevertheless, their obvious assumption that taxpayers would be reluctant to part with more money for educational purposes was perhaps mistaken. The child-centered educational system is based on the assumption that it is planned by, paid for, and operated by people other than its immediate beneficiaries. The student or pupil is not expected to act as ratepayer, voter, teacher, administrator, or politician. The dropping of the age of majority has produced a slight shiver in the secondary system, but the roles are still generally distinct and likely to remain so. In systems of adult education, however, no such distinction is retained. Even sporadic participants are at the same time students, ratepayers, fee-payers, voters, teachers, administrators, and politicians. This fact materially changes attitudes and practices with respect to education, as indicated by evidence from the United States, where school financing is more clearly delineated in the political process. It appears that the adult public is likely to be more generous and cooperative when faced with an increase in school taxes or expenditures for a system which provides actual or potential services for their own education than they are for a system which educates only young people. At the end of the sixties, the Canadian public seemed to have reached an upper limit of tolerance in paying for the education of the young. But there is no reason to assume that the limit was reached or has been reached in terms of paying for educational facilities available to those who pay for them, directly or indirectly. The full implication of this possibility has hardly been considered.

In their efforts at horizontal rationality the commissions tried to deal with many issues. What provided the greatest perplexity for them, and has left their inheritors with the complex issue of "openness" and the "open sector," was their dimly felt awareness that society had translated learning needs far too glibly into educational needs.

Until recently, we tended to ignore or deny the need to include much private adult learning in the public sphere of education. An immigrant society with problems of settlement in an unfamiliar environment could not entirely ignore the need for adult education, but the need was defined traditionally as a small but persistent concern with language, citizenship, and the need to learn new skills of production and consumption. During two world wars we leaped into efforts at training many people in skills and attitudes they had never expected to acquire. After both wars the country also used education policy as a means of reward and veterans' rehabilitation. With the exception of agricultural extension, teacher education, and some limited other vocational training, however, concern for adult learning remained largely in the private sphere until near the mid-century, when an explosion of adult education in the public sphere began and has continued unabated. We must not forget that what we are witnessing is not necessarily a vast proportionate increase in adult learning as such, but an enormous increase in the transfer of that learning from the private to the public sphere.

At the same time, an increasing sophistication about learning is indicated by growing insistence that not all learning needs should be translated into formal educational needs. For example, such systems as "Learnex," an inventory of educational and information resources in East Toronto developed and maintained by the Toronto Board of Education, and the rapid growth of "learning resource centers" seem to indicate that individuals can and will learn many things on their own without resorting to or depending on formal courses, designated teachers, or large educational buildings. In fact it appears that no society could possibly meet its learning needs through formal provisions, psychologically or financially, any more than it can depend on hospitals for meeting its health needs. The legacy of the commission reports is the dilemma of the conflict between conventional government methods of securing both responsibility and accountability in its operations—of which education is a prime example—and the demands of newly self-conscious learners who wish to pursue their own learning, or meet their own needs by means of learning, and who believe they have a right to do so with some public support—meaning access to publicly provided resources.

The balance of public and private endeavor is a serious matter that needs vastly improved information regarding both participation and content of program. Obviously, there has been a mass translation of private individual needs into learning needs on the part of adults. Some of these needs could be satisfied in the private sector by the creation of vast private or segregated training and educational systems like those in the armed services and private industry. However, new social needs, associated not so much with "leisure" as with spare time, which can only be provided for by the use of public or semi-public resources, are increasing their pressure on the educational system. Concerns for retirement activity, child rearing or parenting, home building and access to competent, reasonable services, and a general restlessness with conventional career patterns among the professional middle class indicate some of the needs that individuals are translating fluently into educational demands for enrollment.

One of the most consistent results of research into the participation of adults in education anywhere in North America is that the more formal education adults enjoyed as children and youth, the more likely they are to participate in further education of *all* kinds. In other words, the more their needs as children were translated by others directly into educational needs, the more likely they are, as adults, to continue to do so. There is some indication now of a check to the speed and regularity of that translation, but even this relatively gradual process includes a very high use of public facilities. A very large portion of the population between twenty and forty years of age has had more formal education than any comparable group in our history, and is showing every indication of making substantial demands on both the public and private systems.

Efforts at altering the traditional role of the student so that more people can and will take part in formal college and university education and gain access to formal certification—so far more evident in the United States and the United Kingdom than in Canada—can be regarded on the one hand as a great step forward in the provision of educational opportunity, and on the other hand as a vast act of seduction. There is an aspect of control in such activities: learning, once accomplished privately and individually, is not considered legitimate or of value unless it is associated with the public ritual of education. Centralization, control, and certification seem to have moved upward in our educational system, becoming more evident in the education of adults and young adults than among children. One American adult educator, John Ohliger, has already called attention to the increasing appearance of compulsion in a variety of forms in adult education, and to the danger of people being made to feel so educationally inadequate that they are subtly pressured to seek further education provided by the educational establishment.[13] Ohliger's case seems overstated and entirely without concern for the relationship of social needs, such as competence, to adult education. However, it is clear that a considerable degree of persuasion and encouragement has entered the adult sector.

As this brief analysis indicates, the present educational system is in trouble. A unified vision is required. The Unesco report *Learning to Be* argues that some intellectual clarity is afforded when we shift our focus from "education" to "learning."[14] Since it is now accepted that learning can and does occur at any age, decisions about the allocation of educational resources to other groups and individuals than the young become a clear moral and political choice rather than a safe psychological one. A new perspective therefore must acknowledge the individual and social need of groups other than the young to have free and regular access to educational and learning resources, and it must assume the likelihood that they will demand such access. This approach does not necessarily involve the provision of more expensive and elaborate schools, nor indeed thinking in those simple terms. Rather, a means of analyzing how societies and individuals deal with their needs for any and all kinds of learning must be devised. In this context, learning is used as a term for the steps individuals take, regardless of the content of what is learned. Some learning is entirely private, the concern only of the individual pursuing it. Some learning is public, thereby entering the sphere of "education," the massive collective enterprise in which all societies engage in order to turn the individual capacity for learning to a variety of social or collective uses. A continuum exists with private learning at one end and with education—in its most public and formal sense—at the other. In between the extremes, groups of individuals may provide more or less collectively for semi-private learning, or a society may put extensive resources (such as libraries and museums) at the disposal of private learning.

While resources are obviously being shifted away from the elementary/secondary system, with some being applied to the postsecondary, and while many of the same developments are to be found in both systems, there is a decline in rationalization and communication throughout.

Indeed, there is little hope for rationality or efficiency until the elementary/secondary system recovers its sense of purpose and identity, and that will not happen so long as either of the two systems is defined in terms of age of clients rather than in terms of achievement and access. Age is one of the cruellest bases imaginable for grouping human beings, with the possible exception of those in the prepubescent category. Once that watershed is passed, the variations within any age group in learning terms are as great as any other variation.

A solution to the present dualism might lie in defining the two systems in terms of the skills and levels of knowledge which it would be the primary purpose of each system to foster. The elementary/secondary system would then be the major source of assistance in acquiring the languages of learning —speech, writing and reading, mathematics, music, and dance or physical movement, including athletics. This group of pursuits, resembling the trivium and quadrivium of early western European schools, seem sensible initial areas of development for the young; though the elementary/secondary system would still cater largely to the young, there are also many adults deficient in these skills who in order to achieve them could turn to this system with its widely available outlets. The very lack of some of these skills in our society suggests the need for educational resources resembling the present elementary/secondary system but without its bias of age. Programs in functional literacy or life-skills, for example, would seem better associated with a revised elementary/secondary system than concealed within and tacked onto the postsecondary system. There is no suggestion here of returning to the old pyramid whereby admission to one level is dependent on success (or time spent) in a level below. Rather, the intent is to group skills and resources in the way that most efficiently provides for specific needs. There is no reason why many individuals cannot participate in the elementary/secondary and postsecondary systems simultaneously. In fact, the distinction may gradually disappear.

There is one characteristic of the existing systems that, despite fervent hopes to the contrary, shows no sign of disappearing. Both systems remain principally wedded to the concept of the economic growth of society. What this has meant is that they encourage those students who are the easiest and least expensive to teach, that is, those for whom the movement upward in terms of increased skills and knowledge requires the shortest distance to cover. Others are discouraged from entering, and when they do enter, they are encouraged to leave at the first sign of failure. Devotion to this principle has largely been the cause of the failure of the elementary/secondary system to break the poverty/deprivation cycle. Children of poor and limited backgrounds are encouraged to drop out permanently as soon as the law allows. Poor communities are usually served by schools that, in their middle-class bias, are inadequate to the task, with resultant high rates of student rejection and failure. Deprived individuals' efforts to translate overwhelming economic and social needs into educational needs have been ignored, and so they have learned not to engage in such translation, even though it appears that many of those needs can only be met through education. Such individuals have translated some needs into learning needs, in that they do send their children to school, but learning there seems to reinforce rather than alleviate what has been called the culture of poverty. Although the postsecondary system has in fact offered further schooling to a substantial portion of the population which would not have engaged in it prior to employment, attempts to reach and respond to the really poor through educational recruitment have met with little success. The reason for such failure lies in the attempt to meet learning needs with conventional educational resources. Only by responding, at the learning-need stage, with a variety of informal or non-formal responses (such as, for example, Unesco's functional literacy campaign) can the problem be met.

Any exploration of the postsecondary system and its extension into adult education reveals an even greater tendency to favor the already successful and to do little of remedial value, with the exception of the manpower program. The postsecondary system at the moment bears a close resemblance to the state of the education of children when the common school movement began: there were good schools for those already well-off and little or nothing for the poor. It is essential to recognize that the system now in operation has biases that can be disastrous in the future.

Fortunately hope, like learning, is a hardy plant. It was hoped that the formal school system, by concentrating on children, could contribute massively to equality, justice, stability, and growth, all at the same time. That hope, despite the obvious successes of the system in supporting a technical industrial society by reinforcing the middle class, proved to be false. We have suggested that the weakness of the system lay in its concentration on children, to the virtual exclusion of adult learning or educational needs. The new hope is that the introduction of the concept of lifelong learning will rectify that weakness.

There is substantial evidence to support the contention that children learn more enthusiastically and more effectively in groups, families, or societies in which adults are themselves engaged in learning. But there is also evidence that it will not happen automatically. We have created in recent years the largest and wealthiest educational establishments in history, establishments which for the most part are wedded to a preoccupation with the young and schooling, and which are likely to be resistant to any change in focus. The major issue is whether institutions and professional groups devoted to the learning of others can themselves learn. Unless they can indeed learn to apply their care, attention, judgment, and skill to the evolution of new systems, the vision of the "learning society" will remain a mirage.

In this paper, we have tried to start a process of discovering a new vantage point. We have argued that such a new vantage point must first allow for the concept of continuing education. To remain mired in institutional administrative and jurisdictional distinctions which have little bearing on the aspirations, hopes, and promises of the learner will be destructive and eventually fatal. We must think in global terms of the whole society's response to all its learning and educational needs throughout every individual member's life. We cannot account either intellectually or administratively for what is happening, or what should happen, in the postsecondary sector without being aware of or accounting for what is happening in the elementary/secondary sector, and vice versa. The increase in educational opportunities for adults which is now taking place is not a matter of simple addition. It is an organic development which like learning itself requires recognition and matching change in the entire educational enterprise. We need, first of all, to reconsider in detail the "form" of formal education, since that form educates, or perhaps trains, more relentlessly and surely than the constantly shifting content: what structure or structures will serve greater freedom for both young and old in making broad career choices and experimenting with tastes, attitudes, or perspectives; and what structure will insure that both young and old will acquire the competence on which many lives, indeed a whole civilization, may depend. Second, we should shift our preoccupation from "education" to "learning," a shift that will be as significant in our intellectual history as the shift from Ptolemy's perspective to that of Copernicus.

Focusing at one time on both individual and social needs represents one attempt to simplify our thinking and at the same time be more inclusive of events and activities that relate to both these needs. Both the passionate individual need for learning and the social need to enlist the energy and passion that learning represents, for society's own growth and maintenance, must be taken into account and kept in some balance. The first without the second is naive, the second without the first is terrifying.

In the early sixties, R. W. B. Jackson saw correctly what the needs were and how they might best be balanced. The balance lasted for a short time only, but it was crucial. While it included what we may now in new perspective see as inherited mistakes, nevertheless it served, and the legacy we inherit is considerable. Now in a new time and a new world, with even less margin for error, we must try to do at least as well.

NOTES

1. Hilda M. A. Neatby, *So Little for the Mind* (Toronto: Clarke, Irwin, 1953).
2. R. W. B. Jackson, *The Problem of Numbers in University Enrolment*, Bulletin no. 18 (Toronto: Canadian Education Association and Department of Educational Research, Ontario College of Education, 1963).
3. Ibid., p. 15.
4. Ibid., p. 11.
5. Ibid., p. 1.
6. Ontario Legislative Assembly, Select Committee on the Utilization of Educational Facilities, *Interim Report Number Three* (Toronto: July 1974), p. 1.
7. Philip H. Coombs, *New Paths to Learning for Rural Children and Youth*, ed. Barbara Baird Israel (New York: Published by the International Council for Educational Development for Unicef, 1973).
8. D. J. Baum, *The Final Plateau: The Betrayal of Our Older Citizens* (Toronto: Burns & MacEachern, 1974). In an officer's career (and the same would hold true for enlisted ranks) progression is expected. No individual may stay in one rank for more than a reasonable period of time; there must be advancement, and if it does not come, the service person is given a clear signal of the need to reconsider the forces as his career (p. 24).
9. Economic Council of Canada, Eighth Annual Review, *Design for Decision-Making* (Ottawa: Information Canada, 1971).
10. Allen Tough, *The Adult's Learning Projects* (Toronto: Ontario Institute for Studies in Education, 1971).
11. Province of Alberta, Commission on Educational Planning, Report of the Commission, *A Future of Choices: A Choice of Futures* (Edmonton: Queen's Printer, 1972).

12. Commission on Post-Secondary Education in Ontario, Report of the Commission, *The Learning Society* (Toronto: Ministry of Government Services, 1972).

13. John Ohliger, "Is Lifelong Adult Education a Guarantee of Permanent Inadequacy?" (Saskatoon: University of Saskatchewan, Graduate Program in Continuing Education, March 1974). Unpublished paper.

14. International Commission on the Development of Education, Report of the Commission, *Learning to Be: The World of Education Today and Tomorrow*, Edgar Faure, chairman (Paris: Unesco; Toronto: Ontario Institute for Studies in Education, 1973).

Shifting Ideologies among Youth in Canada

Jack Quarter

In 1971 a government-sponsored commission on youth titled *It's Your Turn* stated the following:

> Young people in Canada show every indication of joining the great refusal taking place throughout the world. Their confidence in the existing order is being undermined on two fronts; not only are they forced intellectually to challenge many of the values inherent in our society, but also the traditional motives or incentives for participation in the "system" are increasingly unavailable. This refusal which ranges all the way from disenchantment to rejection, is manifest in many ways—the growing absenteeism in high schools, the decline in university enrolment (relative to predictions), the demand for storefront or street services and, especially, the marked increase in drug use among all classes of young people.[1]

The Committee on Youth report employed Herbert Marcuse's label of "the great refusal" to describe the outlook of many diverse subgroupings—including youth who have moved to rural communes, those living in urban enclaves, the drug culture, political activists, and perhaps a majority who keep one foot in the door of "conventional" society. In some cases the differences among these groups are greater than the similarities. Moreover, the various subcultures are not the exclusive domain of young people because some adults identify with the sentiment that is being expressed.

If there is a unifying strain among these diverse groups, it is a lack of commitment to stable roles in such institutions as the corporation, school, family, and government. In some cases the lack of commitment may be derived from a counter-commitment that leads to a concerted opposition to social conventions; in other cases it may not involve a firm counter-commitment or opposition, but merely a period of experimenting, observing, and

---

"Shifting Ideologies among Youth in Canada," by Jack Quarter, is reprinted, with slight revisions, from *Youth and Society*, vol. 5, no. 4 (June 1974): 448–72, by permission of the Publisher, Sage Publications, Inc. (Beverly Hills/London).

deciding. Among this latter group there is probably even lack of commitment to fundamental social change.

This pattern of withholding conventional commitment in industrially developed societies has been described by Keniston as a new stage in life called "youth."[2] Although Keniston's description of youth seems to restrict its membership to a narrower group than is referred to by the Committee on Youth report, there is much overlap between the two groups. In contrast to "adolescence," Keniston points out that youth are biologically and socially prepared to assume positions of responsibility, but they withhold a commitment because they cannot reconcile the expectations involved in conventional social roles with their own values.

Perhaps more than any other writer, Keniston has captured the spirit of the youth experience in industrialized societies, but by referring to the desire for an "indefinite prolongation of the nonadult state" as a stage in life, he seems to reduce the social significance of the phenomenon. A stage-of-life concept (e.g., infancy or adolescence) implies that biological factors are of considerable importance in the stage's onset, and that biological factors will in turn contribute to growing out of the stage. Although this may be true in small degree for "youth," the fact that only a minority of young people attempt to withhold a commitment to adulthood would suggest that youth is less a developmental phenomenon than an outlook that is primarily induced by social relationships in industrially advanced societies. Desiring to prolong the nonadult state is important because it is a reaction to existing social relationships. The fact that it is most likely to occur in the late teens and twenties is less a consequence of biological factors operating at those ages than of the position of those age groups in the social order. Because youth have not had to make a commitment, psychologically they are in more of a position to withhold themselves than are adults who have already committed themselves to conventional orientations. Otherwise there is no conceivable reason why a twenty-year-old is more likely than a forty-year-old to withhold a commitment to conventional social roles. The importance of the great refusal is less its relationship to the life cycle than its relationship to social institutions.

The Committee on Youth report has been severely criticized as representing the views of only a small segment of youth; and on the surface this criticism seems quite valid. The report does not include the conformist youth that social critics such as Edgar Friedenberg and Paul Goodman have lamented about and the many conventional subcultures among youth. Yet as valid as the criticism of the Committee on Youth report is, there is a fallacy in weighing the importance of a social phenomenon by the numbers it represents at a given point in time. Such reasoning is reminiscent of the statistician who drowned in the river that was two feet deep—on the average. Notwithstanding the importance of numbers manifesting a pattern of behavior, it is also important to know whether the forces that are stimulating noncommitment are likely to grow, and whether we are witnessing the initial stages of more profound social changes.

CONCEPTUAL FRAMEWORK

To examine the phenomenon of noncommitment among youth, it seems necessary to set out a dynamic conceptual framework through which it is possible to view the relationship between ideas (ideology) and social organization. In this regard we assume, as did Max Weber in 1930, that social organization requires an appropriate motivational pattern to stimulate its development and to sustain its stability.[3] Although Weber's critique of Marxist materialism came forward as one-sided idealism, his argument is well taken that ideology is a dynamic social force, and not just a reflection of the organization of production. As Tawney rightly suggests in his critique of Weber, the ideology and the socioeconomic organization should be viewed as interdependent forces, both of which evolve from independent influences and both of which interact with and stimulate each other.[4] The material conditions in a society make certain types of ideas more probable than others; however, the ideas that evolve have much to do with previous cultural influences, and these ideas in turn influence socioeconomic development.

Whether the predominant ideology in a society represents the interests of one class over another is really of less consequence than the fact that for social institutions to be relatively stable the members have to be motivated to participate. Punitive restraints or coercive rewards enacted in the interests of a dominant class, as is the case in all class societies, are not usually as effective as ideology in sustaining a pattern of social relations.

Weber contended that the ideology of the Protestant Reformation was necessary for capitalism to supplant feudal social organization. People had to believe that their worth in the eyes of God would be measured by their standing on Earth. It was through hard labor, individual initiative leading to the conquest of nature, self-denial, and planning for the future that the individual could best be successful. The working class had to perceive work as an end in itself, and had to experience guilt for excessive leisure. The bourgeoisie, for their part, required an ideology that would allow them to exploit the labor of the working class as well as natural resources, and to have a clear conscience in doing so. The values of the Protestant Reformation were the fuel required by the machines of industrial development.

Once this ideology was internalized, then production could become the goal of human labor and the economy could be organized in accordance with that goal. Although the readiness of the material conditions may have made the Protestant Reformation or a similar ideology very probable, the Protestant Reformation in turn allowed industrialization to take off.

The point is that it is impossible to have an industrializing society with a preindustrial motivational pattern, and similarly a preindustrial society with the motivational pattern of an industrialized society. Pelletier's vivid description of the Indian people's value system and the difficulties they have in adjusting to industrialized settings is an apt illustration of the point.[5] Pelletier describes the experience of Indians working at a sawmill at Longlac, Ontario, who were quite frequently absent or late, and much to the annoyance of their manager did not meet the production quota of the company. On the advice of a Community Development Officer, the manager of the plant allowed the Indians to organize their own production team on a communal basis that was more compatible with the Indian way of life than the highly specialized assembly-line that the company used. The Indians worked very efficiently, completed their quota before the hunting season, and then took off to enjoy themselves. The next year, the manager, who was operating off a different motivational pattern, increased the Indians' work quota by 50%. As a result the Indians rebelled and refused to cooperate.

The example cited by Pelletier is an apt illustration of the motivational differences between preindustrial and industrialized societies. For the Indians, work was a social function that was performed in order to produce things that were needed or to earn the wages to purchase necessary goods. Working in a factory was in and of itself a compromise with the Indian way of life, but the workers seemed able to make the adjustment, provided that they could take some of their way of life with them. For the manager, work was part of a never-ending process—an end in itself. He subscribed to what Max Weber called the Protestant ethic.

As industrialization has proceeded and ideology has changed from religious into scientific garments, much of the work in the social sciences has been devoted to revamping the values of the Protestant ethic into an appropriate secular variant. Social scientists who experienced the process of industrialization and for the most part believed it to be worthwhile have set out "objective" standards to assess phenomena as well as a suitable scientific rationale. Achievement, the secular version of the Protestant ethic, has become the pivotal aspect of the culture. The rhetoric is secular rather than religious, and the exponents are social scientists rather than clergy; however, both sets of ideas are designed for explaining "the social system" and motivating adjustment-type behaviors.

Perhaps the most direct effort to make the connection between the Protestant Reformation and achievement comes from the work of David McClelland.[6] In a monumental study of countries throughout the world, McClelland found that the values of self-reliance, which were a part of the Reformation, led parents to employ independence and mastery training in rearing their children, and this in turn led the children to be disposed to achieving standards of excellence. McClelland's thesis runs parallel to the theorizing of Talcott Parsons and the functional sociologists.[7] These theorists contend that social equilibrium is best maintained by having individuals assigned to highly differentiated roles according to their achievements rather than their ascribed characteristics (such as class, sex, and ethnic group). Through institutions such as the family, school, and peer group, children are socialized to achieve. Then, on a day of judgment, avenues to functions of varying status are opened or closed to them according to their assessed merits.

The ideology of achievement and the various interrelated ideas sustaining it have provided a conceptual framework to explain industrialization—particularly as it has occurred within the capitalist economies. For example, the demand for a highly mobile labor force that would save, plan, and live for the future while suppressing the impeding emotional commitments that are part of the present has been equated with rationality. Within the social sciences the emotional detachment that had previously been referred to as alienation by social critics is now referred to as "affective neutrality" or virtually ignored as a scientifically inaccessible quality of "inner man." The ideology of achievement is in fundamental conflict with other ideologies that are less compatible with the needs of an industrialized society, and it is through the social sciences that the efficacy of these other ideas has been undermined. The experiential psychologies of Freud and the existential humanists, and the social thought of Marx, have received the ultimate criticism of being nonscientific and nonobjective, and along with human nature have been banished to the unconscious forever. In the achieving societies the rational man is one who can anticipate and maximize rewards without any impeding "emotional hangups."

If it can be accepted that achievement provides the ideological foundation of modern capitalism, and that social stability is fostered by belief in this ideology, the question which has to be asked is whether the great refusal does represent a fundamental shift away from this ideology. Without a systematic investigation one can only speculate about the answer to this question. Nevertheless, the durability of the phenomenon and its international character would seem to justify a discussion of the available evidence.

ACHIEVEMENT ORIENTATION AND INDUSTRIAL DEVELOPMENT

In this paper I would like to set out two general hypotheses, and to present evidence to justify a more rigorous test of these hypotheses. (*a*) The achievement orientation is weakening among youth. (*b*) The weakening of the achievement orientation is being stimulated by the very process of industrial development that ironically depends upon the achievement orientation. In other words, with increasing industrial development the orientation to achieve is becoming an obsolete motivational pattern. Let us examine each of these hypotheses in turn.

The Achievement Ethic Is Weakening

There seems little need to say that achievement is not a part of the "hippie" motivation pattern.[8] In many respects, hippies, especially those who have gravitated to rural communes, have established a preindustrial way of life. The spiritual value system emphasizes living in harmony with nature rather than conquering it, living in the present rather than the future, and cooperation rather than individualism. Among the many strains in the youth culture, hippies living on rural communes might be considered as the only group who have formed a unique society.

We are more concerned with youth who remain and live within the mainstream of society but who are withholding a commitment to conventional institutions—either because they oppose the conventional goals and are committed to or searching for alternatives or because they are questioning the goals and experimenting with alternative life styles. They are similar to "counter-cultural youth" who have moved to rural communes only insofar as neither group identifies with or is willing to commit itself to conventional institutions. However, youth who remain within the mainstream of the dominant society have to grapple with the dissonance between their ideas and the available institutional outlets. To deal with this dissonance, a pattern of noncommital behavior is developing.

This point is illustrated by a survey the author conducted among a random sample of 218 arts and science students at the University of Toronto in the spring of 1972. The survey shows that 39.9% of students were totally undecided about a career, whereas 6.4% had decided about a field but not a specific career (1.4% did not respond). The percentages of totally undecided males and females were about equal (41.8% males and 38.0% females). But more important, the proportions did not change appreciably over the years. Among first-year students the percentage of totally undecided was 44.2%, in second year the percentage was 34.5%, and in the third and final year the percentage was 44.4%.[9] The percentage of undecided in the last year was almost identical to that in the first year.

More revealing than the proportions of undecided students were the reasons for indecision. Approximately two-thirds made remarks like: "can't say," or "nothing is appealing," or described the available options in derisive, cynical, and nondescript terms. Indecision sprang less from practical reasons than from a sense of profound dissatisfaction with the available opportunities.

This survey to measure the extensiveness of career indecision was stimulated by the author's thesis research and a longitudinal study that was a follow-up to the thesis.[10] The thesis involved a study of student politics among a volunteer sample of 248 male incoming students at the University of Toronto.[11] It indicated that there was a disproportionately large number of politically left-wing students among those who were undecided about a career. Political attitudes were assessed by a series of scales examining issues inside and outside of the university. The magnitude of the relationship between political attitudes and career indecision was quite strong with an F-ratio ranging from 11 to 26 (the weakest F-ratio had a $p<.001$). Moreover, a three-year follow-up indicated that the undecided students had been radicalized relative to career-committed students during their university years.

A more thorough investigation of the characteristics distinguishing undecided students was also very revealing.[12] On Kohlberg's moral dilemmas, the undecided students expressed more principled responses relative to the career-committed—the largest proportion of whom were very conventionally oriented. Many of the scales on the Omnibus Personality Inventory differentiated the two groups of students. Undecided students were much more esthetic than the career-oriented; they had a stronger appreciation of art, literature, music, paintings, and sculpture. Another OPI scale that differentiated the undecided from the career-oriented and that tapped characteristics similar to estheticism was the Masculinity-Femininity scale. The career-committed students were more interested in difficult subjects, such as chemistry, physics, and mathematics; the undecided students were inclined toward the "soft" esthetic subjects. Supportive of this result is the fact that a disproportionately high number of undecided students studied the humanities and social sciences, as opposed to business, professions, and physical sciences.

A series of OPI scales that measured authoritarianism—Complexity, Autonomy, and Practical Orientation—also differentiated the two groups. The undecided subjects expressed a higher tolerance for ambiguity, a desire for freedom and independence from judgmental authoritarian thinking, and a preference for ideas and the mysterious, as opposed to facts and the concrete. This antiauthoritarian humanistic strain expressed by undecided students has also been found among other youth groups. It has been discovered among student activists and among youth working out alternative cultural options.[13] It has also figured prominently in popular musical lyrics.[14] Like the desire for political and cultural change, the search for career alternatives seems to be hinged to a changing motivational orientation.

Surprisingly, the Religious Orientation scale of the OPI did not reveal a significant difference between undecided and career-committed students, but undecided students did express greater nonreligious attitudes. Of the undecided, 61.6% classified themselves as being atheist or agnostic, or as belonging to a nonsectarian religion, whereas only 39.9% of the career-committed fell within these categories. The nonreligious attitudes among the undecided would seem to be another expression of a changing value orientation.

Another set of characteristics that differentiated undecided youth from the career-committed were personal adjustment and self-satisfaction. Responses to the Personal Integration, Anxiety Level, Response Bias, and Social

Extraversion scales of the OPI indicated that undecided students experienced more guilt, unhappiness, and anxiety, and were more socially withdrawn. In addition, their response to a seven-point scale indicated greater dissatisfaction with school. These feelings may be viewed as the by-products of the motivational change that comes from a dissatisfaction with society, where there are no viable alternatives as outlets for changing orientations. Other data such as those showing marked increases in suicides, alcoholism, drug addiction, and admissions to hospitals for mental illness in the younger age groups indicate the adjustment difficulties among youth.[15] Undecided youth are not manifesting such extreme dissatisfaction, but their professed anxiety and guilt seem to be symptoms of a similar reaction to society.

The distinctive pattern of characteristics manifested by undecided students would seem to indicate that career indecision reflects a unique orientation to life. In a sense, the indecision may be viewed as a defensive posture needed until changing ideologies have institutional outlets.

A similar reaction on the part of youth is illustrated in Beckman's study of the scholastic performance of grade 11 to 13 students in a suburban Vancouver high school.[16] Beckman divided his sample into two groups, "hip" and "nonhip," and then traced back their scholastic performance from grade 1 through high school. The hip students displayed superior performance to the nonhips throughout elementary school, but at the start of high school there was a sharp reversal. Grades among the hip students dropped off markedly while grades among nonhips remained relatively constant. This pattern occurred in spite of the fact that the hip students had higher intelligence quotients and showed a stronger intellectual disposition on the Omnibus Personality Inventory than the nonhips. Beckman concluded: "The failure of the educational system to involve the interests of these intelligent and questioning young people is a point which is both disturbing and worthy of consideration at all levels of educational policy-making."[17]

In addition to declining academic performance, Beckman discovered that over 60% of the hip students, as opposed to 25% of the nonhip students, were undecided about their future careers. Interestingly, the pattern of characteristics manifested by Beckman's hip students on the OPI is strikingly similar to the pattern undecided university students showed in my own research.

This questioning of values also can be found in the changing orientations toward work. Money and status, the traditional job incentives, no longer seem sufficient reasons to perform a job. Youth are searching for ways of life that provide modes of self-expression rather than making sacrifices for extrinsic rewards. There is a reaction against the technological imperative that reduces jobs to insipid components and ignores the need for intrinsic job satisfaction. The reorientation to work among youth can be found in projects submitted for Opportunities for Youth grants. The program was set up by the government of Canada during the summer of 1971 in response to the unusually high unemployment among youth. With unemployment throughout the labor force running between 6% and 7%, and unemployment in the 14 to 24 age group at approximately double that level, the government became concerned at the social and political consequences of high unemployment among the 1,800,000 students coming into the labor force and set aside $57.2 million to employ such students. Applicants had to submit proposals for jobs, and they were rated and funded according to priority categories set by officials. Of the project applications, 38.3% fell into the social-service area and involved activities such as community enrichment, referral agencies, education, pollution clean-up, drop-in centers, legal–medical aid, rehabilitation counseling, and day care centers; 36.6% of the applications involved research in environmental problems, sociology, community service, and historical and ethnic research; 15.0% were recreation projects; and 10.1% involved cultural activities such as theater, photography, music, and crafts.

Although the nature of the submissions was undoubtedly influenced by the fact that one criterion for funding was that the project must involve meaningful work, the instant popularity of the program and the decision to renew it in 1972 testified to the changing work orientation of youth. Approximately four times as many proposals were submitted as were funded; and the applicants seemed to emphasize community, service, and expressive types of activities. The programs provided the opportunity for students to offer services without the constraint of profit or success, and evaluation of the outcome proved quite satisfactory.[18]

Similar and stronger evidence of the changing vocational orientations among youth comes from the United States. In a fifteen-year study of medical students at Harvard University between 1958 and 1972, three primary areas in career selection were discovered.[19] In the 1950s the primary orientation was toward specialized private practice. In 1959 there was a shift toward graduating doctors who would do academic research, with part-time teaching and part-time patient care. There was an emphasis on obtaining a strong grounding in basic science and research, and premedical humanities and social science courses dropped out of the curriculum. Funkenstein suggests that the "Scientific Era" was stimulated by the Cold War competition between the United States and Russia, which made funds available for basic research, as well as for such important scientific discoveries as DNA and a poliomyelitis vaccine.

Then, in the late 1960s a new era was ushered in. Many medical students were distressed by the failure of the conventional medical system to deliver the service properly and to prevent illness. In this present "Community Era," there is an emphasis on making sure that all segments of the population have basic coverage without regard to cost. Students began studying the social sciences and choosing careers in public health and family medicine, in spite of the resistance of the medical establishment to sanctioning this trend. Interestingly enough, the onset of the Community Era in medicine is paralleled by the spread of the great refusal; the values implied by the shift to community service seem to express a shift away from the motivation of the entrepreneur and academic achievement, toward providing the service in the most humane way possible.

A similar emphasis seemed to emerge in the projects funded through Opportunities for Youth grants by the Canadian government. Students in professions such as law, dentistry, and medicine sought to integrate their service into the community and make it readily available to the people.

Yankelovich's study of values among university students throughout the United States also provides further evidence of changing orientations toward career and work.[20] Yankelovich examined the values of the two groups of college students: career-minded and postaffluent. The latter group were more typical of youth withholding a commitment. Some of the statements that differentiate the two groups are an interesting reflection of value orientations (see accompanying table). Again, these items seem to indicate a shift away from the achievement orientation.

The research evidence discussed in this paper, although far from conclusive, would suggest that a more rigorous investigation of the basic motivational pattern among youth is in order. In a technologically advanced society, ideology is an extremely difficult concept to pin down because the diversity of life styles and subcultures allows for a diffusion of values, and because it is possible to arrive at very different conceptualizations or central themes depending upon the specificity or generality of the values that are being considered. However, one central aspect of ideology in a capitalist economy or any economy that is committed to industrial growth as a fundamental goal is the importance of values related to production. We have referred to this as achievement, partly because it grows out of a tradition in the social

Changing Value Patterns

| | % Agreement ||
	Career-minded	Postaffluent
Competition encourages excellence	71	48
Private property is sacred	79	55
Factors important in a career choice		
Self-expression	56	75
Job security	56	29
Chance to get ahead	45	19
Money	54	29
Prestige	28	14

sciences that seems to capture the spirit of this ethic and partly because the idea of "striving for excellence" and the related values of individualism, activism, and future orientation seem essential to a society that is committed to economic growth. The evidence that we have presented to suggest that this ideology is weakening is drawn from the fact that new entrants to the labor force are deliberately withholding a commitment to conventional jobs and are in some cases attempting to redefine the work orientation, and the fact that, in support institutions such as school, capable students are not responding to the usual incentives and are either dropping out or performing poorly. The school system seems to be fragmenting in response to these pressures. These behaviors would indicate that there is a serious questioning of the fundamental value of economic growth as an end in itself, and that youth are attempting to establish social relationships that are directed toward other goals.

Now it could be argued with some validity that it is not the desire to achieve but rather the goals that have weakened. Within the humanistic ideologies that many youth have adopted, the notion of striving for excellence still prevails. In the Maslowian framework, for example, the goal is to strive for "self-actualization," as opposed to operating from "lower" needs. There is little doubt that the idea of achievement that has been central to the culture of societies devoted to economic productivity still is very prevalent, and that it will continue to prevail as long as the basic institutions in society remain relatively stable, but the important point is that there is a serious questioning of values as well as a gradual change, and that the humanistic mutations of the emerging ideological framework are less compatible with the institutional pattern needed to sustain a capitalistic society than their nonhumanistic counterparts. A youth who accepts the importance of "self-actualization" is not likely to adjust to the assembly line at General Motors or to any regimented corporate institution, whether it is a workplace or a school. His strivings require creative outlets, and he is likely to rebel or withhold a commitment to any institution that is incompatible with his outlook.

The exact meaning of the great refusal is an important question that requires further empirical investigation. If further evidence accumulates that suggests the ideological changes among youth represent an outlook that is incompatible with the economic goals of capitalism, then the functional explanation that this phenomenon represents a transition phase from childhood to adulthood has to be dismissed.[21] A reaction to society could hardly be viewed as an adjustment mechanism if it leads to maladjustment to conventional institutions. Moreover, the explanation proposed by Parsons that this extreme reaction by youth is a by-product of rapid technological change does not really come to grips with the implications that the great refusal has for society.[22]

There seems little doubt that the youth cultures in industrially advanced societies are making it increasingly difficult for youth to adjust to conventional roles. However, the more important question is whether this phenomenon will remain what has been called a "2% culture" that has no serious impact on society, or whether the human and social forces that are stimulating youth to withhold a commitment to conventional social roles contain the seeds of revolution that will continue to grow into a more profound social movement. This latter question requires some analysis of the forces stimulating the great refusal.

The Process of Industrial Development Is Weakening the Achievement Orientation

There are two striking features of the uncommitted pattern among youth that immediately come to light. The first—which is most self-evident—is the youthfulness of the proponents. The second is the fact that the strongest opposition seems to be coming from the "successes" rather than the "failures." The most militant opponents of society are concentrated in the universities, and even among the university students there appears to be some relationship between conventionality and social class. Noncommitment is being seeded by wealth, rather than poverty, an anomaly that is difficult to explain using a Marxian class analysis.

If in fact the combination of youthfulness and success is stimulating an oppositional culture, it seems important to examine each of these aspects in a developmental context. The first aspect, youthfulness, is easier to speculate about since the literature is replete with many rich explanations of the biological, emotional, and intellectual factors that make youth a difficult period of adjustment.[23] Youth is a period of reconciliation between the individual and society in which the individual forms a sense of self that allows for a harmonious relationship with others. This reconciliation is most difficult in industrialized societies, where the disjunction between childhood and adulthood is more extreme and the period of transition is lengthier. As the process of industrialization has continued, two factors have made the transition period lengthier. First, the onset of the adolescent growth spurt now comes at an earlier age, beginning at about age 13 in most industrialized countries.[24] This represents a decline of more than four years during the last 130 years in the onset of adolescence. Second, the years of training before entering the labor force have increased. In Canada during 1971, only 50.7% of youth aged 14 to 24 participated in the labor force, and if the projections for the expansion of education prove to be accurate, the participation rate among youth will continue to decline.[25] A student studying for a profession can be expected to attend school until his or her middle or late twenties, and a grade-12-level diploma is becoming a minimum standard for even the most menial of jobs.[26]

Given the present circumstances, there is no apparent reason why the trends toward a lengthier period of youth should change. The forces that are contributing to the earlier onset of the adolescent growth spurt and the lengthier period before entering the economy are continuing to operate. On the basis of these trends, it would have to be predicted that the period of time that biologically mature youth spend in a nonadult state under the influence of dissonant peer cultures will increase significantly, and the tension that is associated with this period of adjustment will be exacerbated in the future.

Although the case can be made that a prolonged apprenticeship may be stimulating identity conflict and tension, and that the degree of conflict might in some way be related to the length of the apprenticeship, this does not explain why the revolt among youth has taken its present form. If a desire to withhold commitment to conventional institutions is the inevitable outgrowth of an extended apprenticeship, why then are those experiencing this reaction a minority among youth, let alone a mini-minority of the total population? Youth of the 1950s also underwent an extended apprenticeship, and in spite of their rebellious pranks and fads were quite conventional in orientation. Rather than prolonging the nonadult state, they desired to shorten this period of life and become adults as rapidly as possible. At present we find the opposite reaction. Youth are undecided about careers when options are available, dropping out of school when the degree is accessible, doing poorly in their academic work when they have the talent, and experimenting with counter-institutions when conventional institutions have the welcome mat out and dusted off. A prolonged apprenticeship may explain identity conflict, but it does not explain the development of an oppositional identity or a deliberate withholding of commitment.

If, in fact, there is a shift in basic motivational orientation, it can be contended that this shift is occurring predominantly among youth rather than among adults because this stratum of society is in the process of being socialized and conflicting social forces are most likely to be acted out within this group. To use a metaphor, the period from puberty prior to the assumption of adult roles could be viewed as a stage upon which a drama is unfolding. But why is the plot one of deliberately withholding a commitment, or in some cases of overt opposition to conventions, instead of a cry for more production, more achievement, and more of the same? And why are those who have volunteered to participate in this drama drawn from the most "successful" stratum in society? Perhaps these two questions are tied together and related to the content of the achievement ideology and to the nature of success.

As mentioned previously, values can be viewed as a fuel that propelled industrial development. When the material conditions were suitable, the idea of proving one's worth relative to others by striving for excellence made the machines of industry turn. For a complex of psychological and social reasons—both rational and quite irrational—this calling had meaning to people and became a driving social force.[27] People accepted the fact that the purpose of their work should be to expand production and that academic training prior to entering the labor force should be to develop characteristics that the great industrial machine requires. The social sciences, for their part, either dismissed human nature, with the exception of its adaptive qualities, or made allowance for competing biological drives that were activated primarily by deficiency. Thus the "good society" was one that could produce more than the "underdeveloped" and overcome human deficits. Humans were socialized to produce, because it was believed that maximizing production was a worthwhile human goal. The ideology of achievement served the purpose of stimulating production and, more importantly, of obscuring other real human deficiencies that this socialization pattern was creating.

Not all segments of society were allured by the ideology of achievement. Indeed, it seems that the "culturally deprived" had the misfortune of having values less compatible with efficient production to guide their development. The socialization pattern of striving for standards of excellence was most strongly adopted by the middle class and contributed to the success of this group relative to others.[28] And at present it seems that this ideology is being rejected most strongly by middle-class youth for reasons that are not easily discernible, unless one assumes that there is more to human nature than competing biological drives—and an inalienable part of human nature is the capacity to rebel against frustrating social relations. The functional social relations most conducive to efficient production seem to be inducing rebellion among those who are best equipped to adapt to them and who have most access to the valued goals of society—including material affluence, academic education, health care. On the other hand, acceptance of the ideology of achievement is most manifest among those who still strive for success—that is, for the goods and services readily available in the middle class. To put it simply, *functional social relations can become chronically dysfunctional when the goal of the organization is perceived as being of minimal value.* And it seems that among segments of the middle class production for the sake of production is treated with an abundance of skepticism, if not outright rejection.

In a society of material scarcity, one can readily believe that the notion of self-denial to achieve excellence has meaning, especially when the rewards allow for the purchase of goods and services that meet real human needs. The ideology provides a rational purpose even if there are irrational and humanly harmful consequences. However, for those who have been liberated from material want, and for those who believe that the productive capacity exists to eliminate material want for all, the consequences of the ideology of achievement can no longer be obscured by any rational purpose that may have been served in the past. As a result, we presently have the anomaly that an ideology that stimulated the material conditions for affluence is making itself obsolete—and is likely to continue to sow the seeds of its destruction the longer it remains intact.

As industrialization continues and material goods and services become more broadly distributed, skepticism directed at the goals of achievement and the adoption of humanistic ideals is likely to spread. Moreover, the fundamental commitment of capitalist economic organization to expanding production means that there are limitations to what institutions can offer as viable alternatives. The corporation, for example, can allay worker dissatisfaction by modifying the highly specialized assembly line into somewhat more complex components and by encouraging workers to participate in reorganizing the tasks, but it cannot abandon its fundamental commitment to maintaining production at a profitable level. In a capitalist society creative expression must always be secondary to the profitableness of labor. Similarly, the school can liberalize regulations and move toward a "free school" model; however, the fact that schools are provided with capital to socialize and select students for the economy places a major constraint on the reorganization of education. As long as the goals of the economy remain unchanged, humanistic orientations that teachers might seek to instill in their students are secondary to the practice of socializing students to excel and selecting the successes and failures. The teacher–student relationship is defined by the functions of the institution—and as long as the functions remain unchanged, variations in the teacher–student relationship are limited.[29] Even in free schools, innovative practice is limited by the awareness that scholastic performance is the major vehicle to valued professional jobs.[30] Like the corporation, schools can make normative changes by placing students on governing bodies or modifying specific regulations in response to pressure from students, but the nature of the society of which the school is a part supports the basic institutional structure.

Schools can allow the teaching of humanistic ideas, but it is more difficult to practice them. And the corporation can endorse all the symbols of youth, but its fundamental commitment to profit means that freedom, ecology, and long hair are peddled like any other product. The conflict between the humanistic ideologies spreading among youth and the institutional commitment to economic production is basically irreconcilable. The institutions can only feign concern and make minor reforms intended to siphon off the pressure.

For those who have divorced themselves from the ideology of achievement, the only options are to withhold a commitment, to join oppositional subcultures, or to move to rural counter-cultures. As long as the basic institutions of society remain relatively stable, viable options will be limited. Counter-institutions operate under great hardship and tend to be very transient.

CONCLUSION

In summary, this analysis leads to the conclusion that the youth revolt is a significant social force. The process of industrialization is extending the period of youth as well as creating greater productivity; and productivity seems to be undermining the motivating force of the achievement ideology. These circumstances are creating noncommitted people who are desirous of a reorientation to life—a condition that eventually must affect the very nature of society.

NOTES

1. D. Hunter, P. Bourdon, and V. Kelly, *It's Your Turn: A Report to the Secretary of State by the Committee on Youth* (Ottawa: Information Canada, 1971).
2. Kenneth Keniston, "Youth: A New Stage in Life," *American Scholar*, vol. 39 (1970): 631–54.
3. Max Weber, *The Protestant Ethic and the Spirit of Capitalism* (1930; reprint ed., New York: Charles Scribner's Sons, 1958).
4. R. H. Tawney, *Religion and the Rise of Capitalism* (Toronto: New American Library, 1963).
5. W. Pelletier, "For Every North American That Begins to Disappear, I Also Begin to Disappear," *This Magazine Is about Schools*, vol. 5 (Spring): 7–22.
6. David McClelland, *The Achieving Society* (Toronto: Macmillan of Canada, 1967).
7. See Talcott Parsons, *The Social System* (New York: Free Press, 1951); Parsons, "The School Class as a Social System," *Harvard Educational Review*, vol. 29 (1959): 297–318; and E. Shils and Talcott Parsons, *Toward a General Theory of Action* (New York: Harper & Row, 1962).
8. See J. Hopkins, *The Hippie Papers* (New York: Signet Books, 1968); K. Westhues, ed., *Society's Shadow* (Toronto: McGraw-Hill Ryerson, 1972); B. Wolfe, *The Hippies* (New York: Signet Books, 1968); and L. Yablonsky, *The Hippie Trip* (New York: Pegasus, 1968).
9. A small number of fourth-year honor arts and science students were also in the sample, but the numbers in this group were too small to be representative of fourth-year students. Of students in fourth year, 32.1% were undecided about a career. When this number is combined with students in third year to obtain a picture of students in their last year, the percentage of undecided is 40.4%.
10. Jack Quarter, *The Student Movement of the Sixties* (Toronto: Ontario Institute for Studies in Education, 1972).
11. The percentage of undecided students in the volunteer sample was 29.3%, which is somewhat smaller than those in the random sample previously referred to. However, this group included professional as well as arts and science students. Three years later a follow-up survey of 186 who participated in the original sample indicated that 26.9% of the sample were undecided. Although there was much shifting about as to who was undecided, the proportions remained relatively con-

stant. In addition, the proportion of students who were decided about a field but not a specific career increased significantly over the three years. In first year it was 9.7%, whereas in third year it was 18.9%.

12. All the differences reported in the paper are significant at the .05 level, and most of the differences are at the .01 level.

13. For student activists see R. Flacks, "The Liberated Generation: An Exploration of the Roots of Student Protest," *Journal of Social Issues*, vol. 23, no. 3 (1967): 52–75; C. Hampden-Turner, *Radical Man* (Cambridge, Mass.: Schenkman, 1970); P. Heist, "Intellect and Commitment: The Faces of Discontent" (mimeographed; University of California Center for the Study of Higher Education, 1965); Heist, "The Dynamics of Student Discontent and Protest" (mimeographed; University of California Center for the Study of Higher Education, 1956); Kenneth Keniston, *Young Radicals: Notes on Committed Youth* (New York: Harcourt, Brace & World, 1968); and Quarter, *The Student Movement*. For youth working out alternative cultural options see L. Beckman, "A Study of the Hip Adolescent, His Family, and the Generation Gap," Report submitted to the Committee on Youth, May 1970; Kenneth Keniston, "You Have to Grow Up in Scarsdale to Know How Bad Things Really Are," *New York Times Magazine*, 27 April 1969, pp. 27–28 and 112–29; C. Reich, *The Greening of America* (New York: Random House, 1970); and Theodore Roszak, *The Making of a Counter-Culture: Reflections on the Technocratic Society and Its Youthful Opposition* (Garden City, N.Y.: Doubleday, 1969).

14. See J. Carey, "The Ideology of Autonomy in Popular Lyrics," *Psychiatry*, vol. 32 (May 1969): 150–64; and J. E. Harmon, "The New Music and Counter-Culture Values," *Youth and Society*, vol. 4 (September 1972): 61–84.

15. See, for example, the statistics reported in Marshall Wilensky, "Self-Destructive Behavior," *Orbit 27*, vol. 6, no. 2 (April 1975): 7–9.

16. See Beckman, "A Study of the Hip Adolescent."

17. Ibid., p. 47.

18. A. Cohen, *Report of the Evaluation Task Force to the Secretary of State* (Ottawa: Queen's Printer, 1972).

19. D. H. Funkenstein, "Medical Students and Medical Schools during Three Eras: A Fifteen Year Study of Medical Students 1958–1972" (mimeographed; Harvard Medical School, 1972).

20. D. Yankelovich, *The Changing Values on Campus* (New York: Washington Square, 1972).

21. See S. N. Eisenstadt, *Modernization: Protest and Change* (Englewood Cliffs, N.J.: Prentice-Hall, 1966); Eisenstadt, "Archetypal Patterns of Youth," in *The Challenge of Youth*, ed. Erik H. Erikson (Garden City, N.Y.: Doubleday, 1965), pp. 29–50; S. N. Eisenstadt, *From Generation to Generation: Age Groups and Social Structure* (Glencoe, Ill.: Free Press, 1956); and Talcott Parsons, "Age and Sex in the Social Structure of the United States," *American Sociological Review*, vol. 7 (1942): 604–616.

22. Parsons, "Youth in the Context of American Society," in *The Challenge of Youth*, pp. 110–131.

23. See Erikson, *Identity*; B. Inhelder and Jean Piaget, *The Growth of Logical Thinking* (New York: Basic Books, 1961); and Keniston, *Young Radicals*.

24. J. M. Tanner, *Growth at Adolescence* (Springfield, Ill.: Charles C. Thomas, 1962).

25. W. Illing and Z. Zsigmond, *Enrolment in Schools and Universities 1951–52 to 1975–76* (Ottawa: Queen's Printer, 1967).

26. For a trenchant commentary upon the relationship between education and jobs in the United States, see I. Berg, *Education and Jobs: The Great Training Robbery* (Boston: Beacon Press, 1970).

27. See Erich Fromm, *Escape from Freedom* (New York: Holt, Rinehart & Winston, 1941) for an interesting discussion of why the ideas of the Protestant Reformation were assimilated.

28. McClelland, *The Achieving Society*; B. C. Rosen, "The Achievement Syndrome," *American Sociological Review*, vol. 21 (1956): 203–211; Rosen, "Race, Ethnicity, and the Achievement Syndrome," *American Sociological Review*, vol. 24 (1959): 47–60.

29. Quarter, "The Teacher's Role in the Classroom," in *Must Schools Fail?*, ed. Niall Byrne and Jack Quarter (Toronto: McClelland & Stewart, 1972).

30. T. Durrie, "Free Schools," in *Must Schools Fail?*

Education and Basic Human Values

Clive Beck

INTRODUCTION: AN INCREASED EMPHASIS ON BASIC HUMAN VALUES

Over the past ten years, thinking about education has for many people been marked by a shift in emphasis from efficiency in achieving accepted goals to a radical reassessment of goals. Whereas in the mid-sixties it seemed that the major task for educational research and development was to provide improved educational technology and administration, now many are wondering whether technology and "the administrative mentality" might not be part of the problem. Programmed learning and computer-assisted instruction, once viewed by many as the solution, are now seen as an important but relatively small part of the *means* to whatever the solution may be (to the extent that means can be separated from ends). Standardized, "objective" educational measurement is under a cloud, with test after test being shown to be biased, or narrow, or superficial, or irrelevant; and fewer people seem to have the motivation (because of increasing doubts about the whole enterprise) to develop such tests. Evaluation is obviously important; but do the conventional educational measurement instruments really evaluate anything of significance in education? What, indeed, *is* of significance in education? The whole issue of the purpose of education is being opened up in such a way that most of the previously established plans for increasing efficiency in education are rendered obsolete. The goals these plans presupposed are being called into question.

This does not mean that the technology-and-measurement era in education was unimportant or even that it is over. Success in any complex human enterprise involves mastery of technique, and any ongoing rational activity requires some means of measuring progress in attaining goals.[1] The mistakes we have made have shown us where solutions do *not* lie, and there have been successes in some specific areas upon which we can build. The chief lesson being learned from the era through which we have just passed is twofold: first, the goals of education are not as obvious as we had assumed, and must be investigated with as much energy and scholarship as we have devoted to finding the means of attaining them; and second, notions of "efficiency," "technology," "administration," and "measurement" in education cannot be defined independently, but must be understood in the light of the goals of education. (*a*) Efficiency in achieving accepted goals of education may not be *educational* efficiency at all if the goals are not appropriate. (*b*) Educational technology, too, must be designed with appropriate goals in mind; otherwise, from an educational point of view, it will be very bad technology. (*c*) Administration of an educational institution may be superb from the viewpoint of one set of goals, and utterly incompetent and irresponsible from the viewpoint of another set. (*d*) Measurement procedures in education must be designed to match appropriate educational goals, otherwise they will serve no useful purpose. Efficiency, technology, administration, and measurement in education are not absolutes: they are relative to the ends of the educational enterprise. And these ends must be looked into more carefully.

GOALS FOR EDUCATION

In attempting to determine goals for education we must press the issue back further and further until we find a basis in ultimate human values. For if an educational enterprise is not ultimately worthwhile, all things considered, then it is simply not worthwhile. We may have thought that it is valuable for a student to master the theorems of classical geometry or to learn the dates and places of battles in the Napoleonic wars, but unless such learning will lead to the significant achievement of ultimate life goals, such as survival, happiness, fulfillment, friendship, the welfare of others, respect from others, self-respect, freedom, and so on, in what sense is it valuable?[2]

Of course, we can artificially ensure that learnings serve such ends by building rewards and punishments into the situation: Johnny will gain the respect of others and a measure of happiness if he receives top grades in geometry. But there are several difficulties with this procedure. In the first place, it is usually only a privileged few who can participate in artificial rewards of this kind. Second, if the students *en masse* become aware of the artificiality of the rewards, one may be faced with a serious problem of morale and motivation in the school. And third, it is difficult to see the wisdom of taking learning activities that are not really worthwhile and *making* them so, when there is so much really worthwhile learning to be achieved. If one is going to reinforce certain learnings—and most societies and educational institutions inevitably do—why not choose at the outset learnings that would be of major "natural" value in a student's life, whether there were supplementary institutional rewards or not? And so we come back again to the need to ground educational goals in basic human values.

If one adopts this realistic, human approach to values in education, what implications with respect to the goals of education emerge? To begin with, education must place students in a better position *in general* to live life well and handle life's problems. A major portion of educational activity should be concerned with acquiring outlooks, skills, attitudes, emotions, and behavior patterns that will enable individuals and groups to attain ultimate life goals of the kind listed above (survival, happiness, and so on). The schools must engage in *value* education to a substantial degree: helping students learn how to achieve fundamental human values, for themselves and others. Since the achievement of such values is the whole purpose of education (and of all other human enterprises), it would be anomalous if education did not involve direct treatment of value problems. It has sometimes been suggested that the best way to achieve happiness and other fundamental values is to forget about them and concentrate on something else; but such advice must surely fall into the category of "old wives' tales," with a grain of truth diverting our attention from the basic implausibility of the position. In an increasingly complex and man-made world, it is unlikely that survival and happiness will be attained by "looking the other way." Careful thought, planning, and action will be necessary, and many of the requisite skills, outlooks, and behavior patterns must be cultivated from a very early age.

A second goal or function for the school is to help students with *specific* life problems. The arguments here are much the same as for the school's general role in value education, but it must be recognized that at particular times and for particular individuals, groups, or communities the school will be able to help with particular value issues or decisions. At present the school is almost overwhelmingly geared to general learning that is meant to be of use as occasion demands or at some time in the future. As a result the school often loses touch with the real needs and indeed the real nature of the child, and is largely unsuccessful even in bringing about general learning. John Dewey was clearly not one to disregard the need to place the child, through schooling, in a position to cope with adult life; and yet he spoke out strongly against the conception of education as *merely* "preparation for life."[3] His point was that helping a child to live life well now is an essential aspect of preparing him for future living, as well as being valuable in the present. What does it mean to help a child to "live life well," now and in the future? My proposal is that there is no alternative to basing such a notion in fundamental human values: survival, happiness, fulfillment, friendship, and so on, for oneself and others.

A third package of goals for the school, as is generally assumed, comprises leading students to basic skills in areas such as reading, writing, and arithmetic and introducing them to academic disciplines, such as history, literature, physics, anthropology, and so on. Basic literacy in these areas may even involve intensive drill to render habitual those responses that are most effective when largely automatic, whether it is a matter of spelling correctly or of knowing a valid argument when one sees one.

However, it is important to make some qualifications with respect to this third set of schooling goals. First, the attainment of knowledge of basic skills and academic disciplines at the level usually achieved in schools, although a demanding task, nevertheless can be achieved with plenty of time to spare for other learnings that are concerned more directly with attaining basic human values. Second, knowledge of the kind in question is only one portion of the knowledge required for the comprehensive attainment of human values: it should by no means be the only concern of the school. And third, knowledge of academic disciplines as it is usually passed on in schools is largely of "cultural" value for students. No more than a small proportion of it is actually used for any other purpose than enabling people to engage in "fellowship" with one another, to have the satisfaction of sharing common learnings, to have a common idiom for sharing ideas. A realistic, humanistic approach to education forces one to face up to the essential limitations of the discipline learning that goes on in schools, while admitting that it does have a place. If discipline-type learning is to play a major part in the comprehensive attainment of ultimate life goals, it must be thoroughly integrated, in a manner not yet common in schools, around general and specific life issues and problems.

This brings us to a fourth goal for the school, namely, helping students acquire a functional, *working understanding* of the world and of life. As I have mentioned, the teaching of literature, history, physics, and so on as it is currently conducted in the schools is of largely "cultural" value. (It does also lead to the issuing of school certificates, but the criteria used in awarding school certificates are largely political and institutional in nature and have little to do with the conditions of achieving basic human values.) In order that the valuable knowledge inherent in the various academic disciplines may be utilized, it must be combined with knowledge from a great many other sources, including the student's everyday experiences since early childhood, and built into a working understanding of the world and of life.

The word "working," here, is meant to draw attention to the functionality of the knowledge, to its relatedness to the solution of specific and general problems, which facilitates the achievement of ultimate life goals. It also suggests a comprehensive set of interrelated insights or pieces of knowledge, of a kind that is an essential background to the performance of life tasks. All practical problems are by their very nature many faceted, and the difficulty with traditional discipline knowledge is that it simply is not organized for the solution of practical problems. The school must restore students' confidence in the value of everyday experience, and, drawing from academic disciplines and other sources, help them to build on it and systematize it in ways appropriate to their various life needs.

A fifth goal for the school is to provide good custodial care (or "day care").[4] This is in fact a major function of the school, evident only when one is realistic rather than merely ideological and sentimental with respect to the role of the school in contemporary society. It becomes especially apparent in the event of a teachers' strike, when the chief concern of many parents is: What shall we do with our children all day? The non-striking teachers rush to "man the ship," above all to keep the students occupied so that day care will be maintained. A faithful principal is found "doing gymnastics" with a hundred or more students, not because he can teach them any gymnastic skills but because that is a solution to the pressing care and control problem.

The results of failing to face up to the custodial care function of the school have been little short of disastrous, both from the point of view of providing *good* custodial care and from the point of view of fostering learning.[5] In cases where valuable learning has been impossible—the teachers are incompetent, the students cannot handle the learnings expected of their age level, the cultural differences between teacher and student are too great, or whatever—students (and teachers) have been kept miserable by a constant round of meaningless activities. If it had been accepted that a major function of the school is day care, attention could have been turned to much more enjoyable and absorbing ways of passing the time, and even to developing human relationships between teachers and students.

On the other hand, where valuable learning has been possible, the quality of learning activities has often been considerably diminished by attempting to make them serve the double function of fostering learning and maintaining control. So much of what is described as teaching is in fact the supervision of "busy-work," designed to keep little hands out of mischief. Every experienced teacher knows—and every beginning teacher soon learns—that the key to "discipline" in the classroom is to have every student occupied. When this insight is combined with lack of recognition of the custodial care function of the school, it is only too easy for school activities to be chosen almost entirely on the basis of their potential for keeping every student occupied (so long as a facade of "respectable" learning can be maintained). Learning the capital cities of all the countries in the world, for example, may be prescribed because it will keep a group of students occupied for several weeks (and it is certainly a very respectable thing to do), even if it is of practically no value to most students and the information will soon be forgotten anyway. Even the students will be "taken in" by its respectability and persuaded to view it seriously. It is important, then, to distinguish the learning function of the school from the custodial care function and set about fulfilling both in effective ways. If one can achieve both optimally through the one activity, that is all to the good, but one must keep the two functions separate in one's thinking in order to be in a position to judge whether or not in fact both *are* being achieved, whether together or separately.

It might be queried whether custodial care *should* be a goal for the school. The school, it might be argued, is after all an educational institution, and any day care function it serves is purely incidental; serving such a function should not be a major positive goal for the school. However, while a legitimate distinction between education and schooling (as currently practiced) can be made, it does not follow simply from this distinction that education should be the sole function of schools, and that provision of good custodial care should not be a major positive goal for schools. Most societal institutions are multi-functional and there is reason to believe that many of them should be even more so. Industrial plants, for example, fulfill functions for both employers and employees at an economic level, and there is a growing body of opinion that they should fulfill functions at social, emotional, and even educational levels as well. Etymologically, the word "school" is by no means tied exclusively to education, and even if it were, one could simply change the meaning of the word, or use another word to refer to the institutions we now call schools.

Illich and Reimer in their respective works have proposed a more flexible situation in which different goals, educational and otherwise, would be achieved by separate institutions (and in some cases through non-institutional arrangements). However, there are many respects in which their proposals are not realistic, given the existence of the current system of "educational" institutions and the problems involved in switching to alternative arrangements. More may be possible in twenty or thirty years' time; but at present schools simply *do* serve a major day care function, and until alternative facilities are provided they must serve this function and, moreover, must serve it well. It is ironic that often the same "reform-minded" people who are clamoring for more day care facilities for one- to four-year-olds are demanding the abolition of schools, which provide day care facilities for children from age five upwards. How can they be so sure that what goes on in the "pre-school" institutions will be more satisfactory than what goes on in schools; and if they are aware of satisfactory principles for conducting pre-school centers, why cannot these be applied equally to schools? (Of course, the hours during which schools are open may have to be extended for some children, if the day care function is to be properly fulfilled.)

It is apparent, then, that a *pure* discussion of education in contemporary society is difficult, for much of formal education is conducted in institutions that have functions other than educational ones. In particular, a discussion of schooling leads to the issue of custodial care or day care, and it is clear that provision of such care at a satisfactory level must be a major goal of schooling, if not of education, strictly defined. And the reasons for having this goal for schooling lie, once again, in ultimate human values. A great many parents in contemporary society need time in which they are free from child care responsibilities so that they can pursue various life goals; and their children in turn need environments in which they are able to survive, be happy, maintain their self-respect, have fellowship with other children and adults, and so on, and they have this need regardless of any educational development that may be planned for them.

One might go on for some time listing additional goals for the school, but the ones mentioned so far are perhaps those most in need of attention at this time, and they serve to illustrate the general point that schooling goals must be developed and justified in terms of basic human values. To summarize: schools must (*a*) help students acquire a general capacity to live life well and solve life's problems, (*b*) help students with specific problems as they arise, (*c*) help students acquire basic skills in "the three Rs" and familiarity with culturally important academic disciplines, (*d*) help students acquire a functional, working understanding of the world and of life, and (*e*) provide good custodial care. All of these goals can be justified in terms of basic human values, but equally their importance is limited to the extent of their contribution to the attainment of basic human values. In particular, the three Rs and various academic disciplines have an important but limited place in the school. They are to be studied efficiently and well, but the amount of time devoted to studying them in isolation should not be such that the other important functions of the school are neglected.

Finally, to return to the efficiency-technology-administration-and-measurement mentality that was characteristic of much educational theory in the mid-sixties, we can see from our brief survey of schooling goals that a broader educational outlook was indeed necessary. The conceptions of efficiency, technology, and measurement were almost entirely centered upon teaching the three Rs and traditional academic disciplines, thus neglecting many other major functions of the school. The conception of administration did extend a little further to include custodial care, but it was "care" in a very stern sense of the word, with connotations of protection and control rather than enjoyment, fellowship, and general well-being. To reiterate what was said in my introductory section, the importance of efficiency, technology, administration, and measurement in education is not in question; the point is rather that they must be conceived in such a way that they promote (and do not hinder) the achievement of the full range of goals of the school and, through these, the basic human values of all concerned.

VALUE EDUCATION

One of the five major goals for the school mentioned in the preceding section was that of helping students acquire a general capacity to live life well and solve life's problems. This is roughly speaking the area covered by value education, or by "moral education" in the broad sense of that term often employed by educators today. I will now spend some time discussing value education by way of illustrating in this particular functional area how the school must press issues back further and further to basic human values in order to determine both the methodology and the content of its activities.

Few educators ten years ago could have foreseen the enormous upsurge of interest in value education that has now occurred and appears, if anything, to be accelerating. At that time, moral education was still closely associated in people's minds with the inculcation of religious dogma, and value education generally was not seen as a major function of the school. Since that time, three main changes have helped pave the way to the current emphasis on value education as a goal for the school: study of moral development by educational psychologists has led to the notion that schools may foster a reflective, non-indoctrinated morality that is of considerable value to students but is not necessarily tied to a particular sectarian religion; broader conceptions of religion that permit a more humanistic, universalized approach to morality have become more widely accepted; and the "quality of life" movement in Western society generally, with its radical questioning of many traditional specific and intermediate-range values, has brought an awareness that people must learn how to *live well* in some basic sense of that expression: we must sort out what is *really* worthwhile in life and not simply continue a mindless pursuit of traditional "success" goals. It is now possible to advocate a major role for value education in the school without being seen as advocating sectarian religious instruction, without being accused of adopting an antireligious or a-religious position, and without being thought to be exaggerating the importance of value issues. Almost everyone can see, now, that the adequate solution of our value problems, including our moral problems, is of crucial significance for all human beings, and that most of the issues cut across sectarian religious and ideological distinctions.

Value education, like education in general, must be grounded in basic human values if it is to overcome the traditional objections to "moral education" and at the same time be genuinely helpful to students (and teachers). It cannot consist simply in the inculcation of specific and intermediate-range moral precepts. The major aspects of a sound approach to the study of values are, first, the identification in oneself and others of fundamental life goals or values, and second, the determination of satisfactory ways of achieving these ultimate goals or values. This *study* of values (as distinct from the activity of learning how to live one's values) is fairly objective in nature, in that students and teachers carry out an objective inquiry into what people ultimately value in life and which means are more effective in achieving ultimate life values. Thus, it is genuinely helpful to students and teachers, in that it assists them in both clarifying and achieving their basic values. At the same time, however, it does not involve the imposition from outside of an arbitrary set of specific moral rules, the process usually referred to as moral indoctrination.

By moving to the level of basic human values, then, one is able to avoid the excesses of value inculcation that have in the past given value education a bad name. However, it should be recognized that all education—and value education is no exception—necessarily involves an element of direction and persuasion, whether it comes from teachers, from books, from films, from outside visitors, or from fellow students. Simply by ensuring that value education is conducted in the realistic, reflective, "ultimate life goals" manner I have proposed is to build certain general value assumptions into the learning process. It is hoped that eventually the process will round on itself and these assumptions will themselves be examined, but with particular students this may not happen for some time. Thus, while one may fairly be said to have avoided indoctrination, in the ordinary sense of the term, one will not have a neutral approach to value education.

In the desperate attempt to avoid indoctrination and hence provide a value education program that is acceptable in public schools, many educationists have proposed what they regard as value neutral approaches to value education. Thus we have the Simon proposal that students merely *clarify* their values (specific, intermediate, and basic) and learn to embrace them sincerely and live by them.[6] We have the Oliver, Shaver, and Newmann approach, according to which students merely learn various reasoning *skills* (and relevant facts) and then work things out from there.[7] And we have the Kohlberg methodology, according to which one merely stimulates *natural* moral development that is taking place anyway.[8] The approach I have outlined would certainly include elements of values clarification, teaching of reasoning skills, and stimulation of natural development—and in that regard it is an eclectic approach that acknowledges the importance of drawing on other approaches—but it does not require the teacher to refrain from attempting to persuade students to adopt his/her position if he/she considers it to be a better one for the students in question. What is right or wrong, good or bad, for a given population is largely an objective matter: it is not true that one person's values are as good as anyone else's, or that a teacher should not, as in other objective inquiries, argue for a particular point of view. The crucial requirement is that the discussion and argument be carried out in a context and atmosphere such that students feel free to disagree, raise objections, construct alternatives, and adopt whatever position they consider most satisfactory. Indoctrination is to be avoided—in values as in other subject areas—not by refraining from teaching but by teaching in a non-indoctrinative manner. In the area of value education a major aspect of teaching in a non-indoctrinative manner consists in carrying discussion to the level of basic human values so that students can explore with the teacher the reasons for more specific value judgments and principles and not simply accept them without understanding or argument.[9]

The topics covered in value education span the whole range of human values, from private questions of diligence and self-control to public issues of political strategy and legal justice, from fundamental issues about the value of freedom and equality to practical questions about effectiveness in decision-making. Because of the breadth of the range of topics, a school program in value education would involve almost every subject area in the school (insofar as the school continues to be organized along subject lines): literature, history, social studies, health and physical education, environmental studies, science, family studies, home economics, and so on. The value topics could be dealt with either as an integral component of topics within these courses or as issues that arise out of topics in the courses but are treated to some extent separately, over one, two, or three class sessions. There is considerable concern on the part of teachers to maintain the integrity of their respective disciplines. This concern can be satisfied (to the extent that it is legitimate) either by restricting the amount of time devoted to value issues or by dealing with values in such a way that the study of the discipline in question is actually enhanced.

The issue of whether teachers should be provided with prepared materials is a very controversial one, but it would seem that unless teachers have at least some materials to "fall back on" they will be reluctant to venture into the explicit study of values. The answer to those who object to the provision of materials on the ground that it is "spoon feeding" or "over directive" is twofold: first, materials are essential in most cases if teachers are to take up curriculum suggestions at all; and second, the problem of over direction can to a considerable extent be overcome by ensuring that teachers have half a dozen different sets of materials to choose from. They have freedom, then, partly in their choice of a given set (or combination of sets) of materials, and partly through their capacity to adapt materials and, eventually, develop their own.

No one type of material is the best vehicle for the approach to value education I am proposing. The crucial factors are the substantive ideas contained in the materials and the manner in which the materials are used by the teachers. Accordingly, in order to amass the range of materials necessary for value education work, it is legitimate to draw on many different traditions, using case study material, textbooks, films, children's literature, values clarification notes, role playing and drama motifs, discussion notes, and so on. Different teachers and different groups of students may prefer different types of materials. The important thing is that, whatever the materials, the approach employed is the reflective, ultimate life concerns approach described earlier.

As with materials, so with teaching procedures; a healthy pluralism should prevail. The field of value education has been ill served by projects that advocate a particular procedure as *the* correct teaching procedure. The case study method—detailed investigation of a particular historical or fictional case—can be interesting and valuable but must be supplemented by other more systematic techniques. Values clarification exercises are an important component in a program, but students must go on to evaluate critically their values in the light of more objective considerations. Simulation activities can be stimulating, but must normally be followed up by discussion; and there is a limit to what can be simulated in the classroom: often it is best to discuss experiences students have actually had, rather than attempt to simulate experiences. Discussion and reasoning skills should be developed in the classroom, but there is much more to value education than acquiring a set of skills.

Value education, as I have described it in this section, will quickly pervade the whole school, in all its activities, its structure, and its atmosphere. For once students (and teachers) have been encouraged to be reflective, at the level of basic human values, about traditional value topics, they will quickly see that there are value assumptions implicit in all subject areas, administrative structures, and so-called extracurricular school activities, and will apply the same outlooks and methodologies to these value assumptions. This does not mean that the other activities of the school will be replaced by value education: all the schooling goals identified in the preceding section obviously must remain intact. But the value education program of the school—both formal and incidental—may be one of the chief means whereby the school as a whole is brought into accord with the basic human values that should guide all educational endeavor.

NOTES

1. For an attack on the use of technique in modern Western society see Jacques Ellul, *The Technological Society* (New York: Vintage Books, 1964), *passim*; and for a critique of Ellul's position see Clive Beck, *Educational Philosophy and Theory* (Boston: Little, Brown, 1974), pp. 66–71.
2. For an elaboration of this "ultimate life goals approach" to educational value, see my *Educational Philosophy and Theory*, chs. 1 and 10, and *passim*.
3. John Dewey, *Democracy and Education* (New York: Macmillan, 1916), ch. 5.
4. This point has been made by Ivan Illich in *Deschooling Society* (New York: Harper & Row, 1971), chs. 1 and 6, and by Everett Reimer in *School Is Dead* (New York: Doubleday, 1971), ch. 2.
5. See *School Is Dead*, ch. 2.
6. See, for example, Sidney Simon et al., *Values Clarification* (New York: Hart, 1972).

7. See, for example, Fred M. Newmann and Donald W. Oliver, *Clarifying Public Controversy: An Approach to Teaching Social Studies* (Boston: Little, Brown, 1970).

8. See, for example, Lawrence Kohlberg, "Stages of Moral Development as a Basis for Moral Education," in *Moral Education: Interdisciplinary Approaches*, ed. C. M. Beck, B. S. Crittenden, and E. V. Sullivan (Toronto: University of Toronto Press, 1971; New York: Newman Press, 1972), pp. 23–92.

9. For a much fuller discussion of value education by myself and my colleagues see *Educational Philosophy and Theory*, ch. 8; Clive Beck, *Moral Education in the Schools* (Toronto: Ontario Institute for Studies in Education, 1971); and Edmund V. Sullivan et al., *Moral Learning* (New York: Paulist Press, 1975).

Trends in Society, Trends in Curriculum

Garnet McDiarmid

EDUCATION IN ITS BROADEST CONTEXT

When we speak of Western society, we include the Mediterranean area, from which our schools have drawn such legacies as language, literature, and art, as well as our fundamental modes of rational and religious thought. It is not surprising, therefore, that Canadian investigative committees on curriculum and other school concerns have without fail included the United States and Great Britain in their tours of inquiry.[1] This deliberate seeking out of ideas from other countries has always coexisted with the more common practices of bringing in visiting speakers on education, encouraging cross-national academic study, and using foreign texts in Canadian schools—which has been a cause for concern ever since Egerton Ryerson spoke out on the use of United States textbooks in 1867.

The adoption of the German term *kindergarten* serves to remind us not only of foreign influences but indeed of the very roots of our schools. When Europeans began to establish counterparts of their schools in North America, they brought to the task the contradictory ideologies of education to meet the needs of the individual and the needs of society. Besides the European classical influence upon both university and high schools, there has been a strong American influence that goes back at least as far as the famous American Committee of Ten in 1892. This committee consisted of six representatives from collegiates and four from secondary schools who organized small subcommittees to review the content and teaching of Latin, Greek, English, modern languages, mathematics, physics, astronomy, chemistry, geography, natural history, history, and civil government and political economy. One historian, H. L. Campbell, has noted that "in most Canadian provinces the findings of the committee resulted in some small curriculum expansion but chiefly in a formalizing and unifying of secondary curriculum."[2]

In view of the interlocked economic development of the U.S. and Canada, and the common language of the greater part of both populations and other media of communication that we share, it cannot be considered accidental that the societal and educational trends that sweep through the U.S. leave on our side of the border both the dust and the glitter such movements engender. During the 1960s the U.S. "curriculum reform movement" brought the modern proclivity for capitalized contractions into Canadian schools with such inventions as PSSC, BSCS, and SCIS.[3] Another indicator of international influence is the Unesco report *Learning to Be*, which describes a wide array of educational techniques, analyses, theoretical formulations and their applications, and the uses of technology now being shared or sought by most countries in the world, developed and underdeveloped.[4] More recently, the January 1975 issues of both the American *Phi Delta Kappan* and Ontario's *Educational Courier* featured articles on community schools and the school climate. Whether or not these parallel events are coincidental products of our mutual historical development, a reaction to the big-is-better ethic, temporary holdovers from a nostalgic past, or the result of diffusion from one country to another is not as relevant to curriculum as the questions they raise: What benefits are such innovations presumed to confer on students? Will schools adapt to local conditions, or become more uniform? Are we willing to evaluate our innovations?

In searching for answers to questions about innovations that look desirable in other countries, we must of necessity seek out their reports, their evaluations. This is a hazardous enterprise because conditions may not be similar. We know, for example, that Ontario teachers differ both demographically and attitudinally from teachers in the U.S.;[5] yet, lacking specific data, we must call upon distant studies, for example, the ground-breaking Coleman report,[6] and treat their conclusions as hypotheses to be confirmed locally.

The Emerging Canadian Identity
Because the notion of being Canadian seems vague to many people, there are likely to be as many points of reference among our citizenry as there are people who think about the matter. Unlike U.S. citizens, with their revolutionary break with the past and their comprehensive, codified constitution (both of them unifying symbols that have always been placed before their young), Canadians seem to have come upon a consciousness of their national identity rather late in life. Some few may have been impressed during their early years in school by references to the Statute of Westminster, others will recall with pride Canada's independent role in World War 2, but most will probably recall the effect of the Centennial celebrations, most particularly those that took place in the highly creative Expo '67.

That these occasions for pride were running more deeply than symbolic attachments was, paradoxically, denied legitimacy by governments until recently. Nevertheless, our combined sensitivities have been sharpened by annual reports of the Economic Council of Canada that continue to generate alarm at our loss of control over Canadian industry, by the speeches and writings of the two courageous professors from Carleton University who persist in their case against the numbers of non-Canadians on Canadian university faculties, and even by French Canadians' vocal demands for equal rights within Confederation. Events such as these have served to heighten our gradually developing awareness of a Canadian identity—which has been mistakenly labeled as "nationalism," a term that became derogatory after World War 1—and it has been reinforced and carried into many areas that impinge on education: TV and radio broadcasts, publishing generally, and, in particular, school textbooks and their use in schools.

Hodgetts summed up his concerns about the whole matter of Canadians' lack of identity in the title of his book *What Culture? What Heritage?*[7] Under Hodgetts's leadership, the Canada Studies Foundation has sought to deal with these concerns in the schools, where Canadian studies, latterly including native studies, have proliferated in response to popular demand.

While these events were still nascent on the Canadian scene, a number of concerned individuals and organizations based in Toronto formed the Ontario Curriculum Institute. Its boldness in concept—dependence on voluntary funding and reliance on popularly recognized excellent classroom teachers as sources for innovative curriculum development—eventually became its largest shortcoming. But the original Institute was the germinating seed of something new in Ontario education.

When the Ontario Institute for Studies in Education was chartered in 1965 as part of the University of Toronto, its mandate was to conduct graduate studies, to engage in research in education, and to assist in the implementation of its findings. In a certain sense its evolution was, as some biologists say of individual development, a recapitulation of the phylogeny of the rest of the province. Just as our earliest settlers from the Old World established their roots, then were joined by a proportionately large influx of United Empire Loyalists and, later on, by immigrants from the U.S. and other countries, so new recruits from such widespread areas as the United States, Australia, India, the Caribbean, Great Britain, and Europe came to OISE and were shaped as a whole by the surrounding geography and culture of Ontario. It is no secret that this formative period was accompanied by a considerable amount of dissatisfaction aimed publicly at the new institute. But if my current impressions are correct, more pleasure than criticism is now expressed, because OISE is visibly striving to meet the needs of Ontario education and is in some instances having a notably wider impact. This is the legacy R. W. B. Jackson leaves with the province as he retires from the first directorship of OISE.

It is entirely appropriate that the surrounding society should make evident what it feels OISE's role ought to be. However, there may not be an awareness that societal mechanisms, ranging from informal to formal, verbal to financial, private to public, have always shaped educational institutions. In any institution, such efforts are often perceived as interference, as "politics"—in its most pejorative sense. This paper is an attempt to explore the influences that have appeared on the Ontario education scene and have eventually come to bear on the curriculum of the public school system.

What Is Curriculum?
An analysis of the relationship between the curriculum of the schools and various shaping mechanisms in society begs the question of the definition of curriculum. In 1941 the *Encyclopedia of Educational Research* stated,

> In recent educational literature and in this report the school curriculum is considered to be all the actual experiences of the pupils under the influence of the school. From this point of view each pupil's curriculum is to some extent different from that of every other pupil.[8]

These words constituted the terms of reference that curriculum developers brought with them when they attempted to integrate new concepts of child development, social trends, and school practices.

A significant change occurred after the appearance of Sputnik in 1957, however, as massive government grants encouraged outside experts to enter the field of education in the lower schools to enhance the quality and quantity of graduates in science and other related fields as a means of increasing the U.S. national effort in the Cold War. In this period, studies in public and school administration proceeded on parallel lines. Canadian education, already stinging from Hilda Neatby's rebuke in *So Little for the Mind*,[9] was drawn into this essentially militarist morass more deeply than anyone realized until the consciousness-raising tragedies of Latin America and Viet Nam.[10] Here were specialists whose occupational lives were devoted to and shaped by an increasingly powerful method of description and control of nature and people: operationalism. They transferred their a-human, amoral world view to the school. The innovators in this period did not question the general purpose of the school, as did curriculum developers of an earlier era; they *assumed* (falsely) that the school had one, and only one, general purpose: cognitive enhancement. As Bruner was later to say, "The prevailing notion was that if you understood the structure of knowledge ... you could know a great deal about a lot of things while keeping very little in mind."[11]

Because of this assumption, the only question that remained was, "How do we accomplish our objective?" This is an engineering question, and the answers that were produced took on such labels as "Social Science Curricula," "Social Studies Curriculum Program," "The Anthropology Curriculum Study Project," "The English Composition Curriculum Project," and

"The Science Curriculum Improvement Study." These misnomers were then carried into discussions and descriptions of general school concerns. Where there had been a common understanding of the meaning of the word "curriculum," the term now took on a confused new meaning, as the following examples illustrate:

—In 1966 John Goodlad wrote, "If anthropology, sociology, economics, political science, and psychology are to have a place in the pre-collegiate curriculum, are they to stand alone or are they to be joined with history and geography in a synthesized social studies program? The combining of several social sciences into a social studies curriculum provides areas for fruitful exploration." Goodlad uses the word curriculum as a whole entity, as a part of that entity, and even as a synonym for "program."

—In 1971 Elliot Eisner wrote, "The problem ... was to make the school's program, the curriculum, more intellectually respectable by developing subject-matter curricula that more accurately represented the values, methods, and content of the academic disciplines." The same confounding of meaning occurs in this statement.

—In 1974 Decker Walker and Jon Schaffarzick state, "for the most part, the new course materials were intended to replace existing materials in standard school subjects, not to add new subjects to the curriculum." And then they proceed, "students using different curricula in the same subject generally exhibited different patterns of test performance."[12]

As linguists have informed us for years, the words we use shape our concepts and our actions. When those who used to inquire into curriculum problems followed the dictates of their training, they asked about intention: What can or should the school contribute to the child? It is not entirely inaccurate to say that they asked "Why?," but later, when a mathematics course became known as a "mathematics curriculum," the question became "How?" In effect, *the misuse of a word preempted a whole field of inquiry.* In a literary sense we could say that this is a perverse example of the tyranny of words; it reflects the hidden effect of the singular world view that engulfed the schools during a period of stress in our competitive, technological society. Not surprisingly a very conservative analysis of U.S. schools by Silberman produced "mindlessness" as their most consistent characteristic:

This mindlessness—the failure or refusal to think seriously about educational purpose, the reluctance to question established practice—is not the monopoly of the public school; it is diffused remarkably evenly throughout the entire educational system, and indeed the entire society.[13]

The problem does not stop with this unconscious drift into the engineering mode. As Toffler has noted, it is becoming institutionalized, part of the very structure of governance.

A far more significant effort to tidy up governmental priorities was initiated by President Johnson, with his attempt to apply PPBS (Planning-Programming-Budgeting-System) throughout the federal establishment. PPBS is a method for tying programs much more closely and rationally to organizational goals.... But who specifies these larger, more important goals? The introduction of PPBS and the systems approach is a major governmental achievement. It is of paramount importance in managing large organizational efforts. But it leaves entirely untouched the profoundly political question of how the overall goals of a government or a society are to be chosen in the first place.[14]

We have a choice. We can permit a methodology brought to a high stage of development as a consequence of the single-minded necessity of fighting World War 2 to dominate our very way of seeing and doing things, or we can bring it under conscious control in the service of a Canadian society with emergent multiple goals. But there is one prerequisite: the goals of society must be found among and developed with the people in a thousand different ways. Such a condition probably applies to all institutions in a society.

THE RELATIONSHIP BETWEEN SCHOOLS AND SOCIETY

To limit a social analysis of curriculum to "what students *learn* rather than what they *do*,"[15] as Mauritz Johnson has urged, would provide us with no more of an insight into the relationships between culture and curriculum than those we can perceive between the society of the early 1900s and the emphasis at that time on the calculation of squares of shingles, pecks of beans, and cords of wood in piles of known dimensions. On the other hand, to take as our term of reference "all the actual experiences of the pupils under the influence of the schools" would involve us immediately in an analysis of far more complex events in which the schools have always participated. Although I accept the proposition that the culture of a society establishes and controls within relatively close limits the practices, materials, and accomplishments of formal education, there is a corollary: some future trends may be perceived in the contemporary concerns of society.

The schools' attempt to meet the social and developmental needs of children and youth is not a simple affair, nor is it a means whereby schools will change society. That was a form of naiveté extant in the early 1930s when Counts wrote *Dare the School Build a New Social Order?*[16] More recent examples of the simplistic belief in the efficacy of textbook and classroom exhortation can also be found. Knowing as we do today that venereal diseases reached epidemic proportions among young people in 1973 and 1974, that pregnancies frequently occur at thirteen years and younger, we can only read incredulously the following remarks made in 1952:

The major hope for improving family life lies in education in the schools. There we must attempt to set an ideal of what constitutes a good husband, a good wife, and a good home in which to bring up future citizens. It is in school that we must attempt to give to the young person some appreciation of the soul satisfactions that come from a well-adjusted and happy family life. *Late adolescence is the time to do it effectively.* Young people are interested in such matters at that time and have formed no permanent or serious emotional attachment to a member of the opposite sex—an attachment which a few years later will warp their judgment. Adolescence is the time when **ideals and standards may be most easily set**—standards of judgment which will be of value when the young person reaches the age of selecting a wife or husband.[17] [Italics mine]

It is a fallacious chain of reasoning that identifies social ills (including poor school achievement), labels these as correctable by education, and then assumes that education is congruent to what goes on within the schools. The Hall-Dennis report was noble in articulation and idealistic in concept. Nevertheless, its authors were quite unrealistic in charging teachers with the responsibility for changing society.[18] The Provincial Committee on Aims and Objectives of Education forgot a lesson frequently taught by a long-time Chief Director of Education in Ontario, J. G. Althouse. In 1945, when the Hamilton Rotary Club wrote to Althouse regarding its concern about the high rate of delinquency, the Director replied in an address as follows:

Public education as a means of combating juvenile delinquency is a kind of educational service which can be realized, in this province, only when the community is convinced that this is possible, desirable, and within the limits of cost which are considered reasonable by the community. The Department of Education believes public education can be used for this purpose, but that this will be effected here in Hamilton only when the people of Hamilton are similarly convinced. When you are convinced, the Department will give you all the help it can in organizing and in carrying out your projects; but if your conviction fails, do not expect the Department to force you to do better than you are willing to do.[19]

Here is the clue we must follow, but with as much sophistication as thirty years of hindsight can give us.

Historical Trends in Curriculum Development
The history of curriculum in both Canada and the U.S. can be conceptualized as consisting of five overlapping periods. These periods can generally be distinguished one from another by the rhetoric used. Changes in curriculum were generally foreshadowed by changes in statements of intent, though, as in many other spheres of life, changes in educational practices dragged behind changing intents.

The first, the *Frontier Period*, can be characterized simply by one quotation that suggests the flavor of the time. It should be remembered, however, that the scene described in the quotation occurred less than five generations ago.

After the letters were thoroughly learned, the first step in advance was promotion to the class which was engaged in the study of the New Testament, the Bible being then the standard textbook for reading. The scholars were thoroughly drilled in the teaching of Bible truths for a long time after learning to read fairly well. Not until the scholar could read and spell well was he allowed to begin to write, and a good deal of pains were taken to teach the scholar to write well. The pens used were goose quills; the ink was made of soft maple bark, oak galls, or something of that nature. To buy ink was impossible at that time, and steel pens had not come into general use. The copybooks were often made of wrapping paper; foolscap paper was very scarce and expensive. A little arithmetic was also taught, and this in the majority of cases was the total amount of education which the pupils had the chance to receive. More advanced pupils were taught a little grammar, geography, and history.[20]

The *Traditional Period* that came next was by far the longest. In Ontario, Egerton Ryerson marked its beginning unambiguously in 1867 when he said that the purpose of elementary schools was to develop facility in practical matters and in the three Rs. It was not anticipated that many children would pursue education beyond eight years. Indeed, it was a long time before even eight years of schooling could be called "universal." Ryerson's secondary schools were to teach such subjects as English, natural history, Latin, Greek, and mathematics in order to "prepare students for University College, or any college affiliated with the University of Toronto."[21] This expectation is one that powerful segments of society still apply to the secondary schools of today. Extra subjects were added gradually from Ryerson's time on, and course content changed very slowly. Indeed, it seemed that the greatest change in elementary science over more than fifty years was the shedding of the label "natural philosophy"![22]

The High School Entrance Examination and the various versions of middle- and upper-school matriculation examinations then in use reflected society's drive for uniform standards of achievement and at the same time, as John Porter has demonstrated, reinforced an elitist view of who should rise to positions of leadership in society.[23] Indians, immigrants, and working-class children in general fared very poorly in the Traditional Period. J. B. Conant was scathing in his criticism of the effects of this type of curriculum, which lasted for approximately three-quarters of a century in the U.S. and until at least 1937 in Canada.

Those who could take it found the formal instruction excellent; those who couldn't or wouldn't dropped by the wayside as a matter of course. From the point of view of those on the receiving end—the professors in the colleges—this was a highly satisfactory situation. What sort of education the rest of the fourteen-to-eighteen-year-olds received was none of their affair![24]

This is a severe indictment of the Establishment, and we may defensively deny that such an unfeeling and structured sorting process operated here. It is instructive, therefore, to read another quotation from the Chief Director of Education in Ontario.

Few ever scaled to its [the educational ladder's] top and, as soon as they did, they tended to lose touch and sympathy with those whose strength or interest flagged ere the top was reached. Indeed, those who reached the top were often suspected of putting up barriers at certain rungs of the ladder to make progress more painful and less easy for their competitors.... Where they went to—these discards—was not regarded as the school's business.[25]

However, in Canada as well as in the U.S., society's concern for children began to challenge the country's allegiance to the traditional institution of the school in the late thirties.

Public pressure to democratize and individualize education ushered in a new era, which I identify as the *Thwarted Progressive Period*. Although progressivism had an ameliorating effect on tradition, it was thwarted because its advocates were far ahead of their time. As Lawrence Cremin has shown, the rising tide of dissatisfaction with contemporary economic and social affairs, which resulted in populist or progressivist political movements in the late nineteenth and early part of the twentieth centuries, also began to challenge traditional child-rearing practices in the home and, inexorably, the schools.[26]

Urie Bronfenbrenner and Celia Stendler have recorded the liberalizing changes in child-rearing practices that gradually permeated society after the turn of the century.[27] Permissiveness, a pejorative term now, originated with the view that mothers should "permit" their infants to schedule their own feeding and toilet routines. Just as it took many years for this radical idea to be accepted by a significant number of parents, so it took many years for an appropriate concern to extend to the developmental needs of school-age children. Naturally, it has taken us many additional years to learn how to translate this concern into proper and *acceptable* practice. Ontario, like the rest of Western society, was very strongly hierarchical in its authority relationships, and this carried into education as unconsciously as the use of language. "There is no evidence of any tendency towards the Progressivism which has alarmed our neighbors to the south," Althouse reassured a convocation at Ryerson Technical School in 1952. And yet in 1956 the same man could write in the University of Toronto *Quarterly*: "In the lowest grades of the elementary school, there is growing recognition of the fact that all children do not manifest the same readiness to learn, or an equal readiness to learn the same kinds of things, at the same age."[28]

When homes and then schools reinterpreted their responsibilities by accommodating somewhat to developmental and individual differences, the recipients of this new form of socialization grew up with the expectation that their children would in turn be permitted and encouraged to express individual preferences. Thus, cumulatively, an evolutionary mechanism of overlapping and succeeding generations brought to the schools and other repositories of tradition in our culture a qualitatively different life style.

As seems always to be the case, initial rhetoric was stronger and went further than the desired changes, but it is now evident that during the late 1920s and on into the 1930s, a great deal of attention, including the new field of empirical research in education, was devoted to justifying the reduction of physical punishment and sensitizing teachers to the conditions that lead to mental ill health.[29] Children's "misbehaviors" were interpreted as consequences to be understood in relation to causes, not as spontaneous willfulness. This process is certainly not complete in 1975, however. At the time of writing, the London Board of Education has just reinstated the use of the strap, a barbaric delusion of educational efficacy, and an admission of failure.

Those who worked in this field in the past were not only psychologists but people who initiated a new role, curriculum development. In all areas of school life they advocated new methods of teaching children for humane reasons, not just for learning efficiency. They also developed new courses, health and social studies, for example. The intention was to make schools less harsh, to modify rote learning practices, and to make schools a little more meaningful to immigrant and working-class children.

Concurrently, educational analysts were gradually uncovering and labeling a whole new realm: the "hidden curriculum."[30] This is a shorthand way of asserting that such structural influences as standards of dress, behavioral codes ("Stand up when you address the teacher," "Don't hold hands in the hall"), homework, terminal examinations, corporal punishment, and other conformity-training processes were at least as important in shaping students' school lives as were such subjects as grammar and Latin. *The climate of a school is a functional part of its curriculum*, and it must be included in discussions of curriculum development, even if teachers and certain members of the general public insist from time to time that this influence on students' lives is and should be "value free." Althouse noted a similar discontinuity in 1942.

No piecemeal subdivision of the child's life can present these vivid, vital experiences. Too many schools attempt the tasks we are considering by a sharp division of the school activities; they maintain the curricular activities, for the sake of knowledge and of skill, and the extra-curricular for the sake of character. To seek to build vigorous citizenship in this piecemeal fashion is just about as sensible as to try to win a race by hopping half a dozen times on the right foot, then half a dozen times on the left, and so on, alternately.[31]

The inextricable aspects of the curriculum that Althouse refers to are now being rediscovered. For example, while Elliot Aronson pays lip service to the indefensible distinction between *what* children learn and *how* they learn, he nevertheless describes what he was able to teach children as an antidote to the hostile and destructive effects that a competitive classroom wreaks upon children in racially integrated schools.

It is important to note that we did no tinkering with the curriculum itself. We did not change *what* the children learned, simply the *way* they learned it.... Thrown on their own resources, they had to learn to teach each other and listen to each other. They would have to realize that none of them could do well without the aid of everyone else in the group, and that each member had a unique and essential contribution to make. It's a whole new ball game.[32]

Indeed! Not to consider the latter intentions as part of the curriculum is to deny legitimacy to the schools' responsibility for human concerns. As long as human beings attend schools they will be guided or herded, supported or ignored, attracted or repelled by the social system that enrolls them. One need only watch nine- and ten-year-olds playing school to see that people are affected by the kind of institution they attend.

It was no accident that convergently oriented lessons, examinations, and rigid promotion practices became the targets of progressivists. The progressive movement identified and attempted to change the conditions of this part of the curriculum by acknowledging the behavior-shaping elements inherent in organizations and by gradually incorporating growth-inducing content and methodology in place of training in conformity. The syllabuses of the period indicate a concern for attitudes, motivation, and attention to the needs of a heterogeneous population that had (and has) a high dropout rate.

W. G. Fleming has meticulously documented the ways in which Ontario's Department (now Ministry) of Education responded to demands for change by successively removing structural impediments to higher levels of education. Nevertheless, there was a countermovement that resisted change by appealing to traditional social values, not the least of which was a concern for "standards." He also records the continuing and adamant opposition raised against changes that would give working-class students an equal opportunity to press toward university, the *raison d'être* of the secondary schools.[33]

Something had to give, and Althouse spoke very plainly in his opening sentence to the Ontario Education Association in 1950:

Three years ago, I urged you, who are practising educators, to devote serious thought to the clarification of the objectives of secondary education, pointing out that, if educators did not succeed in doing this, non-educators would attempt it.

The Chief Director was referring to a report sponsored by the Canadian Education Association in response to growing public concern. It indicated that 59 percent of the boys and 51 per cent of the girls who passed through grade 7 did not finish high school. Quoting from the report, he said, "The school can increase retention by improving its curriculum and instruction, and by guiding students into courses suited to their abilities, aptitudes, and interests."[34]

To the general public it was a relatively simple matter of numbers. Too large a proportion of bright and motivated people were being systematically prevented from entering occupations that required university training. Of course it was not all that simple. Most of those who were admitted in ever-increasing numbers were not motivated in the same way as the upper 2 or 3 percent of the population who could enjoy or tolerate scholastic studies. True enough, the new students wanted to get the carrot, but many could not reach beyond the stick; the relationship between learning Latin, for example, and engineering or banking or managing a shoe store seemed obscure to them. Although the rationalization of Latin's relevance to nursing and to medical careers was accepted for some time, it has since become obvious that the reasoning was fallacious. Terminal examinations were the operants of the screening process, the publicly reportable points where taxpayers or teachers might not understand the Latin but could understand the percents. The learning of Latin and such other subjects as history, literature, and grammar required one characteristic more than anything else: docility. Not all able students had that characteristic.

During a recent public meeting of the Toronto school board, some of the members reminisced about the various methods of control that were applied to them as students. One member recalled a practice most of us have significantly forgotten. When he went to school, he reminded those present, marks were given for subject achievement and also for deportment. A mark of less than 70 percent in deportment meant the student failed his year! The words of two renowned Canadian educators represent the official views of that member's contemporaries. In 1942 Althouse was to say that "willing habitual conformers make ideal Nazis and Fascists," but in 1938 he represented the more authoritarian view that prevailed when he told the Toronto Zonta Club,

> The subordination of selfish considerations to the welfare of something bigger and more compelling than the self is the most urgently needed lesson in democratic lands today. ... educators are deliberately, and successfully, building up the idea that the individual counts only insofar as his effort helps the whole group.

Note how Campbell expresses the same point. We know that he means well, but we also know *what* he means. The growing reciprocity of our own times is completely absent here.

> School can be and should be a society in miniature. It must be a laboratory in which young people learn to live democratically; learn to live harmoniously with their fellows; learn to submit their individual wills cheerfully to the will of the majority even though they are intellectually convinced that their point of view is the correct one; learn, while attempting to convert people to that point of view, to give loyal support to the decision of the majority.[35]

No one could doubt that school teachers represented "the will of the majority"—if they did not, they were invited to leave. Thus, submission to the teacher and to the system was the price paid for continued success up the educational ladder, as Althouse called it. Small wonder that later on, when social undercurrents swept new attitudes into the schools, the strongest teacher reaction to students was "they lack respect."

Teachers had learned over many years to accommodate themselves to the capacities and tolerances for formal study of the upper echelon of a particular kind of student. *They knew intuitively that the entrance of greater numbers would require a qualitatively different kind of education.* Their own motivation and preparation for success in climbing the ladder neither prepared nor disposed them to make changes collectively, but since the students now showing up in the high schools represented a wider range of abilities and motivations and included many individuals who were unprepared and unwilling to accommodate to the existing curriculum, something had to change. Vocational schools apart, the only model that the teachers had was university, thus their recourse was to "water down" the regular curriculum. The substance was much the same, but less was expected of some students.

This obviously led to a lower *average* achievement, and it was misinterpreted as one of the pernicious evils of progressivism. Hilda Neatby's book *So Little for the Mind*, in which she articulated the general public's reaction to perceived changes in the schools, became a Canadian best seller in the fifties. The fact that those changes represented the best that the schools could do in response to the dual pressures of society for university preparation of its young people and for admission of a wider range of students to secondary schools was a complexity that escaped most laymen.

Since the North American culture has always been determined by conditions relating to economic growth, it is only natural that prestige should accrue to business and commercial occupations as well as to the professions, which cater to the needs of the dominant group. With formal education as the gatekeeper controlling entry to these occupations, the struggle for equal access to schools really represented an attempt to achieve equal employment and economic opportunity. Until quite recently, prestige in Ontario was restricted to such occupations as the professions, small firm management, the church, and the armed forces; these occupations served as reference points for parents who sought to provide a secure future for their children. What happened when a greater number of students were forced upon the school system was that they represented the threat of an "oversupply" in the traditionally desirable occupations. Thus, in the unconscious ways in which protective devices work in a culture, the school system was encouraged to siphon off working-class competitors by attempting to raise the prestige of common occupations artificially. Technical and continuation schools were created that would offer credentials as enticements away from the most popularly desirable occupations. Such a ploy was doomed to failure, as Althouse noted as early as 1951:

The continuation schools were established with the avowed object of developing secondary education with a practical agricultural bias. But the rural parents of that day did not want their high schools to prepare boys and girls for rural life; they wanted them to prepare their sons—and a few of their daughters—for the professions.[36]

What would induce parents to want anything other than that? Even failure, as ignominious as it is in our society, would leave their children no worse off than those who successfully took the low-prestige curriculum. And there was always the chance that their children would succeed.

The U.S. attempt at economic and social leveling is instructive. Of course, conditions in the U.S. have been significantly different than in Canada. Even during the Depression in the United States, there existed a much broader range of occupations toward which individual student interests could gravitate; also, there was a publicly professed ideology about equality of educational opportunity, which really meant equal access to good jobs. In brief, the instrumental purpose of schools in the U.S. has always been acknowledged.

Since the power to remove the structural barriers to larger student enrollment did not lie with any one government, the Progressive Education Association accepted the challenge in 1930 of formulating and conducting a bold educational experiment. The preamble to their proposal read as follows:

Students of education in America know that the elementary school has changed fundamentally in organization, curriculum and procedure within the last decade, and that profound changes are taking place in our universities and colleges. But similar reconstruction in the secondary schools is difficult, if not impossible, under the present conditions.[37]

Shortly after, twenty-eight high schools and virtually every accredited college and university in the United States agreed to participate in a plan whereby all students certified by their individual high schools would automatically be admitted to university. This was an experiment to test the socially inspired hypothesis that divergent curricula could lead students from all socioeconomic classes to prestigious careers just as well as the traditional uniform curriculum prepared an elite group. The teachers in these high schools accepted the task of learning how to meet the needs of a greater number and range of students, while at the same time assuming responsibility for applying a new discipline, scientific evaluation. The experiment was terminated because of World War 2, but it lasted long enough to legitimate an ever-increasing admission rate across the continent.

From time to time Canadians have been inclined to make derogatory remarks about the standards of education in the U.S. Admittedly, they have had ample assistance from critics within the country, such as Admiral Rickover and Max Rafferty. Therefore, it is worth noting a distinguished American sociologist's assessment of the American open-access system in 1974, insofar as the overall effect is concerned.

The spread of the common school idea, it should be noted, included a practice which would have far-reaching consequences. These schools, designed in part to Americanize the immigrant and to civilize the lower classes, deliberately set their educational aspirations from the levels upper-middle-class children could attain so as to make it possible for those of "deprived background" to catch up. It was assumed that all would eventually reach higher levels of attainment, of knowledge, in the upper grades and ultimately in college and university. This pattern has continued in U.S. education, so that world-wide comparisons show that American youth study less than their equivalents in upper-level

European gymnasia or lycées. As Max Weber noted in 1918, "The American boy learns unspeakably less than the German boy." By age 20, however, the Americans have more than caught up. And a much greater percentage of them than those of any European country have secured higher education. By going slowly through elementary school and high school, the U.S. system has permitted many more to enter and graduate [from] an institution of higher education.[38]

Thus the first requirement to equality of occupational opportunity—a wider range of graduates—was gradually accomplished in the U.S.

While the battle of numbers was being waged, more profound issues were also affecting North American schools. Part of the motivation of the progressives in education was to place an ever-increasing responsibility on the developing child. By what were then called scientific methods, children were to be taught to inquire into, to form hypotheses about, and to test and evaluate new or evolving forms of *social* relationships. This was the academic side of the amorphous politico-educational movement. The new and therefore much maligned subject of social studies, which was intended to replace academically oriented history and geography, was to be the pacemaker for a series of integrated changes throughout the school.

Consistent with the basic progressive philosophy of teaching responsibility by delegating responsibility, Ontario's Department of Education started in the fifties on the long and as yet incomplete path of withdrawal from centrally defined curricula. The decision was made to involve local teachers and the public, in addition to elected trustees, in the process of developing and approving the new curriculum; this marked the beginning of a trend that can be assigned confidently to the close of the Thwarted Progressive Period. As Althouse said, "three years ago I urged you..."; if secondary schools would not accept the challenge, the Department could try to force the issue.

The habits, expectations, and sanctions of people do not change uniformly with the enactment of new regulations by government. The relatively brief life of this particular accommodation to participation illustrated again, if further illustration be needed, that the general processes of a culture determine the levels of achievement of an educational system. H. Pullen and Floyd Robinson have both documented the inability of both the bureaucracy and local groups of teachers to suddenly change their modus operandi when given newly delegated responsibilities.[39]

A society that includes bureaucrats and teachers and that has difficulty accepting changes in traditional curriculum content cannot be expected to countenance the more radical but complementary expectation that children and young people could or should develop personal responsibility and independent values. Since the teachers were neither permitted nor expected to share decision making with the administrative hierarchy, which in its turn was shaped and kept in line by community expectations, how could teachers help their charges develop a sense of freedom and personal responsibility? In the traditional view, authority must be evident. An injunction of the time was "Get the 'sir' habit"—hardly conducive to the leveling effect portended by progressivism.

The consequence of the progressive movement's inability to change authority relationships, within all but a few private schools in the States, was to leave the content of new school subjects devoid of their major reason for appearing in the curriculum. Thus incomplete, they became formalistic and degraded, and "basket-weaving" became a shorthand denigrating descriptor of courses of the fifties. In 1958, W. H. Swift looked back over the period and described the widespread reaction that had taken place to progressivist intentions, which were blamed for watering down the curriculum: "There has been a significant trend across Canada toward official positions somewhat less free and flexible in both theory and practice. It will remain a moot question whether, had we had the teaching staffs and other requisites essential to success, we might have achieved it and found ourselves on a different road." He went on to note the general indecisiveness of the period:

It is sad, but apparently true, that the demise of Latin is a clear trend in Canadian education. The fact that so little is reportable with respect to curriculum is something of a disappointment to me. I am sure that it arises in part from the fact that we are in a state of uncertainty. There are conflicting views amongst the public, within the educational system, and within the minds of individual thoughtful educators. An inevitable result is that very little by way of significant and controversial change is affected. It is noteworthy in this regard that the Canadian Conference on Education produced no resolutions bearing on the main curriculum problems of the day.[40]

During the time between the Canadian Conference on Education in Ottawa in February 1958 and the Ontario Conference on Education in Windsor in November 1961, signs of the *Intellectual Enhancement Period* began to appear. The Ontario Teachers' Federation started subject-matter committees, and the present writer wrote the first article on the inadequacies of the elementary science syllabus, which was based entirely on an informal study of nature, to appear in any Ontario teachers' journal.[41]

The Ontario Teachers' Federation deliberately organized the Windsor conference in a fashion that placed a maximum amount of pressure on the Minister of Education to revise a very old set of syllabuses. Here the teachers, and in this case a receptive public, were on familiar ground. Bruner's *The Process of Education* became as well-thumbed in education circles as a breviary is in religious institutions.[42] Bruner himself was invited to Ontario several times to elaborate on his notions of matching teaching methods to the cognitive structures of the learner and the assumed intrinsic structures of school subjects. Strong and respected people from assorted disciplines outside the lower schools also began to have a noticeable impact on teaching.

For example, Bentley Glass, a noted authority on biology and particularly genetics, was in considerable demand to assist in formulating new approaches to science education. In Ontario, the work of Howard Mulligan, who chaired the first mathematics committee of the Ontario Teachers' Federation, should be particularly noted as foreshadowing the direction that mathematics education has since taken. When Sputnik appeared, the drive to match school practices with current conceptions was accelerated and generalized to all the sciences, and later to social studies and language teaching.

> The prevailing notion was that if you understood the structure of knowledge, that understanding would then permit you to go ahead on your own; you did not need to encounter everything in nature to know nature, but by understanding some deep principles, you could extrapolate to the particulars as needed.... For the first time in the modern age, the acme of scholarship, even in our great research institutes and universities, was to convert knowledge into pedagogy, to turn it back to the learning of the young.... The schoolboy learning physics did so as a physicist.[43]

Innovators in this period did not question the general purpose of the school as had curriculum developers in the Thwarted Progressive era; they assumed that the school had one general purpose, cognitive enhancement. Even the social studies innovations were structured according to the methodologies of expert practitioners; they were not designed for personal growth—to foster interracial understanding, for example—instead, "thinking" became the target of a mass of research projects in a fashion that implied a kind of disembodiment altogether different from the classical curriculum of the Traditional Period. As the sixties wore on, a body of information on early childhood development and successful short-term intervention slowly began to accumulate. Part of this corpus was derived from Jean Piaget, who developed his own genre in the 1920s and laid the groundwork for Lawrence Kohlberg's later work on moral development.[44]

Then, like a thunderclap came the beginning of the *Period of Personal Autonomy*, which overwhelmed the previous brief decade's innovations. The turning point in North America was dramatized by a black woman who refused to move to the back of a bus, but the issue was worldwide and for the West had been brewing since at least the Magna Carta. Economic conditions, social upheavals after two world wars, and, coincidentally, the coming of age of people who had grown up during a relatively enlightened child-rearing period—another reflection of the progressive era—brought social activism and effective assertions of personal development and equality to the fore. Some of these people became teachers.

When the prevailing social climate is not solidly resistant to assertions of equality, tolerance and freedom acquire respectability. Typically, popular opposition to this new insurgence fastened onto its most extreme expressions, indiscriminately applying the labels "hippie" and "beatnik" to its supporters. But such scapegoating failed to stem the tide, because the excesses of dress and style were merely surface features of a profoundly different set of personal values that were noted in their formative stage during the Thwarted Progressive Period. While the schools were almost obsessive in their refusal to allow miniskirts, pantsuits, beards, denims, and holding hands in the halls, they were not deluded into thinking that this represented the whole of the matter. Even middle-class kids were resisting the old conformities, and what was worse, their parents were encouraging them!

In October 1968, in a last-ditch appeal to a controlling but hopefully supportive society, the executive of the Ontario Secondary School Teachers' Federation placed an ad, "A Letter of Concern Regarding the Secondary Schools of Ontario," in Toronto's *Globe and Mail*:

> We, the secondary school teachers and principals of Ontario, wish to express our confidence in the young people in our secondary schools. We regret that their educational experience has been interrupted in recent weeks by the irresponsible conduct of a few students, trustees, parents and organized pressure groups.
> We believe that the unrest among some students in our schools is symptomatic of the revolt against all forms of authority within our society today, and that this revolt has been further aggravated by sensational reporting by the mass media in some centres.[45]

All the extraneous issues, such as formalistic studies and controlled access, which previously hid under the protective cloak of tradition, were now swept off the stage. In this the age of Aquarius the naked fact stood for all to see: it was the Establishment's attempt to reassert institutional control over personal choice.

It is not surprising that the OSSTF executive should have been so out of touch with the social realities that they should ask for support to hold the line on restrictions; the ad did reflect public sentiment, although to an unknown degree. Letters to the Editor, that popular device of newspapers to stimulate sales, had been saying much the same thing for several years. What was surprising was the response of the general body of secondary school teachers. Irritated and puzzled as they were by these new adolescents, they themselves were far enough along the road toward personal autonomy that they opposed this blatant attempt to reimpose the old standards.[46] The public hardly had time to get into the controversy, so quickly did the secondary school teachers repudiate their own executive.

The teachers' action represented an irreversible watershed in interpersonal relations in the schools. The superficial barriers were knocked down in short order. School boards withdrew the rights of principals to stipulate dress codes and inflict corporal punishment, and teachers started to sport beards, pantsuits, short skirts, and turtleneck sweaters. In that last bastion of "law and order," professional sports, hockey and football players were allowed to have long hair, thus removing from high school coaches their final rationalization in support of conformity.

The Ministry of Education also got into the act, permitting students to choose options in an attempt to force schools to develop more appealing courses of studies. And yet traditional thinking disappears slowly. Parents worried about the lack of history and literature courses, although the new regulations had not had time to have much effect. Moreover, most new courses bore a close resemblance to the old, academically oriented courses, and to that extent they did not enhance the motivation of those who were only marginally disposed to formalistic studies. One new course, Man in Society, represented an attempt to introduce the social sciences into the secondary school curriculum, but it was assigned to teachers who seldom had the background to handle it—a denial of the publicly espoused principle of an orientation toward excellence in secondary school teaching. The low prestige that this course and those who taught it have continued to endure is merely a replay of the treatment that sociologists received in universities as recently as the postwar era: history is respectable, sociology is not. The catchword "relevance," which had been the rallying cry for modernizing courses, was soon assigned to the refuse heap along with "permissiveness."

More profound undercurrents of the Personal Autonomy era surface periodically. Consciousness-raising agitation by women is forcing a realignment of sex roles in our society. Increasing numbers of adolescents cohabit and rear children even while attending school. Yet paradoxically, considering that the family studies course and its variants have existed for some time, and that sixteen-year-olds may apply for abortions and take tests and treatment for VD without their parents being notified, secondary schools had to be forced into allowing pregnant students and pregnant teachers to remain in the classroom.

Another development that may have interesting implications for education is that eighteen-year-olds have now been given the right to vote, not only for members of parliament and the legislature, but also for the school board members who hire their teachers. As is frequently observed, nature and politics abhor a vacuum. On this basis it seems likely that a time will come when, as a group, these new voters will recognize the power that they have; indeed, in Toronto it is possible that their potential force has already been exercised in school board elections. Earlier this year, 22 out of 31 presidents of student councils in Toronto supported the Toronto school board in its opposition to corporal punishment after the board had forced a punitive teacher to resign. Perhaps teachers will now recognize the legitimacy of student participation in school affairs if one of their members again "roughs up" a student and the student council chooses to establish a precedent as the aggrieved party.

The experiences reviewed above lead to the distressing conclusion that if students do begin to organize in what they perceive as their own interests, instead of misdirecting their dissatisfactions at U.S. embassies and superficial fuddle-duddle parades, the schools will evade the issues and attempt to raise the specter of rebellion. If that happens, however, students will find that their teachers have provided them with ample precedents in support of their cause. Early in March 1974, the York County Board of Education placed an ad in the *Globe and Mail* that began as follows:

SOME QUESTIONS:
1. Who should control education in York County? Trustees whom you elect? Or the provincial office of the Ontario Secondary School Teachers' Federation?

And it ends with:

The essence of a democracy is that elected representatives act on behalf of the people. The people retain control because they can change their policymakers at election time. The teachers are demanding an equal voice with trustees in setting board policy, without being directly responsible to the voters.[47]

There is an irony here. There was a time when teachers' organizations attempted to assert the abstract principle of "professional autonomy," claiming that they should not be influenced by current opinion. However, when the prestigious medical associations found that they could not resist social pressure to meet the needs of a changing society, the teachers' associations learned quickly. In York County, they took their case to the public and won the right to be consulted on matters that affect their daily lives, for example, the pupil/teacher ratio. The Board of Education lost: the teachers were successful in their "revolt against authority," as their executive had phrased it in 1968.

This victory by the Ontario Secondary School Teachers' Federation may have implications for responsibility in curriculum development that have escaped attention. Trustees have been the traditional intermediaries between voters and the Minister of Education. Now teachers have won the right to be co-intermediaries. But if the student voters read well the history they are supposed to study, they may learn a lesson from descriptions of the Reformation. During that lengthy historical period a large proportion of people in Western society presumed to dispense with priests as intermediaries between themselves and God. Are trustees and teachers more exalted than were priests during the Reformation, when it comes to dealing with the Minister of Education?

It will be recalled that the advertisement in which the OSSTF executive asked for public support was repudiated more strongly by the Federation's own members than by the public at large. Was it simply superior organization that produced success in the York County dispute? I think not. The common denominator in these events is the move away from traditional values. The OSSTF advertisement could not engender support to resist even the trivial aspects of the move toward personal autonomy; on the other hand, in the York County instance the teachers capitalized on this.

Although society is disaffected by strikes, it is composed of members who are themselves seeking personal autonomy—or involvement—in their own spheres. The excesses of Kent State, the use of tear gas and police dogs to quell student uprisings, the harassment of aldermen and professors on picket lines, all in a climate that was moving toward an attitude of negotiation, reinforced an existing militancy among some and politicized others. But as long as it is not civil insurrection, we have lost our willingness to resort quickly to clubs, tear gas, and court injunctions. In fact public support went to those at the barricades rather than to the police during the most strident days of social activism.

This move away from head-on confrontation is a very important sign of progress in governance of the polity. Previously inflexible bonds in our hierarchical society are becoming pliable and, given the grace of time insofar as military or ecological disasters are concerned, varied peaceful solutions to problems will accumulate and become institutionalized in unknown ways in succeeding generations. The feminist movement is correct in its assertion that emancipating women will simultaneously emancipate men, in the same way that Western society is morally stronger and better equipped to face widespread problems in the world because Blacks everywhere are forcibly freeing the white man of his racist burden. Although the current catch phrase "women's lib" may go the way of "progressivism" and "relevance," it is most unlikely that, short of global catastrophe, the move toward new interpretations of responsibility in this society will lose its momentum.

The proper focus for the future must be on developing skills in anticipatory negotiation and a far more open system of communication than hierarchical authority would have tolerated in the Traditional Period. In education it is inconceivable that responsible curriculum developers should continue to limit their considerations to the comfortable domain of achievement in verbal content. That which used to be called the hidden curriculum has moved into the open and is now prepotent. We still have time to capitalize on the trends in society that impinge on the schools before students again start dropping out in great numbers or are incited by the meaninglessness of it all to "rebel," as the teachers of York County did.

CONTINUITIES FROM THE PAST

The identification of five broad historical periods, by which we may perceive the effect of broad societal trends upon the school's curriculum, does not take account of the superficial pendulum swings of fads in educational practices. There are, however, certain enduring characteristics of previous periods that have extended into the present and that by the nature of things will have an influence on the future.

The first of these is the intuitive, egalitarian spirit of New World expansionism, which still suffuses the culture of the U.S. and Canada. It is a condition that disappoints and sometimes infuriates those who would like to draw clear ideological lines in politics. For example, a former premier of Alberta, Ernest Manning, once suggested a realignment of political parties because they each have members that bridge the spectrum from left to right.

Superimposed upon this generally unconscious feeling that every man is the equal of every other man is an uneasy alliance between our European derived predisposition toward elitism (embodied in one of its forms in the universities) and our assumptions of hierarchical authority, which have developed over approximately the last one hundred and fifty years in our bureaucratic and industrialized economy.

Each of these influences is brought to bear on the schools, which in effect constitute the battleground where people try to but cannot resolve the contradictions among them. The elusive prize of the contest is the right to specify the terms of socializing a new generation. But the enduring dilemma in public education derives from the fact that we have institutionalized each of these contradictory structures of authority.

Equal Access: Does It Work?
The first education policy in Ontario with New World egalitarian implications resulted from Egerton Ryerson's victory over Bishop Strachan. The Ontario public's long-time commitment to the principle of universal access to higher and higher levels of education eventually pitted the lower schools against the universities. This was no less true in the U.S. As Richard Hofstadter tells us, "the belief in mass education was not founded primarily upon a passion for the development of mind, or upon a pride in learning and culture for their own sakes, but rather upon the supposed political and economic benefits of education."[48]

Because they had themselves been trained by professors and been assigned the responsibility of preparing students for university, those who identified most strongly with the academic justification for schools were the secondary school teachers, who found themselves occupying the middle ground, where they are today.

While it has never been popularly acceptable to speak of socioeconomic classes of people in Ontario, the continual reassertions of the principle of equal access clearly rest on the assumption that the children of the poor should have an equal opportunity to work in prestigious occupations, for example, in the professions. The day has finally come when we must ask whether this socially inspired policy actually works. Three basic questions must be differentiated.

1. Have the schools fulfilled their assigned function of occupational preparation?
2. Have people from all socioeconomic levels shared equally in the competition for prestigious occupations?

3. What role do the curricula of the schools play in achieving the social goal of equal access to such occupations?

The answer to the first question must be impressionistic, and while it is overwhelmingly affirmative, it is not unequivocal. There is no doubt that the industrial–commercial economy of North America is prodigious, and that its development has entailed an unprecedented specialization of labor. The schools have certainly adapted to this need, supplying the human resources that contributed to this massive development. We cannot overlook the contributions of skilled technicians and scientists who immigrated to Canada, especially before and after World War 2, but indigenous schooling was the major factor in the technological achievements of North America. These remarks probably apply almost as much to Canada as to the U.S. We have a benchmark in an Economic Council of Canada recommendation that the diversity of the educational base was too restricted to stimulate the economy;[49] within one decade we had produced an oversupply of graduates, demonstrating clearly the responsiveness of the educational system insofar as economic goals are concerned.

The fact that Canadian secondary schools were able to retain an increasing number of persons and that postsecondary institutions could handle them is creditable. However, in answer to the second question of whether students from all segments of society are staying in school in numbers somewhat representative of the size of their respective groups, and if so, whether they are also sharing in the benefits of more schooling, there are disturbing indicators that the principle of equality of opportunity is not working well in Canada. In a study published recently, Wallace Clement demonstrates that the proportion of corporate directorships held by members of Canada's upper class has increased since John Porter published his findings in *The Vertical Mosaic* in 1965. Since then, Porter and his associates have developed a methodology for collecting data that should assist future interpretations of the effect of years of Canadian schooling on particular segments of the population, but precise data are not currently available.[50]

Because of the lack of Canadian data, to seek an answer to the third question of what role curriculum can play we must resort to information from other countries to help us determine whether deliberate intervention in education policies can actually alter the class distinctions that have determined how high students climb on the educational ladder. Most people in the education world will have read at least reviews of the original Coleman report and its five-year reanalysis, the even wider based Jencks study, and the British Plowden report. The conclusions of these large-scale research studies and of numerous smaller but entirely consistent studies are disconcerting, challenging as they do our heretofore simple notions of cause and effect in educational enhancement.[51]

Many educators act as though they wish these reports would just fade away. Their motivations are understandable. It is part of our work ethic to believe that the harder one works the more one succeeds, regardless of background. On this basis, children of the poor should achieve as well as middle-class children, if both work equally hard. Both groups should get equal marks on achievement tests, go equally far in school, and earn similar incomes, on the average, when they graduate. But this is not the case. It simply does not seem to matter what kind of schooling students have. Teachers' education and background, age of school buildings, numbers of textbooks, library facilities, streaming, class size, teaching methods, all of these and more have no significant effect on equalizing achievement. The factors that do explain differences in the achievement of students are such out-of-school conditions as housing, occupation of parents, ethnic background, and the income level of students' neighborhoods.

The findings have been mistaken to mean that schools do not have any effect on students' learning. In fact, they have; but they have not produced a leveling effect. Children of middle-class parents still have the advantage when it comes to school achievement and consequent employment. Since the misinterpretation of research findings has been used to rationalize a decrease in educational expenditures in the U.S., we can understand why many would rather ignore them. However, just as man cannot "undiscover" nuclear bombs, so we cannot wish these findings away.

As noted earlier, there is a positive aspect to the equal opportunity policy. Although the evidence is tentative, as Lipset says, the implications are profound:

In 1973, the U.S. Census Bureau reported one of the most significant statistics in American history. For the first time, the percent of black Americans of college age entering an institution of higher education is identical with the proportion of comparably aged white youth. This is the first major piece of evidence that the United States is finally really beginning to right the ancient wrongs of slavery and racism. Clearly, of course, the education received by many blacks is far from equal, for this indicator of educational equality conceals the fact that a very large proportion of black students are attending the more inferior segments of higher education: junior colleges, black colleges in the South, the less prestigious state colleges, etc. Yet the statistic is very important, for college attendance has a major credentialing function. To obtain a job in the better paid sector of the American economy, one has to go to some sort of college.[52]

The next decade will tell us whether the deliberately pursued education policy of equal opportunity in the U.S. in fact eventuates in the desired payoff of equal access to prestigious employment on the part of Blacks. There are, however, several considerations we must keep in mind when we look at the equal access issue in the context of Ontario education.

In the face of real and practical day-to-day problems and institutionalized opposition, the policy of equal access must not be taken for granted. The elitist but diverting siren song of "standards," which Hofstadter, for example, acknowledges as such, appeals to all of us in education, not just to those who would subvert the historically more recent press toward equal educational opportunity; nonetheless, we must make sure that students are guaranteed equal access to all educational levels. Obvious and direct attacks on inequalities do not seem to work either in education or in other social situations, probably because they are merely symptoms of a more profound disorder.[53] But where structured blockages are identified, as they were in Althouse's day, they must be removed or modified, and policy makers must devote careful, creative thought to the development of alternative routes or goals. It is difficult for taxpayers to see or understand that "do or die" terminal examinations represent such blockages and in fact restrict access to prestigious occupations.

The first practical implication of these considerations is that there should be facilities for lifelong education. Those who leave secondary school at whatever stage and for whatever reasons must be able to return easily. However, it would do them little service if they returned to the same kinds of elitist practices that encouraged them to leave in the first place. Secondary schools must redirect their energies to meeting the needs of students and build from that position.

There are some structured blockages that exist, as the lawyers say, *de facto* but not *de jure*. For example, provision for equal access and equal job opportunities may be carefully designed, but the "every man" sentiment excludes women and at least the visible minorities. In my view, if Blacks in the U.S. soon emerge in fair proportions in traditionally desirable occupations, as Lipset expects, it will have happened because in addition to the equal access education policy there is also *a deliberate legislative policy on the employment side of the equation*. If we are serious about equal economic opportunity in Canada, and our multicultural policy says we are, we must follow through with some sort of action that ensures such equality for Indians, Blacks, women, and others who are now systematically excluded. Primary emphasis on the curriculum, it should now be evident, is a delusion; the curriculum, which is not in any event the property of the schools, must be brought into accommodation with changes in policy. To the extent that this accommodation can be identified with the underlying societal goals noted in the historical section of this paper, the task will be facilitated.

Elitism, Hierarchical Control, and Mutuality

In my view, secondary schools will continue to encounter widespread public indifference and sometimes opposition as long as they maintain their perception of university studies as a primary reference point. It is insufficient for secondary schools to argue that they are meeting universities' demands for uniform standards. Universities change when they are threatened with a loss of income, as we all learned in the late 1960s. Even now, they are quietly moving in the direction of meeting social concerns in order to hold more students longer; however, the process might be more constructively tackled if secondary schools and universities established a committee to deal realistically with the complex problems of equality of access, retention, and prerequisites in curricula.

Most people see secondary schools as simply being instrumental to entering university and the occupations to which university leads. They talk about and support "standards," but when faced with the practical implications of such a policy (i.e., assessing the worthiness or significance of particular academic courses), their support falls into disarray. As for students, they already know about core curricula and other gimmicks that the schools invent as a disguise for traditional programs. Their feelings are consistent with the research cited in the last section of this paper: for most students the program they take does not make much difference when it comes to getting a job. There is no inherent reason why the standards for a Man in Society course (or environmental studies, or urban geography, or child development) should be any lower or less worthy than those for trigonometry or English literature. Indeed, it appears that the paragon of traditional liberal arts, English literature, is becoming transformed simply by virtue of teachers' interpretations, as they themselves move into an age in which personal values are increasingly being examined.[54] The roots of the Personal Autonomy Period are deep, and one should not be surprised that attention to values and people now predominates over the scholarly concerns of preceding periods. Deliberate recognition of this influence, however, would result in more appealing curricula and, indeed, in a demand for teacher education more appropriate to such new curricula. The new curriculum standards suggested in the next section would in consequence grow out of a common interest of our age.

The scholarly view, as valid as it was for a previous time, has to be imposed from the top, so to speak. Thus, the argument for a return to "standards" is seriously misleading. What this slogan really expresses is the desire to keep things unchanged and return to conformity training for recalcitrant youth and some of their sympathetic teachers.

Traditional education had been founded upon a primary conviction about the value of the various subject matter disciplines and ... in so far as the learning process was irksome ... it assumed that the self-discipline that came from overcoming irksomeness would at least be a net gain.[55]

The "self-discipline" of which Hofstadter speaks is quite clearly the internalization of behavioral norms, not of content. It proves again that the so-called hidden curriculum has always been known; the assumptions were simply unquestioned.

Returning to the fundamental question of what we want our schools to achieve, we must ask if there is not more to be desired than the replenishment of the present work force. The schools' traditional answer has always been a simple-minded polemic: "Subjects should be studied for their own sake." Few people ever believed this, as we have seen, but the schools' refusal to accept this fact has prevented them from thinking through properly relevant curricula.

In 1971, the same Jerome Bruner who had so recently emphasized a rigorous intellectualism in the schools wrote:

> In the end, we must finally appreciate that education is not a neutral subject, nor is it an isolated subject. It is a deeply political issue in which we guarantee a future for someone and, frequently, in guaranteeing a future for someone, we deal somebody else out. *I believe I would be quite satisfied to declare, if not a moratorium, then something of a de-emphasis on matters that have to do with the structure of history, the structure of physics, the nature of mathematical consistency, and deal with it rather in the context of the problems that face us.* We might better concern ourselves with how those problems can be solved, not just by practical action, but by putting knowledge, wherever we find it and in whatever form we find it, to work in these massive tasks. *We might put vocation and intention back into the process of education, much more firmly than we had it there before.*

Putting intention into school practices calls upon skills seldom discussed in curriculum matters today. As Jantzen noted in the 1970 Quance Lectures,

> Curriculum planning, like any other social process, requires proper orientation. Those who engage in it must have a clear picture of the society in which the schools operate. They must be able to sense the kinds of skills, knowledge, and understanding required of youth as they face the new world ahead of them. They must adapt both content and method to serve today's distinctly different world and at the same time preserve basic values that have stood the test of time. Professional literature is rich in helping curriculum workers gain such a perspective. It is vital that all those responsible for developing new programs become aware of what is already in print regarding the fundamental changes now taking place in society.[56]

TOWARD A RESOLUTION OF CONTRADICTIONS THROUGH
CURRICULUM DEVELOPMENT

The label "Personal Autonomy Period," which I apply to a noticeably different set of activities in and about schools, has a sociological rather than a psychological connotation because a wide congeries of intentions were and are being expressed in society and therefore also in the schools. The underlying values in this period have revolved around such notions as individuality ("Do your own thing"), liberation ("Freedom now"), enhanced self-concept ("Black is beautiful"), love ("Make love, not war"), autonomy ("Who are you to impose your values on others?"), and, on the negative side, alienated hate ("Burn, baby, burn!"). Slogans they may be, but because they rallied soulmates and exasperated, confronted, or frightened critics, they obviously had real meaning for society.

It would require an empirical study to determine the degree to which these various values expressing what is happening in our culture are "simply" autonomy oriented, that is to say, expressive of a desire to be independent of a controlling person or organization. However, it would be a disservice to the facts and to the future to think that the range of characteristics on the personal-growth dimension run from a dependent or oppressed position at one extreme to autonomy at the other. At the very least, the conceptual scale should be extended from dependence through autonomy, which would fall near the middle, to mutuality, at the opposite extreme from dependence. Mutuality, a condition that permits, indeed encourages, contributions from various levels in the authority hierarchy demands considerable maturity, and it would be too much to expect that every person moving away from dependency can go immediately and painlessly to mutuality. Most of us have to stop not once but several times on a tortuous Parcheesi path, and there are penalties to be paid by the player and his milieu because the match is bad.

Schools could facilitate this movement toward mutuality in a way that they could not have done in previous periods of curriculum development. Heretofore, even if the schools had been so inclined, the controlling society would have prevented any significant relaxation in authority relationships. Now, significant segments of society have matured beyond the level of the schools.

Although teachers are taking part as members of society in the general social movement toward autonomy, few are permitted mutuality in the conduct of the school. In my view, the urge toward participation or consultation is not recognized for what it is. Teachers are unconsciously being diverted from their central goal by administrative accommodations to their claims for participation in such mundane matters as assignments to particular classes and the number of spares or lunchroom supervision periods they have per day. Even here, an observer of the social dynamics of schools may note the continual return of constraining practices after a period of relatively open-ended searching by teachers. Soon after teachers began to get accustomed to the new kinds of possibilities inherent in the option system, someone imposed management-by-objectives, which is an extension of the operationalists' reductionist technique of controlling physical and human events. The ostensible purpose is facilitation, but a latent function is the reimposition of a remarkable amount of hierarchical control.[57]

Manifestly, if teachers are able neither to see a need for nor to show much mutuality, youth cannot learn the reinforcing behaviors that will lead them to express greater maturity in the school. To put it another way, the teachers will continue to invite "rebellion" and dropouts if they cannot develop mutuality among themselves, with the administrators and policy makers in the school system, and with the adolescents they teach.

The principles of mutuality are the principles of participation. It has always seemed to me a supreme irony that teachers so often advance the magnificently idealistic goals of democracy and growth of independence when they teach social studies, then direct students to textbooks and superficial group projects. Since students are already exercising their independence in other areas of their lives (for example, they have the right to apply for abortions at sixteen and vote at eighteen), surely the schools' concern should be to enhance the intellectual and moral decisions students make and to see that their teachers are more mature in their dealings with students. These are issues to be developed in behavioral aspects of the curriculum, not merely presented in an intellectualized form in text books and other informational materials.

The traditional outlook is that independence and the responsibilities it implies must be learned at home and in church. But let us not be misled any longer; the traditional outlook stems not from a neutral, hands-off attitude, but from a definite assignment of responsibility for conformity training to the schools. Social values and responsibilities are learned in social situations, where decisions are made and consequences faced. And since *the whole school is a complex social system in microcosm*, I believe it will increasingly be perceived as a dereliction of duty on the part of the schools if they do not encourage and teach adolescents to participate in all decisions that affect their school lives. Not solely as a preparation for the future is this an important matter, but also because the consequences of policy and personal decisions are met there, every day. The power to teach and to learn mutuality lies in productive interactions with the group, not in isolated study in library carrels, which belong to a bygone age when society could and did dictate norms for individualism—a term that means something else today, as David Riesman presciently told us in 1954.[58]

One must affirm immediately that significant student participation in policy development, however gradually introduced, will alarm some parents while it satisfies others. Thus, concern for mutuality demands that parents and various community agencies also be involved. Emergent socialization goals are different from what they used to be, and are probably irreversible: today's school structures must facilitate growth, since they belong to society as a whole, not merely to the school of which they form a part. Contrary to popular opinion, Bowles and Gintis note the positive consequences of broader forms of participation:

Repeated experiments have shown that in those complex work tasks that increasingly dominate modern production, participatory control by workers is a more productive form of work organization. The boredom and stultification of the production line and the steno pool, the shackled creativity of technical workers and teachers, the personal frustration of the bureaucratic office routine, increasingly lost their claim as the price of material comfort.[59]

Discovering ways to rise above personal accommodations to institutional structures will not be easy; the development of human beings and of social institutions does not proceed by logical steps. It is therefore not possible to plot an invariant sequence of activities that will lead people to assume reasonable responsibility. People who are in or close to the situation, however, and who have the principles in mind and the skills at hand, can incorporate innovations in participatory policy making into the curriculum.

Several OISE projects oriented to non-traditional socialization processes have undergone relatively extensive trials. Not the least of these is the governing structure of OISE. For four years now, seventy people representing various categories of the general public, students, professors, and support staff have carried the responsibility of formulating and articulating general policy. If the Institute's governing structure is not always thought of as a model to be emulated, it is at least a model from which to learn.

To the extent that the representatives are sympathetic to the reasons for universal participation, we must expect them to be discussing the principles with other Ontario educational institutions. I do not mean to imply that there is universal agreement on the principles. Ideologies are forceful differentiators. Some people have been incensed at the notion of secretaries and students sitting on policy-making bodies; such people would also have great difficulty guiding adolescents in identifying issues, assembling data, and presenting and negotiating points of view during the process of formulating policy. And yet acting in a participating role is precisely what adults increasingly find themselves doing. Since our feelings about personal autonomy have been reinforced by the age we live in, we resent decisions in which we have not participated. One consequence we see is the formation of the large number of committees and ratepayers groups that we so often satirize or denigrate. Of all people, educators should understand these relationships. For youth to assume responsibility for their own lives, which is the ostensible socialization goal, they must become involved in administrative policy and curriculum development. Indeed their involvement must be considered a legitimate part of the curriculum.

Several new concepts designed to foster increased community and student participation are now being tried out in Ontario schools. The effects of high-school-based students' participation in the social-service sector of three Toronto boroughs and several Indian communities are currently being studied by OISE researchers. The greatest problems they have found so far inhere not in the adolescents, but in the difficulties adults and organizations have in adapting to their increased participation. Another new concept being tried out with the purpose of identifying and testing the kinds of structures that would facilitate new forms of socialization among the young is the establishment of several broad-based community schools that offer a wide array of locally developed activities.[60] Also under way is a lengthy and intensive evaluation of the consequences of open-plan schooling in comparison with traditional schooling. This study is providing important information to Ontario, which has shown remarkable tolerance in the development of such an ostensibly different form of schooling. All these activities, while valuable in their own right, are designed to discover the governing conditions that are involved in linking the curriculum to broad societal forces.

The traditional aloofness of professional organizations and their members was once described by George Bernard Shaw as "a conspiracy against the public." In our increasingly secular and suspicious age the public has reacted against this aloofness, seeking broader participation. Even where research results overwhelmingly confirm a theory, as in the case of physical punishment having a negative effect on learning, the remedies immediately project the curriculum developer into that part of human affairs in which competing values get resolved, distorted, or ignored—the public arena. The curriculum developer can no longer arrogate to himself or to a limited organization the right to make changes. He must have a base of public legitimacy. This is only one of the reasons why the "teacher-proof" packages developed in the brief Intellectual Enhancement Period failed. Although the inrush of students and the appearance of Sputnik caused an anxious society to vent its feelings on the schools, the alphabetical, cognitively oriented remedies provided by the acme of scholarship were not anchored in the real causes of dissatisfaction, which were socio-emotional.

It seems safe to assume that innovations in the curriculum will continue to be informed by studies of cognition. However, those who are working at the frontiers of knowledge are conceptually far ahead of classroom teachers and the people who pay the bill for education. Therefore, a sense of the human level at which different groups of people communicate is one of the essential skills that the curriculum developer must bring to his task. This is no less true for teachers than it is for researchers. The fact that teachers have felt increasingly compelled to take their grievances to the public is a tacit acknowledgment that, in the final analysis, the public controls the operation of the schools. And, as we have seen, this control extends to the rejection of content and procedures that may be valid for learning but unacceptable to the prevailing mood or climate of belief.

The Ontario Ministry of Education's encouragement of community participation in extending the use of school facilities is an affirmation of our changing times. However, the inability of many people either to develop or to understand the potential that lies in school–community relations will undoubtedly become more apparent and thereby reinforce the schools' already widespread alienation from social concerns. Ontario's professed interest in multiculturalism will provide a rigorous test of the skills and attitudes that we have developed in our society to date.

Education for Minority Groups
In my early years of teaching OISE's graduate classes in general curriculum, I used to distribute comparative data from census reports. The trends toward urban concentration and a decreasing percentage of Anglo-Saxon residents

were unmistakable, but to the teachers of the time this information meant little because the impact had yet to be felt. Now we have special classes to deal with the education of minority groups. Although there are still some parts of the province that seem to deny this new responsibility, the facts are ineluctable. The accompanying table indicates the changing origins of all Ontario residents over the last three census periods.

Data for the city of Toronto are particularly illuminating. By 1970 the Toronto school system discovered that more than 40 percent of its students had learned some language other than English as their mother tongue; and by 1972 only 54 percent of Toronto's population could claim British origin. In the Toronto school system today there are
— over 10,000 who speak Italian
— over 4,000 who speak Portuguese
— over 3,000 who speak Greek
— over 2,700 who speak Chinese
— over 1,200 who speak Polish.[61]

In my view, minority-group education has four general facets, one or more of which will increasingly concern all curriculum planners.
1. Education of specific minority-group members, both children and adults.
2. Education of all students about minority groups, prejudice, and discrimination.
3. Problems related to combined classes.
4. Career-ladder education, allowing social mobility to occur if desired. There is a particular problem that arises from the increasing trend toward the erection of barriers (sometimes called "professionalization") that prevent Indians, immigrants, and working-class children in general from access to established occupations:
    a) to teaching—parent volunteers, aides, certified teachers.
    b) to other careers.

Two other points should be noted. Since Ontario is officially committed to the concept of multiculturalism, mutual understanding and tolerance is an obligation to be accepted by all, not merely by the dominant culture. This means that Old World divisions and antagonisms must be just as subject to review and modification as relations between citizens and immigrants.

From my own observations of the attention that various ethnic groups get at conferences on multicultural concerns, I would assert that native Indians continue to be ignored by all except a few individuals. Undoubtedly there is a complex interaction between the Indians' current status and the threat they present in terms of economic competition, but the persistent fact of a social distance between Indians and all others remains a test of the sincerity of those who espouse the cause of multiculturalism.

It will be a long time before we will be able to judge the depth of Canada's commitment to multiculturalism and its consequences, but it will be in the schools that we will observe the effects most directly. In this period of emphasis on individual development, a conflict is emerging between two sets of values. On the one hand, the dominant segment of society and the schools are deeply involved in working out the implications of profoundly changing life styles; instrumental to this cause is the need to get communities rather than central sources to discuss and define educational objectives. Immigrants, on the other hand, do not share some of the motivations of the more egalitarian yet alienated segment of society. By and large, they expect that teachers will reinforce such traditional values as clearly distinguished and dependent age and sex roles for their children. The more emphasis that is placed on

Population of Ontario by Reported Origin

	1951 N	1951 %	1961 N	1961 %	1971 N	1971 %
British Isles	3,081,919	67.03	3,711,536	59.52	4,576,010	59.40
French	477,677	10.38	647,941	10.39	737,360	9.57
Austrian	8,126	.18				
Czech and Slovak	29,025	.63				
Finnish	29,327	.64				
German	222,028	4.83	400,717	6.43	475,315	6.17
Hungarian	28,182	.61				
Italian	87,622	1.91	273,864	4.39	463,095	6.01
Jewish	74,920	1.63	65,280	1.05	135,195	1.76
Netherlands	98,373	2.14	191,017	3.06	206,940	2.69
Polish	89,825	1.95	149,524	2.40	144,115	1.87
Russian	16,885	.37	28,327	.45		
Scandinavian	37,430	.81	63,653	1.02	60,225	.78
Ukrainian	93,595	2.04	127,911	2.05	159,875	2.08
Other European	70,048	1.52	349,797	5.61		
Chinese	6,997	.15				
Japanese	8,581	.19	39,277	.63	112,780	1.46
Other Asiatic	6,560	.14				
Native Indian and Eskimo	37,388	.81	48,074	.77	63,175	.82
Other and unknown	93,034	2.02	139,174	2.23	569,015	7.39
TOTAL	4,597,542		6,236,092		7,703,110	

Source: Dominion Bureau of Statistics, *Census of Canada, 1951*, vol. 2, p. 5-26; *Census of Canada, 1961*, vol. 1, part 3, p. 82-13. Statistics Canada, *Census of Canada, 1971*, vol. 1, part 4, p. 5-4.
Note: Blanks in this table indicate that the categories varied across census years.

What about the Three Rs?
Some readers may be reassured that I share their intuitions about the need to take account of social interrelationships in the curriculum of institutions to which children and youth are required to spend many hours a day. Nevertheless, they may wonder about the rest of the curriculum. Is it moving with the times, as must happen with other institutional adaptations in our society?

The most dramatic changes in subject matter in recent years have come with the introduction of the so-called new math, which marked as much of a break with the past as the move to metric measures that is now taking place. The controversy that is now arising over the use of mini-calculators in the classroom stems from the age-old fear that doing things the easy way makes achievement less worthy; it is reminiscent of Plato's lament that introducing the general population to writing would destroy man's memory, or, more recently, of the concern that replacing Sprott's no. 2 steel nibs in schools with fountain pens and somewhat later with ballpoint pens would destroy penmanship. Teachers are only human and, as with most of us, find it easier to decry the passing of a familiar routine than to develop new procedures that extend our capabilities.

Both elementary and secondary schools have seen a gradual shift from nature study and general science to courses in specific sciences. Grade 13, which still exists in Ontario (perhaps because of the prestige that still inheres in anything leading to university), seems to have adopted the Physical Science Study Committee's course of studies in physics, a successful carryover from the Intellectual Enhancement Period. Regrettably, the course has failed in its primary purpose of creating a broadly based, scientifically literate population, but it remains challenging to those who are initially inclined to study physics.

A more unfortunate consequence of the introduction of sophisticated approaches to teaching physics in senior grades, at least as far as the U.S. is concerned, is that it has brought about a rapid decline in the selection of science options. Traditionalists generally bemoan this fact on the grounds that students are evading "hard work." More important, however, is the question of whether there are sufficient people remaining with the motivation and capacity to profit from special-interest courses. I believe that there are. We do not have a shortage of scientists or engineers. The best answer to those who worry about students' refusal to tackle an array of courses that may later become prerequisite to further study is that students can return to school when their motivations are stronger, in keeping with the worldwide trend toward lifelong learning. If it becomes acceptable to return to school at any age (and if the schools are attitudinally prepared to accept mature students), the frenetic and obsessive pressure on adolescents to make basic career decisions and pursue the hopeless task of identifying courses that *may* have great use later in life may let up, permitting students to study and work fruitfully on more immediate but equally worthy areas of concern.

A remarkably versatile and stimulating innovation in social studies for eleven- and twelve-year-olds, known as *Man: A Course of Study*, was produced in Canada and the United States by Canadian and American advisors working under the direction of Jerome Bruner.[62] This course is still considered somewhat of an "import" and is therefore being introduced rather tentatively. But its recurring theme—What makes man human?—makes it both relevant and appealing to teachers and pupils in the elementary school. It is particularly appropriate for Canadians because of extensive National Film Board coverage of the Netsilik Eskimos.

Jean Piaget's investigations, which led to a new conceptualization of learning processes, has suggested to many psychologists a new theory that might provide a basis for enhancing instruction. Following Piaget's early findings that children invariably pass through several maturational stages in their ability to make value judgments on rules and sanctions in interpersonal relationships, Lawrence Kohlberg went on to demonstrate that value decisions implicit in adolescent and adult interpersonal behavior could similarly be conceptualized as developmentally sequential. It is possible to teach people to make more mature judgments than those they made in the past. In recent years several members of the Institute's staff have done follow-up work on Kohlberg's research and have developed both new approaches and materials for moral education in the schools.[63]

Besides their work on moral education, Institute staff have initiated several projects that are in keeping with the current emphasis on personal and social development in the schools; notable among these projects are several that deal with the question of women's roles and the treatment of various minority groups in our society.[64]

In previous sections it was demonstrated that an anxious society focuses its concerns upon the schools because the assertion of varying life styles generates unconscious fears of loss of control. As the witches of Salem discovered long ago, when a large section of a fearful public refuses to look at evidence, the powerless suffer. This has also been the lot of elementary teachers, who are periodically told that they are not teaching reading properly. Since one can always make the claim that children should be able to read better than they are presently doing, evidence that they are doing well remains unpersuasive. Nevertheless, a 1972 report by the Toronto Board of Education indicates clearly that children in this city are achieving reading scores according to their grade level and consistent with norms established over several decades of measurement in Ontario, immigrant children excepted.[65]

The manner in which the press commented on a recent U.S. survey, reported in *Reading Achievement in the United States, Then and Now*, is indicative of the unfounded nature of much of the criticism of school achievement. The strongest finding of the researchers was that reliable information is scattered and difficult to find; nevertheless, they hazarded a tentative conclusion on the evidence available that there had been a *steady* rise in achievement levels during the forty years prior to 1965, although "over the last ten years there may have been a very slight decline in reading achievement." They went on to observe that "of all our hesitant interpretations, we feel less certain about the last one." What their report does show is that, whether or not the decline in fact exists, the level of achievement is still higher than during the 1950s.[66]

The *New York Times* reported this research under the heading, "H.E.W. study cites a possible 'slightly negative trend' in children's reading ability" although the following story did refer to the important qualification noted above. *Time* magazine stated, without any qualification whatsoever, "public school students' reading levels have been falling since the mid-1960s." "The cure," *Time* pontificated, "lies in the classroom." Obviously the reporters for these magazines did not heed the observation that the authors of *Then and Now* made at the close of their report:

One of the interesting hobbies we have engaged in during the past several years in which we have been compiling these data, is to write to all those who make statements about the declining literacy in the United States. We have done this first to determine if those who are making such statements would direct us to their data sources; and secondly, we wrote to them because we felt they had little evidence on which to base their claims. We are now convinced that anyone who says that he *knows* that literacy is decreasing is a very unsure person. Such a person is at best unscholarly and at worst dishonest.[67]

The Humanities in an Age of Personal Autonomy
When medieval metaphysics had run its course, new scholars gradually emerged to draw attention to the actor in the cosmic panoply. Man's history, literature, and language became predominant in the academic curriculum of the universities, and eventually, as we have seen, in secondary schools also.

Since succeeding ages are always influenced by events that have gone before, it is only natural that these new humanistic studies should still be abstract, removed from everyday life and from everyman. As Hofstadter has shown, when everyman demanded a share of the prestige and position that such studies *seemed* to guarantee, he brought his common concerns with him and degraded the bases of classical studies. They were simply irrelevant to his purposes, and since he paid the taxes, he bent them to the best of his understanding.

Although it has been demonstrated in this paper that the form and the ritual of the traditional disciplines remain, the content has little semblance to that of a previous age. The qualitative change in society's values now requires that the form of the disciplines become dynamic, part of the process. Just as the relativistic age of Einstein eroded the mechanistic world of Newton, so also, the many new aspects of human interrelationships in the social world are becoming evident in the unconscious ways in which culture is evolving. Hence the several suggestions in this paper that the social processes of schooling can and should be seen as rich potential ground for curriculum development instead of as a reason for restraint.

The classical form of present university-oriented studies turns such unavoidable questions as sexual experimentation, venereal disease, birth control, and abortions into abstract discussions *about* these matters. A reinterpretation of the humanities would induce responsibility by employing the natural conditions of involvement. For several years, for example, I have involved male and female high school students in nursery school programs. They have obviously benefited from learning practical applications of child psychology while concomitantly preparing themselves for responsible parenthood.

The creative, dramatic, and performing arts are also subjects that have too often been studied in the abstract. A transformation in the meaning of the humanities would invite participation in a participatory age; drama and art would have increasing appeal if the students' urge for expressing personal values were not suppressed by vested interests in the measured didactics of the curriculum of another time.

Since our society is not particularly noted for mass appreciation of the arts, the suggestion that they should form a fair proportion of a new curriculum requires some justification. There are several levels of consideration.

The proposition that the time is ripe is not sufficient. For curriculum matters to be successful, there must apparently be a sizable community demand, one that is realistically founded, not based on projections of anxiety or utopian ideals. Ontario's new Ministry of Culture and Recreation may play a major role in this area, developing the potential that is undoubtedly present in this age of participation. When it becomes "respectable" for adults to enthuse about such new-found joys as painting, putting on skits and concerts for, let us say, institutionalized patients, and hiking and other participatory sports, it will become apparent that these are activities with social applications worthy of the curriculum in the schools of the future.

Once people have accepted the idea of taking an active role in sports and the arts, a second, highly desirable goal, could be brought into focus. It will be recalled that school became more meaningful—that is, it retained ever-increasing numbers of students—when the utility of schooling became more apparent. A wider array of occupations stimulated the interest of a wider array of students. However, under new conditions in society the meaning of equality of opportunity need not be restricted to alleviating the competition for admission to the traditional professions.

Occupational and socioeconomic class lines in our society have developed as a consequence of the commercial and industrial base of the economy. An emphasis on personal development through the arts would attract people with interests and skills that do not readily fit into our present hierarchical scale of levels of prestige. And if such a movement were sustained, a wider array of emotionally satisfying, prestigious occupations could well emerge, not only in the arts themselves, but also in the management of the arts, making room in the traditional professions for capable and task-oriented people who are not ordinarily recruited today.

A society that could deliberately adopt such measures for the greater fulfillment of personal potential would be unique. A multicultural population could identify common goals in such a society without feeling that an integration of purpose means a loss of identity. Perhaps we could even reverse the trend of always being influenced by innovations started in other countries. When representatives of educational committees on new practices start visiting us, we will know that we are finding good answers to some of the new problems in society.

NOTES

1. The foreword to the Hall-Dennis report (Provincial Committee on Aims and Objectives of Education in the Schools of Ontario, Report of the Committee, *Living and Learning* [Toronto: Ontario Department of Education, 1968], p. 4) notes that members of the committee included in their review a study of school systems and programs in the United States, Europe, and Asia.
2. H. L. Campbell, *Curriculum Trends in Canadian Education* (Toronto: W. J. Gage, 1952), pp. 31–32.
3. PSSC, *Physical Science Study Committee Course on Physics* (Boston: D. C. Heath & Co., 1960); BSCS, *The Biological Sciences Curriculum Study* (New York: John Wiley & Sons, 1973); SCIS, *The Science Curriculum Improvement Study Units on Elementary Science* (Chicago, Ill.: Rand McNally, 1970–71).
4. International Commission on the Development of Education, Report of the Commission, *Learning to Be: The World of Education Today and Tomorrow*, Edgar Faure, chairman (Paris: Unesco; Toronto: Ontario Institute for Studies in Education, 1973).
5. Garnet L. McDiarmid, "How Do Teachers View Their Profession?," *Educational Courier* (May–June 1969): 47–53.
6. J. S. Coleman, E. Q. Campbell, C. J. Hobson, J. Partland, A. M. Mood, F. D. Weinfeld, and L. R. York, *Equality of Educational Opportunity* (Washington, D.C.: U.S. Government Printing Office, 1966).
7. A. B. Hodgetts, Report of the National History Project, *What Culture? What Heritage? A Study of Civic Education in Canada* (Toronto: Ontario Institute for Studies in Education, 1968).
8. O. I. Frederick, "Curriculum Development," in *Encyclopedia of Educational Research* (New York: Macmillan Co., 1941), p. 374.

9. Hilda M. A. Neatby, *So Little for the Mind* (Toronto: Clarke, Irwin, 1953).

10. See Irving Louis Horowitz, *Rise and Fall of Project Camelot: Studies in the Relationship between Social Science and Practical Politics*, 2nd ed. (Cambridge, Mass.: M.I.T. Press, 1974).

11. Jerome S. Bruner, "The Process of Education Revisited," *Phi Delta Kappan* (September 1971), p. 21.

12. John I. Goodlad, *The Changing School Curriculum* (New York: Fund for the Advancement of Education, 1966), p. 106; Elliot W. Eisner, ed., *Confronting Curriculum Reforms* (Boston: Little, Brown, 1971), p. 2; and Decker F. Walker and Jon Schaffarzick, "Comparing Curricula," *Review of Educational Research*, vol. 44, no. 1 (Winter 1974): 83.

13. Charles E. Silberman, *Crisis in the Classroom* (New York: Random House, 1970), p. 11.

14. Alvin Toffler, *Future Shock* (Toronto: Bantam Books of Canada, 1971), p. 472.

15. Mauritz Johnson, Jr., "Definitions and Models in Curriculum Theory," *Educational Theory* (April 1967): 127–40.

16. George S. Counts, *Dare the School Build a New Social Order?* (New York: John Day Co., 1932).

17. H. L. Campbell, *Curriculum Trends in Canadian Education* (Toronto: W. J. Gage, 1952), pp. 93–94.

18. See *Living and Learning*, p. 9.

19. J. G. Althouse, "Providing Opportunities for Wholesome Development" (Address to the Rotary Club, Hamilton, November 1945), in *Addresses by J. G. Althouse* (Toronto: W. J. Gage, 1958), p. 118.

20. "Reprint of Articles from the *St. Thomas Journal* on Schools and Dominies in the Township of Aldborough," in *Documentary History*, vol. 1, p. 166 (cited in Campbell, *Curriculum Trends*, pp. 28–29, footnote).

21. See "News Report," *Journal of Education* (Toronto), vol. 20, no. 5 (May 1867): 81.

22. See Garnet L. McDiarmid, "Science and the Child," parts 1 and 2, *Educational Courier* (October 1960; November 1960): 20–21; 29–32.

23. John Porter, *The Vertical Mosaic: An Analysis of Social Class and Power in Canada* (Toronto: University of Toronto Press, 1965).

24. James B. Conant, *The Education of American Teachers* (Toronto: McGraw-Hill, 1963), pp. 4–5.

25. Althouse, "Awakened Interest in Our Schools" (Address to the Ryerson Institute of Technology, April 1952), in *Addresses*, pp. 50–51.

26. Lawrence A. Cremin, *The Transformation of the School* (New York: Alfred A. Knopf, 1961).

27. See Urie Bronfenbrenner, "Socialization and Social Class through Time and Space," in *Readings in Social Psychology*, ed. Eleanor E. Maccoby, Theodore M. Newcomb, and Eugene L. Hartley (New York: Holt, Rinehart & Winston, 1958), pp. 400–425; and Celia Stendler, "Sixty Years of Child-Training Practices: Revolution in the Nursery," *Journal of Pediatrics*, vol. 36, no. 1(1950): 122–34.

28. Althouse, "Awakened Interest in Our Schools," p. 48; and Althouse, "Significant Trends in Education in Ontario," in *Addresses*, pp. 63–64.

29. See, for example, E. K. Wickman, *Children's Behavior and Teachers' Attitudes* (New York: Commonwealth Fund, 1928); and Manfred H. Schrupp and Clayton

M. Gjerde, "Teacher Growth in Attitudes toward Behavior Problems of Children," *Journal of Educational Psychology*, vol. 44 (1953): 203–214.

30. See Jules Henry, *Culture against Man* (New York: Random House, 1964); Philip Wesley Jackson, *Life in Classrooms* (New York: Holt, Rinehart & Winston, 1968); and Benson R. Snyder, *The Hidden Curriculum* (New York: Alfred A. Knopf, 1971).

31. Althouse, "Education Today and Tomorrow" (Address upon the Occasion of Receiving an Honorary Degree from the University of Western Ontario, 1942), in *Addresses*, p. 20.

32. Elliot Aronson, Nancy Blaney, Jev Sikes, Cookie Stephan, and Matthew Snapp, "The Jigsaw Route to Learning and Liking," *Psychology Today* (February 1975): 47.

33. W. G. Fleming, *Ontario's Educative Society*, vols. 1–7 (Toronto: University of Toronto Press, 1971–1972).

34. Althouse, "Arousing and Holding Student Interest in the Secondary Schools" (Address to the College and Secondary Schools Department, Ontario Educational Association, April 1950), in *Addresses*, pp. 223, 224. The report Dr. Althouse refers to was prepared by the Canadian Research Committee on Practical Education and published under the title *Your Child Leaves School: A Study of 12,124 Graduates and 14,219 Drop-outs from Canadian Schools during 1948* (Report no. 2, Toronto, February 1950).

35. Quotations are from Althouse, "Education Today and Tomorrow" (Upon the Occasion of Receiving an Honorary Degree, October 1942), in *Addresses*, p. 19; Althouse, "Some Troublesome Questions about Our Schools" (Address to the Zonta Club, Toronto, February 1938), in *Addresses*, p. 11; and Campbell, *Curriculum Trends*, p. 100.

36. Althouse, "Educational Objectives" (Address to the Ontario Association for Curriculum Development, October 1951), in *Addresses*, p. 42.

37. Wilford M. Aikin, *The Story of the Eight Year Study* (New York: Harper, 1942), p. 140.

38. Seymour Martin Lipset, "Education and Equality: Israel and the United States Compared," *Society*, vol. 11, no. 3 (March–April 1974): 58.

39. H. Pullen, "Curriculum—1961," in *Ontario Conference on Education* (report on the conference sponsored by the Ontario Association for Curriculum Development, November 1961), pp. 96–100; Floyd Robinson, *Teacher Influence on Curriculum*, Research Study no. 4 (Ottawa: Canadian Teachers' Federation, December 1959).

40. W. H. Swift, *Trends in Canadian Education* (Toronto: W. J. Gage, 1958), pp. 62, 65–66.

41. McDiarmid, "Science and the Child."

42. Jerome S. Bruner, *The Process of Education* (Cambridge, Mass.: Harvard University Press, 1960).

43. Jerome S. Bruner, "The Process of Education Revisited," *Phi Delta Kappan* (September 1971): 18–19.

44. See, for example, Jean Piaget, *The Moral Judgement of the Child*, trans. Marjorie Gabain (London: Routledge & Kegan Paul, 1932), and Lawrence Kohlberg, "Moral Education in the Schools: A Developmental View," *The School Review*, vol. 74, no. 1 (Spring 1966): 1–30.

45. *Toronto Globe and Mail*, 15 October 1968, p. 9.

46. See Kenneth Keniston, *Young Radicals: Notes on Committed Youth* (New York: Harcourt Brace, 1968). Keniston was one of the first commentators to take seriously the notion that something new and constructive was developing within the apparent anarchy of youth in the 1960s.

47. *Toronto Globe and Mail*, 13 March 1974, p. 3.

48. Richard Hofstadter, *Anti-Intellectualism in American Life* (New York: Vintage Books, 1966), p. 305.

49. Gordon W. Bertram, *The Contribution of Canada to Economic Growth*, Economic Council of Canada Staff Study no. 12 (Ottawa: Queen's Printer, 1966).

50. See Wallace Clement, *Canadian Corporate Elite: An Analysis of Economic Power* (Toronto: McClelland & Stewart, 1975).

51. See Coleman et al., *Equality*; Christopher Jencks, *Inequality: A Reassessment of the Effect of Family and Schooling in America* (New York: Basic Books, 1972); and *Children and Their Primary Schools*, Report of the Central Advisory Council for Education, Lady Plowden, J.P., chairman (London: H.M.S.O., 1967).

52. Lipset, "Education and Equality," pp. 59–60.

53. See, for example, Peter Marris and Martin Rein, *Dilemmas of Social Reform, Poverty and Community Action in the United States* (New York: Atherton Press, 1969); Daniel T. Moynihan, *Maximum Feasible Misunderstanding: Community Action in the War on Poverty* (New York: Free Press, 1969); and "A Safe Streets Act, But Few Safe Streets," *New York Times*, 13 April 1975, p. E5.

54. A doctoral thesis by Michael Holden ("Literary Theory and the Education of English Teachers: An Analysis of the Theories of Literature Presented in Selected Textbooks on Literature and Its Teaching," University of Toronto, 1973) shows clearly that as far as recommended texts are concerned, teachers in training do not come into contact with vital scholarly questions on the role of English literature. Following Holden's investigation, Ernest Russell Wall identified in his thesis ("The Development and Application of an Instrument for the Substantive Analysis of Literature Teaching in the Secondary School," University of Toronto, 1974) the various ways in which teachers interpret a standard piece of literature. A significant finding was that teachers pursue psychological and sociological cues and develop with their students such topics as the motivation of character to a far greater extent than they attend to "purely literary" concerns.

55. Hofstadter, *Anti-Intellectualism*, p. 355.

56. Bruner, "The Process of Education Revisited," p. 21; H. Jantzen, *Curriculum Change in a Canadian Context* (Toronto: W. J. Gage, 1970), p. 83.

57. See Paul Hersey and Douglas Scott, "A Systems Approach to Educational Organization. Do We Manage or Administer?," *OCLEA* no. 2 (September 1974): 3–5.

58. David Riesman, *Individualism Re-considered* (New York: Doubleday Anchor, 1954).

59. Samuel Bowles and Herbert Gintis, "I.Q. in the United States Class," in *The New Assault on Equality, I.Q. and Social Stratification*, ed. Alan Gartner, Colin Greer, and Frank Reissman (New York: Harper & Row, Perennial Library, 1974), p. 81.

60. A number of professors at OISE are interested in various innovations in the lower schools. I am currently involved with the development of a curriculum to help solve a severe dropout problem among both Indian and white students in Northern

Ontario, a work–study program that also provides for increased involvement in decision making and in integrated studies has been designed. For published reports of other OISE ventures into alternative forms of schooling, see David W. Brison, "Out of School Education in the Social Service Sector," *Phi Delta Kappan* (December 1973): 237–39; and R. Simon, M. Levin, S. Trieger, and G. Cressey, "For the Sake of Argument: Brief for the CELT (Community Learning and Experiencing Together) Alternative School," *Educational Courier* (January 1975): 17–19.

61. From Loren Jay Lind, *The Learning Machine* (Toronto: Anansi, 1974), p. 28.

62. Education Development Centre, *Man: A Course of Study* (Cambridge, Mass.: Education Development Centre, 1968–70).

63. Mention might be made here of *Moral Education: Interdisciplinary Approaches*, by C. M. Beck, B. S. Crittenden, and E. V. Sullivan (Toronto: University of Toronto Press, 1971), as well as of such Institute publications as *How to Assess the Moral Reasoning of Students: A Teachers' Guide to the Use of Lawrence Kohlberg's Stage-Developmental Method*, by Nancy Porter and Nancy Taylor (1972), *Moral Education in the Schools: Some Practical Suggestions*, by C. M. Beck (1971), and the booklets in the Canadian Critical Issues series, edited by John Eisenberg and Malcolm Levin.

64. A recent Institute publication for women's studies is *The Women's Kit* (1974), by Pamela Harris, Becky Kane, and others—a multimedia collection of materials on women past and present, with the emphasis on Canadian women. In the Institute's Critical Issues series is *Native Survival* (1973), by John Eisenberg and Harold Troper, and a forthcoming book on the status of women by Paula Bourne. One OISE study of social studies textbooks, which I undertook in collaboration with David Pratt, demonstrated that there were many discriminatory references to ethnic groups in the textbooks authorized for use in Ontario schools and led Ontario's Ministry of Education to take positive action in modifying current policies on the production of new texts. Published under the title *Teaching Prejudice* (Toronto: Ontario Institute for Studies in Education, 1971), this study has since been replicated in most other provinces, with similar results.

65. See N. Wright and C. M. Reich, *Language: A Study of Fundamental Skills*, Research Report no. 108 (Toronto: Board of Education, 1972).

66. Roger Farr, Jaap Tuinman, and Michael Rowis, *Reading Achievement in the United States, Then and Now* (Bloomington: Indiana University Press, 1974), p. 139.

67. See "H.E.W. Study Cites a Possible 'Slightly Negative Trend' in Children's Reading Ability," *New York Times*, 18 March 1975, p. C23; "Learning Less," *Time Magazine* (Canada), 31 March 1975, p. 52; and Farr et al., *Reading Achievement*, p. 140.

370   From quantitative to
.193   qualitative change in
09713   Ontario education.
F931